Greenhill Books

FEARFUL HARD TIMES

'We had fearful hard times of it at Eshowe.'
Corporal F. W. License, Royal Engineers

Life at Eshowe during the early part of the siege. Pearson's cattle are guided by the few black auxiliaries who stayed with the garrison, and by the scratch force of mounted men nicknamed 'The Uhlans'. The view of the fort shows the main western entrance.

FEARFUL HARD TIMES

The Siege and Relief of Eshowe
1879

IAN CASTLE
AND
IAN KNIGHT

Greenhill Books, London
Stackpole Books, Pennsylvania

Greenhill Books

Fearful Hard Times
First published 1994 by Greenhill Books, Lionel Leventhal Limited,
Park House, 1 Russell Gardens, London NW11 9NN
and
Stackpole Books, 5067 Ritter Road, Mechanicsburg, PA 17055, USA

British Library Cataloguing in Publication Data
Knight, Ian
Fearful Hard Times: Siege and Relief of
Eshowe, 1879
I. Title   II. Castle, Ian
968.045

ISBN 1–85367–180–0

Library of Congress Cataloging-in-Publication Data available
Castle, Ian.
Fearful Hard Times: the siege and relief of Eshowe/
Ian Castle and Ian Knight.
p.   cm.
Includes bibliographical references and index.
ISBN 1–85367–180–0
1. Eshowe (South Africa)—History—Siege, 1879.   2. Zulu War,
1879—South Africa—Eshowe.   I. Knight, Ian, 1956–   .   II. Title.
DT1875.C37   1994
968.4′045—dc20   94-12030
                                                              CIP

Typeset by DP Photosetting, Aylesbury, Bucks
Printed and bound in Great Britain by Clays Ltd, St Ives plc

Contents

Illustrations

Line Drawings

Maps and Plans

Zulu Pronunciation

For readers with no direct contact with southern African languages, many of the Zulu words used in this book may prove difficult to pronounce, based as they are on other different orthographic codes and practices from those used in European languages. The following suggestions are intended as a rough guide for those who have no opportunity to develop an ear for the sound of Zulu words by listening to the language in use.

Perhaps the most obvious feature of Zulu is that it uses several sounds not found in western speech. These are the famous 'click' sounds, made by tutting the tongue against various parts of the palate. To represent them on the page, they are conveyed by the letters 'c', 'q' and 'x'. The 'c' click is made by pressing the tongue against the back of the upper teeth – it is the same sound used in English to convey disapproval, and is sometimes then written 'tsk tsk'. Thus the name of the Zulu king in 1879, Cetshwayo kaMpande, is pronounced '(tsk)-etsh-*why*-o'; the common name component 'wayo' is pronounced '*why*-o'. The 'q' click is a deeper sound, made by withdrawing the back of the tongue from the top of the palate – it is the sort of sound sometimes used by children to represent the clopping of a horse's hooves. The 'x' click is a similar, slightly lighter sound, made against the side teeth; it is the sound often used by riders to 'gee-up' their horses.

Another aspect confusing to non-African readers is the use of capital letters other than at the beginning of the word – for example, the iNgobamakhosi regiment. This is because many Zulu words have prefixes, and the capital is used to denote the root of the word, and the first stressed consonant. Often the prefix can hardly be distinguished in speech, and merely serves to stress the capitalised letter. Generally, Zulu pronunciation lays stress on the penultimate syllable, so iNgobamakhosi would be pronounced 'Ngoba-ma-*khaw*-si'. The letter 'l' conveys a slight slurring sound, rather like the Welsh 'll'; a softer, more fluid version of the English 'shl'. Thus the famous battle of Isandlwana is not *ee-san-dler-warna*, but 'Sand-shl-*wah*-na, whilst Hlobane mountain is Shlo-*barn*-eh.

The letter 'p' and 't', when followed by 'h', remain hard; *ph* should be pronounced 'p', not 'f', and *th* is 't' rather than as in the English '*the*'. Thus the Zulu commander Phalane kaMdinwa is Pa-*larn*-e, not 'fallane', and the uThulwana ibutho is similarly uTul- *warn*-ah. The Zulu name for age-grade regiments is amabutho – ama-*boo*-tow. Finally, 'g' is hard and 'k' is soft, making them sound almost indistinguishable; the Thukela river is therefore pronounced Too-*gay*-lar, rather like the old phonetic spelling, *Tugela*. Gingindlovu is Gin- gin-dsh*loh*-vu. The name Eshowe – the events surrounding which form the basis of this book – used to be pronounced in old-fashioned Zulu e-*Shaw*-eh, but is now generally known by the anglicised version, *ee-show-ee*, with the middle 'o' pronounced as in 'howl'.

Introduction and Acknowledgements

The siege of Eshowe is, perhaps, the forgotten campaign of the 1879 Anglo-Zulu War. It is not hard to see why: on the very day that Colonel Pearson brushed aside Zulu resistance to his advance at Nyezane river, a major British force was annihilated elsewhere in Zululand at Isandlwana. This was one of the worst defeats suffered by a British army during the Victorian Colonial era, which sent a thrill of horror through the Empire at the time and has continued to exercise a particular fascination ever since. Indeed, the story of Isandlwana is all the more dramatic since it was followed just a few hours later by the successful defence of the mission station at Rorke's Drift – an action which was recognised by the award of no less than eleven Victoria Crosses, more than for any other single-day battle in British military history. The operations of Colonel Pearson's Right Flank, or No. 1 Column were effectively overshadowed, and the action has not really received its due among historians as a result.

Yet there is much that is extraordinary about the Eshowe campaign. It was bracketed by two pitched battles; the first, at Nyezane, was fought according to the same Standing Orders, issued by the British commander, Lord Chelmsford, which led to such fatal consequences at Isandlwana – yet Nyezane was a British victory. The second, Gingindlovu, provided Lord Chelmsford with an opportunity to put to the test the lessons he had learned from Isandlwana, and which would ultimately win him the war. In between, eighteen hundred men were cooped up for seventy-two days in a fortified former mission, unable to break out, low on food, and subject to disease which thrived in the cramped and unhygienic conditions. Of course, the Zulus did not prosecute the siege in the manner of European armies of the time; they possessed no artillery and lacked the technology to allow them to undermine the British defences, nor did they launch any mass attacks on the post. The siege was, none-the-less, extremely effective; the Zulus surrounded Eshowe with a flexible cordon of patrols, who were able to summon reserves quickly and in sufficient numbers to threaten any British sortie. The fighting around Eshowe was characterised by constant skirmishing, much of it examined here for the first time. The Zulus effectively neutralised Pearson's force by the simple expedient of daring him to leave his trenches to fight in the open – something which, in the aftermath of Isandlwana, no British commander was keen to do.

This book has been based entirely on first-hand material. Since Pearson's garrison often found time hanging on their hands, many of the officers kept diaries or notes on the siege. We have been fortunate to obtain access to a number which are not only previously unpublished, but which have not before been available for study. As a result, it has been possible to reconstruct for the first time something of the life of the garrison at Eshowe, of their adventures, and of the personalities involved. We have also attempted a detailed study of the battle of Nyezane, an unusual fight in the context of the Zulu War because of the fluid – and sometimes confusing – movements of the British troops. We have similarly relied on official and unofficial accounts to reconstruct the movements of Lord Chelmsford's relief column, and in particular of the battle of Gingindlovu. Although Gingindlovu appears at first glance to have been an easy British victory, eye-witness accounts suggest that the Zulu assault was more determined than has sometimes been supposed, and reveal a wealth of incidental detail.

Unfortunately, it has not been possible to examine the Zulu perspective as fully as we would have liked. The long-standing emphasis on the Isandlwana saga amongst collectors of oral evidence has meant that the fighting on the coastal sector has produced fewer Zulu accounts than for any other sector of the war. Some golden opportunities were missed; the traveller Bertram Mitford interviewed the Zulu commander Prince Dabulamanzi kaMpande in 1882, but, despite the fact that Dabulamanzi had achieved considerable fame among his enemies as a result of his leadership at Rorke's Drift, Mitford left no detailed account of the conversation. A verbatim description of the objectives and methods of the Zulu commanders on the coast would have been invaluable to modern historians; it is indicative of our lack of knowledge in this field that it is not even possible to identify the dispositions of the individual *amabutho* at the battle of Gingindlovu. Nevertheless, contemporary British reports do suggest something of the Zulu movements, and we have relied heavily on John Laband's synthesis, *Kingdom In Crisis*, to place them in the wider context of Zulu political and military reactions to the British invasion. We have also endeavoured to standardise the spelling of Zulu names in line with this seminal work, even to the extent of adopting here the marginally more correct form oNdini for the royal homestead generally known to British historians as Ulundi.

This book has grown out of more than fifteen years' research into the Anglo-Zulu War in both the United Kingdom and South Africa. It does not attempt a general history of the war, which can be found in Ian Knight's *Brave Men's Blood*, and has deliberately avoided the Isandlwana campaign and Rorke's Drift, which can be found in the same author's *Zulu* and *Nothing Remains But To Fight* respectively. Many people have shared their time, knowledge and collections with us, without which it would not be possible. Both authors acknowledge a tremendous debt to 'SB' Bourquin of Westville, Durban, who took us camping around the sites, and shared with us his lifetime's knowledge of the Zulu people and their history. Graham Dominy, the Historian at the Natal Museum, Pietermaritzburg, allowed us full access to the museum's archives, and with his wife Anne and son James proved the most entertaining of hosts. Gillian Berning and George Foster at the Local History Museum, Durban, and everyone at the Killie Campbell Africana Library in Durban proved consistently helpful. Lynn Oakley of the Zululand Historical Museum, Fort Nongqai, Eshowe, made her collection available to us, whilst Mr Bill Robarts of Empangeni allowed us access to the invaluable letters of his forebear, Lt William Robarts of the Victoria Mounted Rifles. In the UK, the staff of both the Museum and Library of the Royal Engineers at Chatham were always helpful, as were all at the National Army Museum in Chelsea, and Tom Hodson of the Buffs Museum in Canterbury. Paddy Griffith gave us access to the Wynne papers, even as he was preparing to publish them, and Rai England allowed us to use some of his unrivalled archive of contemporary newspaper engravings. Cliff Meek, himself a veteran of the KRRC, helped us with aspects of the regimental affairs of the 60th Rifles. Keith Reeves, a regular travelling companion and fellow explorer of Wombane hill, was as generous as ever with his magnificent collection of Zulu War memorabilia, which includes the Shervinton papers; Keith's wife, Veronica, has always tolerated the undue time we have spent with Keith discussing Zulu War topics.

Finally, but by no means least, our respective partners have been constantly encouraging, and tolerant beyond the call of duty; our sincere thanks are due to them both.

Ian Castle
Ian Knight

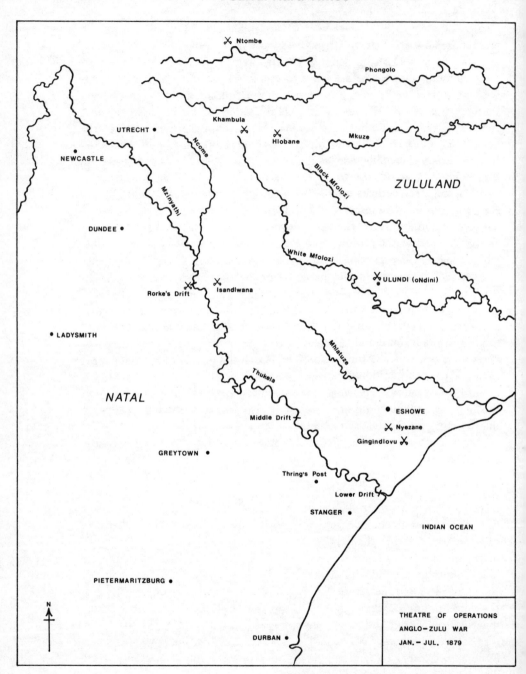

THEATRE OF OPERATIONS
ANGLO—ZULU WAR
JAN. — JUL. 1879

CHAPTER 1

Confrontation

On 11 December 1878, the southern African sun shone down clear, bright and hot on a group of men huddled beneath the shade of a spreading wild fig tree on the banks of a broad, brown river. The men were locked in conference; a meeting that was perhaps typical of the interaction between any one of the European powers with indigenous groups across the world in the great age of Imperial expansion. Here, the representatives of a white colonial power were dictating terms to the representatives of an independent black African state. The outcome of the meeting would be momentous; it would foreshadow the destruction of arguably the most famous kingdom in nineteenth-century Africa – the Zulu.

The meeting had been called by Sir Henry Bulwer, the Lieutenant-Governor of the British colony of Natal, a month before. It followed a period of increasing tension between Natal and its northern neighbour, the independent kingdom of Zululand, which was the result of a protracted border wrangle. The Zulu Royal House had traditionally maintained a good relationship with the British, and the present king, Cetshwayo kaMpande, had agreed to Bulwer's request in the hope of resolving the crisis amicably. He had appointed a number of important *izinduna*, the state officials of the Zulu kingdom, to attend the meeting, and they were accompanied by the king's white friend and adviser, John Dunn.

The British delegation had arrived at the rendezvous site two days earlier. They had been carefully selected for the task by the most senior British representative in southern Africa, the High Commissioner himself, Sir Henry Bartle Frere, and his choice reflected Frere's own secret agenda. He had more in mind for the meeting than the resolution of a border dispute, and his four representatives were all men who prided themselves on having some knowledge of the 'native mind', and who shared Frere's own expansionist vision. They were John W. Shepstone, Secretary for Native Affairs in the Cape Colony, Charles Brownlee, Commissioner for Native Affairs Cape Colony, Henry Francis Fynn, magistrate of Msinga and son of one of the earliest British settlers in Natal, and Brevet Colonel Forestier Walker of the Scots Guards, who was Frere's Assistant Military Secretary. To lend their mission a proper air of importance, their deputation was accompanied by a sizeable military escort.

It was fitting that the Lower Thukela Drift had been chosen for the meeting, as it was perhaps the most important gateway into the Zulu kingdom. The kingdom had emerged under King Shaka kaSenzangakhona following a period of conflict and upheaval in the 1820s. At that time, the internal affairs of the south-eastern seaboard of Africa were largely unknown to the outside world, cut off as it was by a forbidding coastline on one side and by mountain ramparts on the other. Yet rumours of the Zulu rise filtered down to the Cape, where the British had replaced the Dutch as the resident colonial power in 1806, and the promise of new and lucrative trading markets lured a group of predominantly British adventurers into Zululand. Originally, Zulu influence extended across large parts of the area known to Europe as Natal – so called because it had been discovered by the Portuguese explorer Vasco da Gama on Christmas Day 1497 – but King Shaka granted his British visitors land rights around the bay of Port Natal, and the Zulu kingdom retreated to a line north of the Thukela river and its tributary, the Mzinyathi. Natal had been recognised as a British colony in 1843. For most of its length, the border was marked by rugged and difficult country, and could be crossed at only a few manageable points. The Thukela flowed into the sea just three or four miles below the Lower Drift, and in the winter months the current was so sluggish and the water level so low that it could usually be crossed here on foot. As a result, white hunters and traders had used the Lower Drift as their portway into the Zulu kingdom since the 1820s, and in 1878 a ramshackle wayside hostelry, Smith's Hotel, founded by an old soldier of the 84th Regiment, stood a few hundred yards away to cater for the passing traffic. So important was the crossing that in the 1850s Natal had appointed an official, Captain Joshua Walmsley, to watch over it as Border Agent. To the local Africans the crossing was known as Mantshonga's Drift, after Walmsley's African name.

Even before the British commissioners arrived, the spot had become a scene of energetic military activity which boded ill for the future negotiations. Lieutenant Thomas R. Main of the Royal Engineers had been sent to this rather lonely but beautiful spot in advance of the army, with a handful of black labourers. Main had been ordered to erect a defensive post commanding the drift, and he had chosen the crest of a steep knoll on the right bank. On the Natal side, the slopes of the knoll were easy to negotiate, but from the Zulu bank the bluff presented a sheer cliff face which dropped 300 feet to the river below. The heavy work of digging out trenches and piling up ramparts had been carried out by a detachment of the 2nd Battalion 3rd Regiment, 'The Buffs', about 170 strong, who had been stationed there since the beginning of November 1878; the position was christened Fort Pearson, after their commanding officer, Colonel Charles Knight Pearson. On 24 November 'The Buffs' had been relieved by a naval brigade, about 230 sailors and Marines from HMS *Active* under the command of Commander (Acting Captain) H.J.F. Campbell, which had landed at Durban on 19 November. Such was the extent of the British Empire's commitment to policing its overseas interests that it was by no means unusual for the Royal Navy to put men ashore to assist the local land forces: indeed, the *Active*'s party were delighted to find Lieutenant Main in residence; they had served together earlier that year in the Eastern Cape Frontier campaign. The landing party's strength belied any peaceful intent; they brought with them two 12-pounder Armstrong guns which were installed permanently in the fort, as well as two 24-pounder rocket tubes and a Gatling gun.

The British intended the meeting to be an exercise in intimidation. Four chairs and a table were placed beneath a canvas awning which the sailors had spread across the tree – they were for the Imperial representatives, of course, not the Zulus – and a bodyguard had been organised for the commissioners. Twenty bluejackets and twenty Marines had been appointed to the task, and issued an extra ten rounds of Martini-Henry ammunition; considerable fire-power, given that the commissioners could hardly have been expecting to be attacked. At the last minute, on the evening of 10 December, the military force was augmented by the arrival of twenty members of the Stanger Mounted Rifles, one of the local volunteer corps formed from among Natal's white settler population. The Natal Volunteers had already been mobilised for service on 1 December in anticipation of trouble with the Zulus.

The Zulu ambassadors had been waiting at John Dunn's Mangethe residence, a few miles across the river into Zululand, and when they received the British invitation to cross on Wednesday, 11 December, they walked slowly down to the river in accordance with the dignity of their rank and mission. The Zulu party consisted of three important *izinduna*, led by one of the king's advisors, Vumandaba kaNtati, eleven subordinate *izinduna* and between forty and fifty attendants. John Dunn himself accompanied them in an unofficial capacity. It had been raining recently upstream, and the Thukela was in flood, a broad, smooth, fast-flowing expanse of brown water some 300 yards wide. The exhausting task of ferrying the Zulu envoys and their entourage over to the Natal bank fell to the sailors of the *Active*, who rowed back and forth in a number of small boats. When all were safely over, the commissioners took their places at the table while the Zulus squatted, as was their fashion, on the ground in front of them, under the watchful gaze of the naval guard.

The meeting began with the announcement of the boundary commission's findings. Since the 1860s, the Zulus had been locked in a dispute with Boer farmers, who owed their allegiance to the inland Transvaal Republic, over a stretch of land on Zululand's north-western border. In 1877, the British had annexed the Transvaal, and had thereby inherited the border dispute. Frere had appointed a commission to examine the evidence on both sides, and, to his surprise, it had found almost entirely in favour of the Zulus. Frere had known of the commission's report five months earlier, but since it did not fit in with his broader political strategy, he had suppressed it. Now, however, he had manipulated events sufficiently to his own ends as to be able to make the findings known to King Cetshwayo.

It is worth pausing, before the meeting progresses further, to consider who Frere was, and what those ends were. Sir Henry Bartle Edward Frere had been appointed High Commissioner of South Africa and Governor of the Cape Colony in 1877. South Africa had long been a drain on the Imperial purse-strings, a cockpit of ethnic antagonisms. Most of its nation-states had been born in bloodshed, and out of a deep-seated antagonism towards their neighbours; the Boers, the descendants of the old Dutch settlers, had felt oppressed by the British, and had tried to establish their own republics. In doing so, they had fought bitterly against the various black groups who occupied the land before them, and who were themselves internally divided. Britain had been dragged in the wake of the Boer treks, and had already shed rather too much blood in the role of Imperial policeman. When diamonds were discovered at Kimberley, just north of the Cape Colony, in the 1860s, and South Africa at last offered the prospect of economic growth and development, the Colonial Office decided to grasp the nettle and resolve the region's political differences once and for all. The result was a policy called Confederation, which was intended to bring all South Africa's disparate groups together under British authority so that they could more smoothly be administered. It was Frere's task to implement the Confederation scheme.

It was not, of course, an easy task. South Africa was in such a mess precisely because many of its inhabitants did not want to be ruled by the British. Frere, a highly respected Imperial Civil Servant who had cut his teeth administering British India in the difficult years after the Mutiny, did not shirk the implications; some groups would have to be persuaded to accept Confederation, while others might have to be forced. The Transvaal was the first, and perhaps most important, part of the Confederation jigsaw. The British annexation had been swift and audacious, so much so that the Boers had hardly had time to object, yet Frere was well aware that there were rumblings of discontent orchestrated by a strong republican element within the country. Against this background, Frere also found himself faced with a shudder of discontent which passed through South Africa's black population. Their political power and independence eroded by decades of conflict with expanding white settlement, many black South African groups found themselves restricted to cramped reserves, and their anger expressed itself in a series of unconnected flare-ups directed against the further imposition of white authority. Frere quickly came to see that there was much to gain by breaking the power of the largest independent black group in South Africa, the Zulus. By destroying the Zulus, whose army was a legendary bogy-man in settler society, Frere could decisively resolve the border dispute in favour of the Transvaal, and thereby demonstrate to disaffected Boers that something tangible had come from British rule. A little surgical wielding of the British sabre would, at the same time, warn the same Boers of what might happen if they did not toe the line, and point out to other African groups that armed resistance was hopeless. The quickest way to implement Confederation, in other words, was by waging a quick and successful war against the Zulus.

Unfortunately for Frere, Britain had very little cause to quarrel with the Zulu kingdom. True, the Zulu army, over 30,000 strong, did pose a potential threat to the exposed settler communities along the Natal/Zulu border, but only if the Zulu king chose to unleash it. Since King Shaka's time, relations between Britain and the Zulus had generally been good, and there is no evidence that the attitude of Cetshwayo was any different. Nevertheless, the border issue led to an increase in tension, and Frere claimed to see Zulu aggression behind a number of minor transgressions which afflicted the up-country districts in 1878. The most serious and celebrated of these was an incursion in June 1878 by the sons of a Zulu border chieftain, Sihayo kaXongo, who crossed the border to arrest two of the chief's runaway wives who had sought refuge in Natal. If the remarkably even-handed report of the boundary commission provided Frere with no opportunity of provoking a confrontation with Cetshwayo, the actions of Sihayo's sons, at least, did.

Frere now carefully manipulated the boundary award adding conditions that were tantamount to a declaration of war. Here Frere was on sensitive ground politically, for the Colonial Office in London accepted that Confederation might, one day, lead to war with the Zulus, but it did not want it in early 1879; in the Balkans and Afghanistan far more threatening war clouds were gathering. The Colonial Secretary, Sir Michael Hicks Beach, instructed Frere to deal with the Zulus in a spirit of forbearance, but Hicks Beach was two weeks away by steamer and telegraph, and Frere had been trained to act on his own initiative; he sent the terms of his ultimatum to London only when he knew it would be too late for them to intervene. When Frere's ultimatum reached Hicks Beach on 2 January 1879, he knew it for what it was, and had little choice but to accept that Frere's invasion of Zululand would have begun before it could be stopped. The Colonial Office could only hope it would be over quickly.

At the Lower Thukela, the fateful meeting began in the middle of the morning. As Cetshwayo's representatives settled themselves in the shade John Shepstone came forward and began to read out the award of the Boundary Commission. So that the Zulus could understand it fully, it was translated for them by a Natal Border Agent, H.B. Fynney. The award stated that the Zulu claim to the disputed territory had been upheld. Although the confirmation of the strength of their claim was tempered by a condition that any Boer farmer now finding himself on the wrong side of the border would have to be compensated by the Zulus should he wish to leave, the decision was generally well received by the envoys. The only disquieting aspect of the whole proceedings so far was the arrival of Mr Lloyd, a photographer from Durban, who set up his equipment to record for posterity the historic moment. A report in the *Natal Mercury* stated that the Zulus were a little unnerved by this development: 'The spectacle of this strange, three-legged instrument, with its polished tube, directed seemingly at himself, caused Vumandaba, the portly leader of the party, to nudge his neighbour, as though telling him to look out.'

The Zulu party then rose in the belief that the meeting was now over. On the contrary, they were told that there would be a short lunch break, after which the British had more to say. With lunch over, the envoys returned to their former positions. The sun was now at its height, and the tarpaulin afforded welcome shade from the scorching summer heat. The Zulu deputation listened attentively to Shepstone's next speech. They listened solidly for three hours, and at the end of it, they were stunned. To the award of the morning, Frere had added a series of demands which amounted to an ultimatum. The Zulus were told to surrender the sons of Sihayo, and several other individuals whom the British held guilty of border violations. The Zulu army was to be abolished. White missionaries who wanted to practise in Zululand were to be allowed to do so, and a large fine in cattle was to be paid in reparation for the border incidents. Lieutenant Main, who was watching the proceedings, thought 'The faces of the old chiefs (called "ring koppies" from the fact of their wearing a plaster ring around their skull) was a study as Sir B.F.'s speech was translated to them, and their constant whow! whow! showed their astonishment.'

The Zulu representatives were indeed astonished, but as they tried to protest, they were told curtly that the British envoys had no power to discuss the terms of the demands, or to negotiate. The dignity with which the Zulus accepted the blow stirred a sense of fair-play in some of the watching troops. Main thought Shepstone had 'spoke to them like stern parents' whilst Fleet-Surgeon H.F. Norbury of the *Active* noted that 'the bearing of the Zulu indunas was on the whole dignified, collected and courteous, without the least exhibition of temper or bravado'. Yet the Imperial party's adherence to the ethics of the public school was just a touch cynical, since the Zulu envoys were given, for the record, a copy of the British demands – despite the fact it was known full well that no one at the Zulu court could read English. The envoys were told that the British expected some of the demands to be met within twenty days, and full compliance with the rest within thirty days. Failing that, the Zulu kingdom would be at war with the British Empire. The envoys knew at once, of course, that absolute compliance was impossible; the king might have been prepared to surrender Sihayo's sons and to pay a cattle fine, but to abandon the military system would strike at the political, economic and social roots of the kingdom. This was precisely what Frere had intended; whatever the Zulu decision, he would break the kingdom's power.

The Zulu army lay at the heart of the Zulu king's dominion. The kingdom was a conglomerate, made up of a patchwork of formerly independent clans, ruled by hereditary chiefs, who had either allied themselves with Shaka or had been conquered by him. To bind the nation together, the king extracted tribute from his people in the form of guilds known as *amabutho*. These guilds were formed at regular intervals from men of a common age, regardless of their clan origins, and they owed their allegiance directly to the king. They were required to give service until such time as the king gave them permission to marry, at which time they passed out of active service and on to a national reserve. The *amabutho* performed many services for the king; they were tactical units on the battlefield, they took part in royal hunts, and they served as the kingdom's police force. They were armed with a variety of spears for throwing and stabbing, and with hide shields cut to a uniform pattern from the king's own cattle herds. To prise the king from the army, or the army from the king, would undermine the most highly developed structures of the state.

The Zulu dignitaries departed, with heavy hearts, to take the British message to their king, and the British deputation rode back to the Natal capital, Pietermaritzburg. The stage was set, and sands of time began to trickle slowly away for the Zulu kingdom.

Frere, however, was not sitting idly by. In March 1877, a new British commander, Lieutenant-General the Honourable Sir Frederic Augustus Thesiger, C.B., had arrived in the Cape Colony to take command of British troops in South Africa. Thesiger, a career soldier in his fifties who had seen active service in the Crimea, India and Abyssinia, arrived in time to wrap up a small but trying campaign against the Xhosa people on the Eastern Cape Frontier. When it was over, in August 1878, Frere asked him to travel north to Natal, to assess the military prospects of a war against the Zulus. The border with Zululand stretched for some 200 miles, and to defend so rugged a frontier with the limited troops at his disposal would be impossible. In any case, Thesiger's political brief was to overthrow the Zulu kingdom, and this was only likely to be achieved by an offensive campaign. Thesiger formulated a plan of campaign which utilized five independent columns each crossing the border at separate points and advancing on Cetshwayo's principal homestead, known variously as oNdini or Ulundi.

Thesiger typified the Victorian gentleman; he was dignified and aloof, but his manners were impeccable, he was kind to his men, and certainly not a fool. Furthermore, he was experienced in African warfare, but that, sadly, was to prove his undoing, for he had formed his impression of the African's fighting ability on the Cape Frontier. The Xhosa had been unable to sustain attacks on fortified British positions, and had instead waged a guerilla warfare. Despite the fact that Thesiger knew, intellectually, that the Zulus preferred a more aggressive style of warfare, he could not free himself from the belief that they were basically of the same mettle as the Xhosa. His greatest worry was that the Zulus might refuse to give him battle, and by invading in converging columns, Thesiger hoped to pin down the Zulu army and force it into hostilities.

Yet the number of troops at his disposal were severely limited for such a task. Because the home government would not sanction open aggression towards the Zulus, Thesiger was compelled to make do with those troops already stationed in South Africa, plus a handful of reinforcements from home. These troops had to be concentrated on the Zulu border from all over South Africa. He had at his disposal the 2nd Battalion 3rd Regiment, known as 'The Buffs' after the colour of their regimental facings, the 1st Battalion 13th Regiment, the 1st and 2nd Battalions 24th Regiment, and the single battalion 80th and 90th Regiments. At least all these battalions had some experience of the conditions which prevailed in the field in South Africa; the 2/3rd, 1/24th, 2/24th and 90th had all fought against the Gcaleka and Ngqika Xhosa during the Ninth Cape Frontier War in 1878, whilst that same year the 1/13th and 80th had seen action in the northern Transvaal against the Pedi warriors of King Sekhukhune. If most of his officers were therefore experienced in African warfare, they also shared their commander's unfortunate over-confidence and misconceptions about the Zulus. On 28 September 1878 Thesiger wrote to the home government asking for two further battalions to supplement those already available; this was reluctantly approved but with the proviso that they were 'not to furnish the means for any aggressive operations not directly connected with the defence of Her Majesty's possessions and subjects'. The troops accordingly dispatched in November 1878 were the 2nd Battalion 4th Regiment and the 99th Regiment, and two Royal Engineer companies. By that time, Frere was committed to his confrontation with the Zulus, and Thesiger — who had succeeded to the title of 2nd Baron Chelmsford on the death of his father in October — gave him his unreserved support. As a result, Chelmsford displayed a very loose interpretation of the home government's strictures.

While Lord Chelmsford now had the infantry battalions he required, he still faced a glaring lack of mounted troops. Experience gained in the Ninth Cape Frontier War had led to the creation of two mounted infantry squadrons, volunteers who could ride drawn from the Imperial infantry battalions, but with no regular cavalry stationed in South Africa at this time, Chelmsford was forced to look elsewhere to overcome this worrying deficiency. A limited solution was provided by the Natal Volunteer Corps. The Natal government had been informed as early as the 1850s that it was unlikely that there would be sufficient British troops to provide a permanent garrison, and they were advised to make preparations for their own defence. The white inhabitants of Natal enthusiastically responded by forming numerous small, glamorously titled, part-time Volunteer units, whose ranks were filled with good riders who could shoot and knew the country well. When, as occasionally happened, enthusiasm for a particular unit fell and numbers dwindled, it would be disbanded, but inevitably a new unit would spring up in another part of the colony to take its place. In 1878, when Chelmsford requested the services of the Volunteers, there were eleven mounted corps, three infantry and one artillery. Most of these operated under legislation which allocated them a defensive role, and Chelmsford needed both the permission of the civil authorities, and the will of the men themselves, to use them across the border in Zululand. To that end he promised farms in Zululand to anyone willing to accompany the invasion forces, and most of the corps, whose ranks were made up from the white settler farming community, were happy to agree. A total of eight of the mounted units were to serve in Zululand during the war, whilst the rest remained on reserve in Natal. Chelmsford, incidentally, had no authority to promise these farms, since the future of Zululand was clearly undecided, and in the end none of the Volunteers received their reward. Chelmsford also called on the services of a number of irregular cavalry units from the Cape and Transvaal, some of which were specifically formed for the forthcoming conflict. Although they attracted the widest possible cross-section of recruits, not all of whom took naturally to army discipline, these units effectively proved their worth throughout the war by providing the eyes and ears of the army on campaign.

Chelmsford's force, however, remained under strength. As soon as the advance began, he would have to leave strong pockets as garrisons to protect his lines of communication. In order to supplement his force further he approached Sir Henry Bulwer, the Lieutenant-Governor of Natal and head of the civilian administration, and requested permission to raise 7000 levies from the black population of the colony. Natal had an estimated population of over 300,000 black Africans, many of whom had a history of antagonism towards the Zulu Royal House. Militarily, it made sense to utilise this resource, yet Bulwer had misgivings. Although wary of the Zulu power, Bulwer did not support Frere's aggressive action, and was opposed to the impending war. Raising an armed levy from among the Natal blacks offered the fearful prospect of fuelling an internal insurrection, or at the very least of stimulating a bitter vendetta between the majority of Natal's population and the Zulus north of the Thukela. Bulwer procrastinated, but at last gave way in the face of pressure from Frere and Chelmsford, and in late 1878 authorised the raising of a black auxiliary force.

The task of organising this influx of raw material fell to Lieutenant-Colonel Anthony Durnford of the Royal Engineers. Durnford, who was to play no small part in the coming conflict, was already a controversial character in Natal. He had arrived in South Africa in 1872, and had been wounded in a skirmish with rebellious blacks in the Bushmen's River Pass in 1873. As Assistant Colonial Engineer he had been a member of the Boundary Commission that had recently sat and analysed the claims to the disputed territory. Durnford was selected because he admired local African cultures and spoke some Zulu. The force, to be known as the Natal Native Contingent (NNC), was to be organised along European rather than ethnic lines. It was to be divided into three regiments, the 1st of three battalions, and the 2nd and 3rd of two battalions each. Each battalion was to consist of ten companies of a hundred men each under white officers and NCOs. In addition a number of troops of mounted men were to be formed. Appointing suitable senior officers for the seven battalions did not prove too difficult, but finding the sixty European NCOs required by each battalion proved a much tougher proposition. Most of the best colonial volunteers in Natal had already signed up in some capacity or another, and with an air of desperation Chelmsford recruited heavily among the hard-bitten irregulars who had recently been disbanded on the Cape Frontier, and among the dregs of colonial society. Most NCOs in the Native Contingent felt little more than contempt for the men under their command, had no knowledge of their culture, and less of their language. Indeed, some NNC NCOs, recruited from itinerant labourers who had recently come from Europe to make their way in the colonies, could not speak much English either. Nor was there time to train the soldiers properly – there were only two months between the announcement of the formation of the NNC and the expiry of the ultimatum – and there were insufficient uniforms and guns to equip them. Only one man in ten was given a firearm, often of an obsolete type, while the rest mustered with their own traditional weapons. The men were given a blanket, but the only uniform was a distinguishing red rag twisted around the head. With these diverse elements thrown together at such short notice it is hardly surprising that the performance of such units was sometimes less than steadfast.

As his armies marched to their respective assembly points, Chelmsford was forced to re-evaluate his planned strategy. It was proving extremely difficult to concentrate the vast quantity of transport wagons and oxen necessary to keep the proposed columns in provisions, and it soon became obvious that the original plan of five converging columns was unworkable. A new plan was drawn up, and instead of all five columns advancing, only three of them would move on oNdini, the other two – one of which was composed almost entirely of levies – were to remain on the border in reserve. Not until these plans were well advanced did Frere feel able to summon the Zulu king's representatives to hear the award of the Boundary Commission. And he had no intention of letting Lord Chelmsford's efforts go to waste.

The Zulu envoys, burdened by their catastrophic news, had returned slowly to oNdini, reluctant to pass on the terms of the ultimatum to the king because of the terrible implications for the nation. John Dunn had returned to Zululand with them, and, aware of the urgency of the situation, had sent messengers of his own on ahead. The political crisis held a bitter twist for Dunn, whose extraordinary adventures had made him one of Cetshwayo's closest confidants.

Dunn's father Robert, a native of Inverness in Scotland, had come to Natal in 1834, and Dunn was born that same year. Those were wild days for the fledgling white community in Natal, and most of them led a rugged lifestyle, hunting, trading and adopting much of the local Zulu culture. Robert Dunn accumulated several hundred African dependants, and his son grew up equally at ease in both worlds, and with a hardy constitution and a taste for adventure. Robert Dunn was trampled to death by an elephant while on a trading expedition in 1847, and John, then seventeen, began to earn a living for himself as a professional hunter. After being cheated of his wages by a transport rider for whom he worked briefly, John Dunn turned his back on colonial society, and secured permission from the Zulu king Mpande to hunt in Zululand. He adopted a Zulu lifestyle, and operated principally in the coastal sector, opposite the Lower Thukela Drift, where he met the Border Agent, Walmsley. In 1856, Zululand was wracked by a terrible civil war, as the Princes Mbuyazi and Cetshwayo struggled to secure recognition as heirs to their father, Mpande's, throne. In late 1856 Mbuyazi gathered his followers together and fled to the Thukela, hoping to persuade the Natal authorities to support him. They would have none of it, but Walmsley gave Dunn permission to intervene in a private capacity. Dunn offered his own services and those of his small band of trained African hunters to Prince Mbuyazi. It proved an unwise decision; when Prince Cetshwayo swept down to attack Mbuyazi on 2 December, Mbuyazi's followers were overwhelmed and slaughtered. Dunn, who had commanded a wing of Mbuyazi's supporters, only just managed to escape by swimming his horse across the flooded Thukela at the Lower Drift.

Dunn's participation on the losing side might have been enough to ruin a lesser man, especially as he had also compromised himself in the eyes of the Natal authorities by getting involved in a purely Zulu dispute. Undaunted, Dunn volunteered to return to Zululand to confront Cetshwayo, to raise the subject of some cattle belonging to white traders, which had been carried off in the confusion following the battle. The meeting was apparently cool at first, but the prince was impressed by Dunn's audacity, and a genuine rapport sprang up between them. Cetshwayo, who was preparing for the day when he succeeded to the throne, asked Dunn to become his adviser. Cetshwayo felt he needed someone who understood the white world and could deal with it on equal terms; furthermore Dunn's trading connections enabled him to procure goods for the prince which bolstered his power-base. Chief among these were firearms, which Dunn imported through Mozambique in the north; ever pragmatic, Dunn reasoned that by arming the heir apparent, he made the political situation in Zululand more stable than it might have been if other factions had been capable of challenging the succession.

Dunn thrived under Cetshwayo's patronage. The prince established him as an *induna* with control over the district north of the Lower Thukela, the

John Dunn, the 'White Chief of Zululand', Chelmsford's principal scout, who confirmed the Zulu presence before Gingindlovu.

Guy Cuthbert Dawnay, hunter and gentleman adventurer, who fought at Gingindlovu as a volunteer officer.

gateway into Zululand. Dunn vetted the whites coming into the country through his territory, and the prince allowed him to trade on his own account and conduct professional shooting parties. Dunn even secured a contract with the Natal authorities to recruit labourers from the Tsonga kingdom around St Lucia bay in the north, and secure them safe passage through Zululand to Natal where cheap workers were in great demand. As Dunn grew rich in cattle, he accumulated followers, and he was soon able to maintain two establishments on the coastal belt, Mangethe and eMoyeni. In each case, Dunn's personal residence was built in a European style, while his retainers lived in Zulu huts around him. Dunn had married at an early age, his first wife being a mixed race girl, Catherine Pierce, who had accompanied him to Zululand. As his fortunes grew, however, and much to Catherine's disgust, Dunn began to take in Zulu wives. In this respect he had adopted Zulu custom utterly; as an important chief, he sought to ally himself to the influential families within the kingdom by marriage.

His acceptance of polygamy made Dunn something of an outcast in the race-conscious settler society of the 1870s, yet visiting British gentlemen found his lifestyle intriguing. It was a curious mixture of the Zulu grandee and the English country gentleman. He imported his furniture and cutlery from England, dressed in tweeds, and led regular shooting parties, usually composed of visiting officers. By 1878 he was approaching middle age, balding slightly, and bearded, and in his manner he was reserved, particularly on the question of his multiple marriages. Lieutenant Main, when he met him, described Dunn simply as a 'dour Scot', while the traveller Bertram Mitford, writing shortly after the Zulu War, gave a rather more complete and appreciative description:

John Dunn is a handsome, well-built man, about five feet eight in height, with a good forehead, regular features, and keen grey eyes; a closely cut iron-grey beard hides the lower half of his bronzed weather-tanned countenance, and a look of determination and shrewdness is discernible in every lineament. So far from affecting native costume, the chief was, if anything, more neatly dressed than the average colonist, in plain tweed suit and wideawake hat. In manner he is quiet and unassuming, and no trace of self-glorification or 'bounce' is there about him.

For Dunn, the prospect of war offered an unwelcome choice between his adopted nation, and that of his birth. He owed everything to his association with Cetshwayo, yet already many Zulus regarded him with suspicion, simply because he was an *mlungu* – a white man. Yet if he fought in support of the Zulus, he would be regarded by Natal as a traitor, and he knew enough of the outside world to guess what the probable outcome of the war would be. Dunn urged Cetshwayo to comply with the ultimatum where possible, but he found himself isolated by the crisis as many of the king's advisers blamed him for not having done more to ward off the confrontation. Privately, the king advised Dunn to 'stand on one side' and be neutral if the crisis broke, and Dunn returned to his homesteads near the Thukela to contemplate his next move.

In the meantime, the British had almost completed their preparations for the invasion, and the five columns were now taking shape on the borders. The troops already stationed at the Lower Drift would form the basis of the newly-designated No. 1 Column, under the command of Colonel Pearson of 'The Buffs'. No. 2 Column, commanded by Durnford and consisting almost entirely of black auxiliaries, was placed on the steep Thukela escarpment, above the Middle Drift of the Thukela, in the wild country fifty miles upstream of Pearson. No. 3 Column, which Chelmsford intended to accompany himself, was situated at Rorke's Drift on the Mzinyathi. Further north, No. 4 Column, commanded by Colonel Evelyn Wood, was to cross the Ncome (Blood) river at Balte Spruit, and finally, Colonel H. Rowlands' No. 5 Column was based at Luneburg. Chelmsford intended No. 3 Column to be his main thrust into the heart of Zulu country, supported by No. 1 Column on the right, and No. 4 on the left. Initially, Chelmsford was unsure how to use Durnford and Rowlands, but he expected them to be flexible, and to support the main columns as the need arose.

At the Lower Drift, a relative calm presided temporarily as the soldiers and sailors marked time until the ultimatum expired. The sailors certainly made themselves at home, and according to Norbury, 'nearly every tent had its little garden, in which radishes, mustard and cress, and other quickly growing vegetables flourished; coops were also erected which were stocked with fowls', and timber was cut to make sentry boxes and sheds. Having completed the work on Fort Pearson, Lieutenant Main then turned his attention to a large flat-bottomed ferry, known as a pont, which was needed to ship the troops across the river. The pont had been designed by Durnford, and it required no little ingenuity to build it according to plan with local materials, but Main accepted the task as a challenge, and was delighted by the practical help offered by the carpenters of the *Active*. The work was not without its excitement:

> Moving about in the bush here was dangerous, on account of the number of big snakes (mambas) which would attack you, a rare action with snakes. John Dunn told me that one had risen up while he was riding and struck at his horse and it was dead in ten minutes. I only saw one mamba. It came out of the bush on the river bank and proceeded to advance on a body of bluejackets who were making up my barrel raft on a dry sandbank, but it was very foolish as, on the dry sand, it could neither advance nor retire, and so they easily killed it and bore it up in triumph to the camp, 9 feet long.

As the pont neared completion, Main took advantage of some free time and, together with three officers of HMS *Active*, decided upon an expedition down river to explore the mouth of the Thukela. Main was a young man, twenty-eight years old, who had served through much of the Cape Frontier War, but who seems to have relished the adventurous life active service in Africa afforded. Climbing aboard one of the rowing boats, the intrepid band pushed off and began their journey of about five miles to the sea. In his journal Main described the difficulties of navigating the river and the abundance of wildlife which was still present along its banks:

We had some difficulty in getting down, as we constantly grounded on sand-banks, and the place was alive with crocodiles, who made it an unpleasant job to get out and push the boat off, as we constantly had to do. At the mouth was a big long sandbank formed since the last freshet and a big sort of lagoon above it some 200 yards or so across. As we approached this we saw 2 or 3 hippopotami slide down into the water and also turtles floating about on the surface, and the dorsal fins of sharks. Very soon Natives began to collect too on the Zulu side, so we were glad to turn tail and to get back to our camp.

Christmas 1878 came and went, and with no sign of a Zulu response to the ultimatum, there was time to indulge in a few festivities. The Naval Brigade from the *Active* enjoyed a Christmas dinner of roast and corned meat, and were fortunate to share in a plum pudding made by Gunner John Carroll of the Royal Marine Artillery. Carroll records that they washed down their meal with 'plenty of english ale' purchased at 1s 6d a quart, made possible by a generous advance in pay of 5s per man by Captain Campbell. Gunner Carroll's plum pudding was highly praised; whether as a testimony to the qualities of the pudding or not, the Marines seem to have had the better of the sailors in the following day's sporting activities. While the sailors enjoyed their beer, the officers sampled with delight the 'cases of champagne and huge plum puddings' sent up by the people of Durban. Probably as a result, the Christmas afternoon's entertainment that followed took on a rather dangerous complexion. Lieutenant Main wrote:

Eventually a wise man suggested that we should spend the afternoon shooting, so we extended the whole camp in skirmishing order with guns at intervals and marched across the country to put up buck. No buck were killed, and none of the skirmishers were shot which was fortunate as whenever a buck was moved the firing became fast and furious regardless of the position of the beaters.

John Dunn crossed the river about this time, and Main, who whiled away some time with him at Smith's Hotel, found him

a very interesting companion, with endless tales of big game and his shooting experiences and [he] used to sit on the verandah of our hut to shoot at crocodiles who lay basking on the opposite side of the river. For my amusement he used to get over a party of young girls (intombis) who danced on the lawn like a lot of children and never seemed to cease laughing. The young Zulu girls have a very fair figure, which they soon lose. Their only garment, strings of beads around the waist, didn't leave much to the imagination, but their innocent gambols made one think of them as jolly children.

On 29 December, Lord Chelmsford rode up to the Lower Drift for the first time. Here he met Dunn to discuss the latter's position, and told him bluntly that he must decide where his allegiance lay. If he opted to stay with Cetshwayo, he would have to be prepared to take the consequences. It was a stark choice, but Dunn, who was nothing if not pragmatic, must have known that it was coming, and seems already to have made his decision; he confided to Main that 'his present object was to withdraw his tribe back to Natal'. It was a busy day for Chelmsford, since two Zulu messengers had arrived seeking clarification of the British intentions. Chelmsford was similarly stern, and told them that he was firm in his intention to cross the border on 11 January if the first part of the ultimatum – the surrender of the individuals named in connection with border transgressions – had not been complied with. According to Norbury, Chelmsford regarded the Zulu embassy as a ploy to gain time, and he reflected that 'in a couple of months' or so their mealies would be ripe, and then they would be secure with regard to food, and did they think him such a fool as to permit them to do this?' Before he left, Chelmsford made a revealing address to the men of the *Active*. According to Gunner Carroll, Chelmsford remarked:

> ... on the pleasure he felt to have us under his command once more, and that he wished to impress on our minds that when we crossed the river into the enemy's country, we should always be on the alert when on outpost and that although the enemy might not attack us for the first, second or even third week we should not abate any of our watchfulness or become careless, for come they assuredly would sooner or later and that we should not be afraid if sometimes opposed by ten or even fifteen times our number for we should remember that they know nothing of discipline.

The bluejackets gave Chelmsford three hearty cheers, but the commander-in-chief and all those under his command were soon to learn a much greater respect for Zulu discipline.

Chelmsford prepared a set of initial orders for each of his column commanders to guide them through the first stage of the campaign. To Colonel Pearson, commanding No. 1 Column, he issued the following details:

> Fort Pearson, which commands the drift of the Lower Tugela, will retain its garrison of Bluejackets. The remainder of the column will cross the river and

camp on the Zulu side under the protection of the guns of the fort. If a further advance of the column is ordered, it should be to the Ekowe Mission Station, or to such point in its neighbourhood where the road to Entumeni branches off; here should be an advanced depot well entrenched. It will be held by a portion of one of the new battalions from England.

These initial orders also marked Lieutenant-Colonel Durnford's No. 2 Column in a supporting role to Pearson. On 31 December, however, Chelmsford amended his orders to Pearson, instructing him to:

> ... advance as rapidly as possible, and occupy Ekowe so as to prevent the buildings being burnt. Having occupied that post, unload all your wagons and send back for supplies. Ekowe should be filled up as quickly as possible with as much commissariat stuff as you can cram into it. Place Ekowe in a state of defence, so as to be safe against any attack that may be made upon it. The men of the *Active* should be placed in it as garrison with such addition of redcoats and natives as you may consider desirable. The remainder should accompany the wagons back to the drift as an escort. The men should be allowed to ride in the wagons, and the return journey should be made if possible in two days ...
> You will probably have to remain some time at Ekowe or rather between that place and Lower Tugela, as your column must not advance from there until the two left columns have made some progress. You will have plenty to do however and the troops, European and native, should be kept hard at work entrenching and escorting supplies or improving roads.

Although it is probably true that Chelmsford had a limited choice of candidates of sufficient rank to command a column, Colonel Charles Knight Pearson, the man who was to be responsible for seeing that these orders were carried out, had all the right credentials. He was a career soldier who had some experience of the country, and who was considered sound, reliable, and not prone to rash decisions. He had been born in 1834. He had joined the 99th Regiment as ensign in 1852 but transferred to the 31st Regiment a year later. In 1855 he purchased his lieutenancy and served in the Crimea with the regiment as adjutant, taking part in the siege and fall of Sebastopol and the storming of the Redan. A year later he purchased his captaincy but towards the end of the year he went on half pay for nine months. Returning to the active list in 1857, Pearson joined 'The Buffs' as a captain, eventually purchasing the rank of major in 1865. Two years later he became lieutenant-colonel, assuming command of 2nd Battalion of 'The Buffs'; in 1872 he became full colonel. On the journey out to South Africa in 1876 the ship carrying the battalion, the *St Lawrence*, ran aground at Paternoster Point, about ninety miles north of Cape Town. The ship was wrecked and the battalion spent two very uncomfortable days exposed to the elements on the shore before they were rescued by HMS

Active. Pearson was commended for his calm handling of this difficult situation. In November 1876 Pearson was appointed Commandant of Natal, a position he held until September 1878. With a Zulu war looming, Pearson retired from 'The Buffs' on half pay to take up his staff post in Lord Chelmsford's invasion plans. His farewell speech to his men, just prior to the invasion, had been tinged with an obvious regret, although circumstances now contrived to place his old regiment under him in the field once more.

The command of the 2nd Battalion 3rd Regiment now rested with Lieutenant-Colonel H. Parnell. The battalion had been marched up to Thring's Post, about twenty miles up river from the Lower Thukela Drift, where they waited for three companies who had been detached in Mauritius, and who landed at Durban on 29 October, to join them and bring them up to full strength. On 3 January they were ordered to move to Fort Pearson. After a hectic morning loading up wagons, the column marched off shortly after noon, advancing about twelve miles on the first day. They were badly delayed by the poor condition of the road, which broke up as soon as a handful of wagons had passed over it, and by the weakness of their transport oxen; this was the first taste of a problem with transport which was to dog the British forces throughout the war. Very few of the wagons made it into camp that night, and since most of the tents were with those still on the road, many of the troops were forced to seek what shelter they could under those wagons that had completed the journey. Only A and F companies were fit to continue their march early next morning, and the remainder of the battalion followed later; everyone had arrived at the Drift by 7.30 in the evening; they were welcomed into the rain-drenched camp by the rousing cheers of the men of HMS *Active.*

There were other new arrivals, too. Earlier that morning HMS *Tenedos* had appeared on the horizon at the mouth of the river, from where she fired two guns as a salute, these shots being returned by the two 12-pounders in Fort Pearson. *Tenedos* had arrived at Durban on 1 January and put ashore three officers and fifty-eight men, who were ordered to march up to the Thukela. They arrived on 6 January and joined the men of the *Active.* With them they carried a large anchor from the ship, to assist with the river crossing arrangements, and a Gatling gun. The Native Contingent, too, arrived at about this time. The 2nd Regiment had been attached to Pearson's column, 1700 men drawn mostly from chiefdoms of the coastal strip between the Thukela and Durban. They were commanded by an officer seconded from 'The Buffs', Major Shapland Graves, who led the 1st Battalion himself; the 2nd Battalion was led by Commandant W.J. Nettleton. The NNC were something of an unknown quantity, but Surgeon Norbury thought they looked rather smart, with their red head-bands and blue blankets.

On the 4th, the same day that 'The Buffs' had arrived, John Dunn had come down to the river with about 2000 of his adherents and 3000 cattle. He had made his decision; he still hoped to avoid taking an active part in the fighting, but he had taken Cetshwayo at his word, and decided to abandon his territory in Zululand. The men of the *Active* had a hard day rowing Dunn's followers over the river as the pont was not yet in working condition and there were only five boats available, of varying degrees of usefulness. The oxen were driven into the water and had to swim across, accompanied by their drivers, and several oxen and three of the drivers were swept away and drowned. As they arrived on the Natal bank, the Border Agent Fynney disarmed them of their spears and guns. The whole incident struck several observers as being like a biblical exodus, and once across the river this new influx of people added to the sprawling camps that were taking shape on the gentle hills of the south bank.

By now, the weather was having a significant effect on Pearson's military preparations. The late 1870s had seen one of the droughts which occasionally affect south-eastern Africa but, ironically, it broke in November 1878, just as Chelmsford began to marshal his troops. The summer – November, December, January – can be uncomfortable enough on the coastal belt at the best of times, with daytime temperatures frequently topping 100°F, and a greasy, breathlessly high level of humidity. The most intense days often give way to thunderstorms of tremendous violence, the sky boiling purple in the afternoon light, and unleashing great spears of lightning. An ordinary downpour can turn the driest of dongas into a raging torrent in a matter of hours, whilst the major rivers carry great surges of water down from the inland heights, bursting the sandbars at their mouth as they escape to the sea. Occasional hailstorms lash the countryside with blocks of ice the size of marbles, and it is a frequent occurrence for livestock left out in them to be battered to death. Unpredictability is the key to summer weather; extremes of heat and rain alternate with pleasantly cool, breezy days, or stifling, grey, overcast days. In all, the weather can make life a misery for men camping out in it, and it now proceeded to do so to Pearson's command. The rain continued to fall throughout the night of the 4th and the following morning, a Sunday, it was so bad that the church parade was abandoned. Not until late afternoon did it begin to ease.

The next morning, the 6th, the weather was fine enough for Captain H. Macgregor, 29th Regiment, one of Pearson's staff, to cross the river to prepare some sketches of the surrounding country. It was noticed from the fort that a group of Zulus were moving towards Macgregor out of his line of sight, and an alarm gun was fired which brought him swiftly back to the Natal bank. This incident was regarded as the first sighting of potentially hostile Zulus, and later that morning more were observed on the distant hills. When, that same day, the *Tenedos* contingent arrived, with their precious anchor, plans were laid to complete the arrangements for crossing the river. A picquet of Naval Brigade men rowed across the fast-flowing river and extended on the Zulu bank to cover the area around the drift. There were no Zulus in sight apart from a few scouts on nearby hills, and the anchor was brought across; laying a steel hawser over the river, the sailors attached one end to the tree under which the ultimatum had been read, and the other to the anchor itself. They then withdrew, and the first attempt was made to test the pont the next day. A strong party of men assembled on both sides of the river, and the pont was attached to the hawser by means of sliding tackle. The system proved extremely efficient, and sixty men of 'The Buffs' in heavy marching order were pulled across the 300 yards of river in four minutes.

The rain returned that evening and continued throughout the next day, cancelling all parades including a flogging. Flogging had been abandoned in the British army as a punishment during peacetime, but it was still employed on active service. On this occasion, two men, Privates Craney, H Company, and Bowman, G Company, 'The Buffs', were found guilty of drunkenness, and they each received twenty five lashes the following day, although one of the regiment's officers, Lieutenant Julius Backhouse, commented that '... it did not affect either of them at all'.

The rain turned the Thukela into a torrent; on the evening of 8 January the river rose ten feet in one hour. The sheer force of the water on the hawser, according to Lieutenant Hamilton of the *Active*: '... wrenched the anchor to which it was secured on the opposite bank out of the ground, and all our work for the last week was destroyed in a few minutes; away went all our hawsers out in the middle of the stream, the anchor being dragged like a feather'.

Luckily the tree on the Natal bank held firm, and with it one end of the hawser. The following day a fatigue party of four companies of 'The Buffs' joined the Naval Brigade on the riverbank, and together, with much effort and encouraged by the drums and fifes of 'The Buffs' band, they hauled the anchor inch by inch through the thick soft sand of the river bed and back on to the bank. By now, the force of the current had abated a little, and another attempt was made to transfer the anchor to the opposite bank. Lieutenant Craigie and three sailors of the *Active* placed it aboard a barrel raft and rowed it across. While still in midstream the hawser slipped and swept both Craigie and Able Seaman Dan Martin into the river. Craigie was dragged under by the current but managed to struggle to the surface where he was picked up by a boat. Despite the efforts of his two comrades on the raft, Leading Seaman Perrin and Ordinary Seaman James, who dived after him, and other searchers in the boats, Martin drowned and his body was never recovered. It was, presumably, washed out to sea, or taken by one of the crocodiles which lurked among the reeds that lined the riverbank. Some months later Perrin and James were awarded the Bronze Medal of the Humane Society for their actions. The force of the water took the raft down and the anchor was lost, too, but the raft was later recovered. Able Seaman Martin was the first of many lives to be lost in the cause of the Anglo-Zulu War.

The following day, 10 January, the weather improved markedly, and a convoy of wagons came in; they had been held up by the bad state of the roads at the hamlet of Stanger. The better weather also allowed another attempt to be made to fix the hawser, and this time the task was successfully completed and the line was made fast on the Zulu bank once more. Some of the officers noted that parties of Zulus on distant hills had once again watched the proceedings. Amongst all this hustle and bustle at the camp, amidst the lowing of cattle and the creaks and groans of heavily laden wagons as they lurched to their assigned places, there was a lull in the proceedings at the camp of 'The Buffs', as the men fell in for the funeral parade of Private Jellie of H Company. Jellie had succumbed to the effects of typhoid which he had contracted – like a number of his comrades – during the battalion's service in Mauritius. Jellie's death was particularly noted by 'The Buffs' because his body was the first since the battalion had embarked in Britain to be buried without a coffin. Private Jellie was their coffin maker.

During the day news came in that Colonel Wood's column in the north had already crossed into Zululand about four days earlier, and made camp at Bemba's Kop on the Ncome river. Wood justified his actions on the grounds that King Cetshwayo had not complied with the first part of the ultimatum. Wood's actions were confirmation, were it needed, that a negotiated settlement was unlikely and that war was only a few hours off. As the troops took to their tents that night there must have been a great many varying emotions – apprehension, elation, nervousness and excitement – all of which must have contrived to cause many a sleepless night, for at midnight Sir Bartle Frere's ultimatum expired. With no word having been received from Cetshwayo, his diplomatically engineered solution to the Confederation problem could be put in motion; the British army was at war with the Zulu king.

CHAPTER 2

'What Do You Red-Jackets Want?'

The expiry of the ultimatum on 11 January was greeted by a fine, hot day, but this auspicious start proved to be something of an anti-climax; No. 1 Column was not yet ready to advance into Zululand. The poor state of the road meant that many of Pearson's transport wagons had not yet arrived at the Drift, and nor, indeed, was the column yet up to strength. It would be a few days yet before Pearson would be able to begin his initial movement towards Eshowe.

The stretch of Zululand that beckoned Pearson from across the Thukela, empty and enticing, was perhaps the easiest terrain to be crossed by the various British column commanders. The high weathered ridges and plunging gorges that characterised the more rugged inland reaches as Zululand dropped from the Drakensberg heights had largely spent themselves by the time they reached the sea. The geography of the coastal strip was distinguished by a jumble of interconnected downland hills, bisected regularly by the broad barriers of mature rivers emptying into the sea. While Pearson sat uncomfortably on the border, waiting for the ultimatum to expire, the rains had probably added as much as 2 feet to the height of the lush carpet of grasses, which frequently grew to waist-height, and sometimes above 6 feet. Long-dried vleis soaked up the moisture, turning hollows into tracts of marsh, and every donga became a potential obstacle, while the surface of the track became painfully vulnerable to the lightest of traffic.

It is twenty-five miles as the crow flies from the Lower Drift to the Eshowe heights, but ten miles longer by the winding track. For two-thirds of the distance the country was open and undulating, shaded here and there by a patch of tangled bush. The last ten miles, however, rose steeply up the heights themselves, flanked here and there by offshoots of the Dlinza forest – whose name translates evocatively as 'The Gravelike Place Of Meditation' – a primordial tangle of ancient green trees wrapped with ropes of creeper and dusted by a ghostly froth of moss. Eshowe itself was clear of the bush, situated on the breezy top of the rolling hills.

The coastal belt was one of the few areas of Zululand of which the outside world had some knowledge. When King Mpande had allowed Christian missionaries to establish posts in his country from the 1850s, he had directed many of them to the coast, and it was this area in which Cetshwayo had settled his white adviser, John Dunn. Dunn knew the area intimately; he had hunted every inch of it, and he regularly allowed safe passage across it, both to Tsonga labourers from the north, and to hunters and traders crossing into Zululand at the Lower Drift. As a result, the region boasted one of the few tracks in Zululand that could be dignified by the term road, and it is a reflection of Dunn's influence in the area that it was known as Dunn's Road.

Yet if the Lower Thukela Drift was the most open door by which Europe was penetrating Zululand, the region had also seen something of the price to be paid. In 1838, when the Boers who had broken away from British rule in the Cape had arrived in Zululand, a particularly bitter war had broken out between them and the Zulu king Dingane. A handful of British settlers established at Durban — then Port Natal — had raised a large army among their African dependants, and had crossed the Thukela to support the Voortrekkers. They had been caught just inside Zululand by a much larger Zulu army, and, after a desperate fight, had been scattered to the four winds. The battle had taken place on the slopes of a hill called 'Ndondakusuka, a few miles upstream of the Lower Drift; the battlefield is clearly visible from the top of Fort Pearson. In 1856 the cataclysmic battle between the Princes Mbuyazi and Cetshwayo had taken place on almost exactly the same spot, and the struggle had raged right down to the Lower Drift itself. It was in this battle that John Dunn had had his first, and most dreadful, experience of action. In January 1879, the stage was set for another bloody tussle over the same ground.

The KwaMondi Mission Station at Eshowe, Pearson's first objective, had been established in 1860 by Bishop Schreuder of the Norwegian Mission Society. The first missions had been established in Zululand almost thirty years before, but had foundered in the aftermath of Dingane's war with the Voortrekkers. King Mpande had allowed them to return largely for his own political reasons; he used them as a means of fostering contact with the white world to counterbalance the growing internal threat posed by his heir, Cetshwayo. The king had carefully considered the siting of each mission, and it is no coincidence that there were no less than eleven in the coastal strip before the war began. The king preferred to keep them together, away from the real centres of Zulu royal power, and in an area both sparsely populated by blacks and already exposed to the white world. The origin of the name Eshowe remains obscure; it was originally pronounced *ee-shaw-way*, leading some analysts to suggest that it was an onomatopoeic word representing the whisper of the wind among the grass along the exposed hill-sides. Less romantically, it has also been suggested that it was a corruption of a Zulu name for a distinctive shrub which thrived in the vicinity. In any case, the Norwegians rendered it Ekowe, pronounced with a guttural slur on the 'k' which made the name recognisably similar to the original Zulu; the British, taking this name from the few maps of Zululand available in Natal, adopted this version of the name, but pronounced it literally.

To the Zulus themselves, the post was known as KwaMondi, after the Christian name of its missionary, Ommund Oftebro.

In fact, Christianity did not thrive in Zululand. The Zulu kings tolerated the missions, but were suspicious of any creed that preached an allegiance to a greater power than their own. In any case, the Zulus had a complex web of spiritual beliefs involving respect to the ancestral spirits, and a dread of witchcraft. With its insistence on monogamy, a concept alien to Zulu society, Christianity had little to offer in competition. Most of the Zulu missions had therefore been settled either by immigrants from Natal, or by social misfits who had alienated themselves from Zulu society. The frustration felt by the missionaries was intense and, although wracked by their internal demonina- tional rivalries, they united in their hostility towards the Zulu Royal House, which they felt was blocking their efforts. In the 1870s, as tension between Natal and Zululand had developed, the missionaries had openly called for armed intervention. Not unnaturally, their relationship with the king became strained as a result, and in 1877 most of them fled the country following a highly publicised attack on a Christian convert, Macumusela Kanyile, who was murdered on the KwaMondi mission land. King Cetshwayo apologised for the incident, which had almost certainly occurred without his consent, but the missionaries were convinced it was the first manifestation of a pogrom. They expected their abandoned property would be destroyed by the Zulus, but in fact it had been left intact. As a result, although neither Chelmsford nor any of his staff had seen the Eshowe mission, it was selected because of its situation along the projected line of advance, since the buildings offered potential storage for the huge quantities of supplies that would inevitably have to be stockpiled.

Preparations for the crossing continued throughout the morning of the 11th, and when, at about 8.00am, a group of Zulus were spied some distance off, it was determined to show them that the British had every intention of fulfilling their threat. Orders were issued to the 12-pounder Armstrong guns positioned on the top of Fort Pearson to fire one round each at the target. The two shells exploded unpleasantly close to two or three of the Zulus, and the whole group withdrew hurriedly from view; No. 1 Column had fired its first shots in anger. About an hour later six Zulus appeared at the river asking to be brought across, but when questioned they could offer no account of their business and were immediately taken prisoner as spies.

Later that day the excitement and anticipation of those at the Drift was boosted by a fresh arrival of troops. Into camp rode five of the mounted Volunteer Corps allocated to the column, and later in the day they were joined by four companies of the 99th Regiment. This was an advance party from one of the two Imperial battalions which had been sent out from Britain in response to Lord Chelmsford's request for reinforcement. Two companies had been left as garrisons on the march up, one at Durban, the other at Stanger. The 99th were a young inexperienced battalion, a product of the Minister of War Cardwell's famous Reforms, part of which had been designed to improve conditions of service for Other Ranks. Instead of serving twelve years on active service, a new recruit now signed on for six years with the Colours and six on reserve. This was a change bitterly criticised by many in the army establishment, on the grounds that it filled the ranks with inexperienced men, and deprived them of the steadying influence of the 'old salts'. In the Zulu War, at least, many who held this view were to feel experience proved them correct. For most of the 99th this was to be their first taste of active service. The new arrivals were played into camp by the band of 'The Buffs', but the experienced officers of 'The Buffs' were not generally impressed by what they saw. Lieutenant Backhouse dismissed them as 'a very young lot of men'.

About a hundred men from the Natal Volunteers were now gathered at the Lower Thukela. The Victoria Mounted Rifles and Stanger Mounted Rifles rode in from Thring's Post, while the Durban Mounted Rifles, Alexandra Mounted Rifles and Natal Hussars arrived from Potspruit, where they had enjoyed a pleasant Christmas. All these mounted units were now placed under the command of Brevet Major Percy Henry Stanley Barrow of the 19th Hussars, who also commanded No. 2 Squadron Mounted Infantry, which had a strength of about 120 men. Barrow was a fine cavalry officer who had purchased a commission as a cornet in the 19th Hussars in 1868, and become a lieutenant in 1870. In January 1875 he became captain and Commandant of the School of Instruction for Auxiliary Cavalry, followed in 1877 by the position of Brigade Major of Cavalry at the Curragh. Sir John French, another distinguished cavalryman, who met Barrow a few years later, described him as 'the finest and best character I ever met. He was small in stature, spare and light. I think he had the reddest head of hair I ever saw on any man. His face was expressive of power and intelligence'. Barrow had volunteered for special service in the Cape, and as a result found himself responsible for all mounted troops assigned to No. 1 Column. The arrival of the Volunteers brought his command up to strength, and that evening orders were issued to cross the river the next morning. That night, however, martial ardour was once again dampened by yet another thunderstorm.

The bugles sounded at 3.30am, almost two hours before dawn, to herald the start of an exhausting day for the Naval Brigade. After a quick breakfast eighty men of the *Active*, under Lieutenant Hamilton and Sub-Lieutenant Fraser, crossed the river in boats at 4.30am and prepared to haul the first company of 'The Buffs' over at 5.00am. The working arrangements on the Natal bank were under the command of Lieutenant Craigie, who had almost drowned a few days earlier, and Midshipman Coker, while the pont itself was supervised by Chief Boatswain Cotter, all of the *Active*. Midshipman Lewis Cadwallader Coker was only eighteen in January, but already had an impressive record of service behind him; he began his naval career at the age of twelve aboard the training-ship *Britannia*, and from the age of fourteen he had been at sea, serving on board the *Invincible*, *Tourmaline* and finally the *Active*. Coker was regarded as a fine and promising officer, and his engaging personality – 'cheery', according to Main – was apparently appreciated by all who knew him. When the advance began he was placed in command of the Naval Brigade's Gatling gun.

Once the leading company of 'The Buffs' were safely ashore they extended to protect the landing point while the pont returned to the Natal bank. Next across were a company of the Natal Native Contingent, who then replaced the Naval Brigade personnel on the hauling line. This in turn freed the bluejackets to return to the five rowing boats that plied to and fro across the river. Fortunately the day had dawned fine and warm after the recent rain, and by 6.30am half 'The Buffs' had crossed along with the Victoria Mounted Rifles. The mounted men spurred half a mile forward to form a line of outposts beyond 'The Buffs', and part of the force moved on a further half mile to act as vedettes. These men were ordered to fire on any group of Zulus that approached and refused to withdraw, but in fact they were not troubled. The Zulus did not oppose the crossing, and the only warriors visible were a few huddled on distant hills, silently watching. Lieutenant Robarts of the Victoria Mounted Rifles, with perhaps a tinge of disappointment, commented, 'Nothing happened, nobody attempted to approach us'. The remaining companies of 'The Buffs' were over by 8.00am followed by their baggage. Gunner Carroll wrote in his diary: 'I was much struck at the baggage necessary for a few thousand men, such as provisions, clothing, blankets, picks, shovels, ammunition etc. With this column alone it will take wagons enough to reach five miles long.'

In the afternoon the *Active* men were ordered to strike and pack their tents away before making the crossing. An administrative mix-up which followed allowed the four companies of the 99th to cross in their place, much to the anger of the exhausted sailors, who then had to re-erect their camp on its previous site. The crossing operation was suspended for the day at 8.30pm, an hour and a half after sundown. It had been a long day, but much had been achieved; encamped on the Zulu bank were eight companies of 'The Buffs', four companies of the 99th Regiment, two Royal Artillery guns, half the Mounted Infantry, the Victoria Mounted Rifles and the Field Hospital. Approximately a thousand men, over a hundred horses and a vast amount of baggage had been moved across the troublesome Thukela with no mishaps. Lieutenant Backhouse of 'The Buffs', who had been on signalling duty at Fort Pearson all day, had a fine view of the activities at the river and noted in his diary, 'I never saw such a scene as the crossing was, a picture should have been taken of it'. One of the Volunteers, less used to such military displays, was also impressed:

You should have been at the Thukela drift the day we crossed into Zululand.

That last night spent on the riverbank! That crowd that came to see us off! The cheers that were raised as we passed! The seeming chaos! all gradually finding its own place. Blue Jackets working the pont, commissariat stores piled up on the banks, strings of wagons continually arriving and departing; cattle lowing, horses neighing, trumpets sounding calls in all directions and men hurrying in obedience to them. The shouting of various commands, the galloping of orderlies, and the tramp of large bodies of men made up a wonderful spectacle.

The emphasis on transport matters in all these accounts was by no means coincidental. Unlike its Zulu counterpart, which could sustain itself in the field by foraging alone, the British army had to carry all its baggage, ammunition, supplies, and even its fodder with it on campaign. A battalion of regular infantry – eight companies of a hundred men apiece, and the band and headquarters establishment – needed at least seventeen wagons to transport its necessities, and often many more. Since the army's transport and supply infrastructure was woefully inadequate, it had been the practice to augment the army's own mule wagons with local ox-drawn transport. These had been purchased or hired from civilian contractors, usually at grossly inflated prices, by young and inexperienced officers who volunteered for the unenviable job of Transport Officer. The South African ox-wagon was an enormous wooden beast, 18 feet long with a maximum rear axle span of 5 feet 10 inches. The rear wheel was over 5 feet in diameter, and the front wheel nearly 4 feet, and the wagon weighed 3000 lb. Fully loaded, it could carry 8000 lb on a good road – Zululand, of course, had no good roads, and the average load during the campaign was 3000 lb – which were protected from the elements by a 'tent', a canvas sheet stretched over a wooden frame. Some wagons were half-tents – with only the back part protected – and others 'buck wagons', with no tents at all. These wagons needed an average of sixteen oxen each to draw them, yoked in pairs, and two men to drive them, both usually Africans; a driver, who sat on the box and directed the oxen with a long whip, and a voorlooper, who walked on foot and led them from the front. On the march an ox wagon and team would take up thirty-two yards, with a recommended interval of eight yards between vehicles, although with bad driving individual wagons often occupied as much as sixty yards of road space. To try to manage the unwieldy convoys, the British appointed a conductor to oversee every ten wagons. Whenever possible wagons were driven five or six abreast to shorten convoys and ease wear on the track. Apart from the cumbersome nature of the vehicle itself, the main disadvantage of the ox wagon was the ox itself; to keep a beast healthy it needed to spend eight hours a day grazing and a further eight hours resting while its digestive system broke down the food intake. That left just eight hours a day for work, and it was advisable to rest the oxen for a further two hours in the middle of the day. As a result, the most that a conductor could hope to cover on a good dry road would be fifteen miles, and in Zululand that expectation was reduced to ten. If the track ran across boggy ground, through streams or dongas, or up a steep hillside, the span of oxen might have to be doubled to keep it moving. In the rain any progress would be reduced to a crawl. Mule wagons were smaller and lighter, with a proportionately smaller carrying load. Eight mules were needed to pull a fully laden wagon, but the disadvantage of the mule wagon was that the mules would only eat fodder, and this had to be carried as part of the load. As a result of these limitations, the practical problems involved with simply keeping the British army in Zululand fed and supplied soon came to dominate all strategic decisions.

Nevertheless, Pearson at last managed to get his baggage across the river, and Commander Campbell was full of praise for the zeal and perseverance of the men from the *Active*, and to his superiors he confided, with a certain inter-service smugness, that he felt if the army had handled the operation it would have taken a week to complete.

While all this activity had been in full swing there were further arrivals at the camp. At about 4.30pm Captain Warren Wynne of No. 2 Company Royal Engineers reported for duty, although it was midnight before all his wagons were in camp. Warren Richard Colvin Wynne, a rather doleful-looking man in his early forties, with a receding hairline and a heavy moustache, and a rather earnest, God-fearing personality, was destined to become Pearson's chief engineer. Wynne had graduated from the army's professional training school for Engineer and Artillery officers, Woolwich Academy, in 1862, and been gazetted into the Engineers as a lieutenant. He had served for five years in Gibraltar before returning to England for an appointment with the Ordnance Survey. With just one day's notice he was appointed to the command of No. 2 Company, RE, in December 1878, and ordered to sail to Natal to join the Zululand expedition. Wynne was an extremely hard-working officer and soon earned the respect of those who, at such short notice, found themselves under his command. His arrival, however, caused a certain awkwardness with Lieutenant Main, who had undertaken Pearson's engineering work so far. 'This was their first taste of Colonial life', recalled Main, 'and they had a lot to learn, but were as keen as mustard. I found they were a little put out at my joining the company ...' To ease the situation, Main was given the responsibility of overseeing the work of the Natal Native Pioneers. These men were formed from the pick of the Native Contingent; unlike their comrades in the NNC infantry battalions they were all armed and uniformed. They were commanded by Captain G.K.E. Beddoes whose knowledge of military engineering, according to Main, 'was but slight'.

The rain returned during the night, a fact cursed by the men when nervous picquets of the 99th sparked off an alert at 3.00am. Orders had been issued that no one was to undress when retiring for the night, so as soon as the bugles sounded every man turned out fully accoutred. There were, however, no Zulus to be seen, although the unpopular picquet steadfastly maintained that they had seen about 300 hundred of the enemy. An attack this early in the campaign could have proved interesting as it appears that no attempt had been made to entrench the rambling new camp, nor even make it defensible.

The men of the *Active* were back on duty at the river by 4.30am on the 13th. The remaining half of the Mounted Infantry were ferried over, followed by more baggage. At 5.30am Wynne was ordered across to the Zulu bank, where Pearson informed him that Commissary General Strickland of the Head-quarters Staff had requested that a storage depot be established and entrenched on the Zulu bank. A small house belonging to a Mr Pearce, about 600 yards from the crossing, was selected as the site, and Wynne promised to have plans ready for approval the next morning.

Because of the alarm in the night, Pearson ordered Barrow out on a reconnaissance with the Mounted Infantry and Victoria Mounted Rifles to see if there were indeed any Zulus in the vicinity. Near the deserted St Andrew's mission a few miles ahead on the track, the patrol surprised a small group of eight men, taking two of them prisoner. One of the prisoners asked the patrol, 'What do you red-jackets want in our country?' Shortly after this encounter, a larger body of between forty and fifty Zulus was spotted, and the mounted men set off in pursuit. Eleven more men were cut off and taken prisoner. Yet another group, as many as forty, were seen in the distance at John Dunn's Mangethe homestead, but it proved impossible to intercept them. Barrow's party reconnoitred a radius of about five miles from the river, but saw no signs of any further bodies of the enemy. When questioned, the prisoners said that they belonged to local homesteads and had been directed by Cetshwayo to remain in the area 'to watch the white people'. Eight of the prisoners were then released, whilst five were taken back to the camp along with eleven outdated, loaded firearms which had also been taken. These men were further questioned in camp, and when one very assured individual was knocked to the ground by his guard during the interrogation, he drew himself up, twirled the end of his moustache and replied menacingly, 'You have taken me but there are plenty more waiting for you over there' as he swept his arm across the distant hills.

At the end of the day, Pearson was no clearer about the whereabouts and intentions of the Zulus than he had been when he crossed the river the day before.

The men of the *Active* finally transferred their camp over to the Zulu bank at about 8.00am on the 13th, leaving about seventy of their crew, with the *Tenedos* men, to garrison Fort Pearson. The 2nd Battalion of the 2nd NNC crossed during the morning, followed at 2.00pm by the Royal Engineers, who left a small party behind to make urgent repairs to the overworked pont. The five boats that had been used in the crossing were rapidly reaching the end of their serviceable life, and a message was sent to the *Active* and *Tenedos* to send up three or four extra boats to replace them. When the last elements of the Natal Volunteers, eighty strong, crossed the river, leaving behind only part of the 1/2nd NNC to help the naval garrison at Fort Pearson, a relative calm settled over the Lower Drift.

As he had promised, Captain Wynne delivered his plans for the new fortified depot before breakfast on 14 January. Colonel Pearson approved them at once. Wynne proposed the erection of a large storage building, 50 feet by 60 feet, big enough to hold all the foodstuffs for No. 1 Column. To protect it he intended to surround it by a hexagonal entrenchment with earth ramparts. The length of the fortification was to be approximately 220 feet, and it was to be 195 feet across at its widest part. Although Pearson approved the plans, the position of the entrenchment was not ideal, since it was overlooked by a long ridge 300 yards away to the north. Wynne, however, was determined to do the best job he could in the short time available to him, and he immediately organised work parties which began digging out the earth and piling it up ready to be formed into ramparts.

As the seemingly endless task of ferrying the wagons and stores over the river continued throughout the day, a sudden thud of gunfire at the river mouth announced that the *Active* and *Tenedos* had returned from a patrol up the Zululand coast. Fort Pearson's guns answered the signal, but when both ships attempted to land parties ashore, they were thwarted by a heavy surf that threatened to dash boats, stores and men unceremoniously against the beach.

To speed up the process of transferring the wagons and stores across the river, landing stages had been improvised on either bank. The Naval Brigade offered to keep the pont operating throughout the night, and this was gratefully accepted, but their good intentions were thwarted by the unpredictable river. A sudden flood came down in the dark and swept away the landing stages. Repairs to these were carried out through the night to ensure work could resume again in the morning. As part of the measures to ease the strain on the ponts, various attempts to swim the oxen over had been tried, generally with little success. The majority had to be taken over by pont, two spans at a time. A notable exception were two or three spans of oxen which the army had bought from John Dunn, and which took to the water with such enthusiasm that it was felt for a moment that they would keep on going until they reached their home at Mangethe!

The build-up of supplies on the Zulu bank encouraged Pearson to hope that he might soon start his advance. Accordingly, on 15 January, he instructed Major Barrow to conduct another reconnaissance with the mounted men, along the planned invasion route and towards the Nyoni river, a distance of nine or ten miles. The country through which the patrol moved was mainly grassy, with undulating hills and little or no cover. Barrow reported back that once again he had observed no large bodies of the enemy in the area. A group of about twenty had appeared in the distance but these had soon melted away as the patrol approached. A little more disconcerting was the fact that Barrow's movements had been announced by a series of beacon fires lit on hill tops as he advanced. The spoils for the day amounted to nine looted cattle and confirmation that, if the weather held, the first movement of the column should be relatively straightforward. Pearson was hopeful that the strong breeze that had blown up during the day would help to dry out the wagon tracks.

The huge tented camp that had sprung up on the Zulu bank was formed in an arc, with the 1st Battalion 2nd NNC on the left, then the Natal Pioneers, Royal Engineers, 'The Buffs', Naval Brigade, Royal Artillery, 99th Regiment and finally the 2nd Battalion 2nd NNC. The tent lines of the mounted men were formed behind the infantry. The final element of Pearson's invasion force marched into camp between 2.30pm and 3.30pm on 15 January; the Headquarters of the 99th, its band and two more companies, who joined the four companies which had arrived a few days earlier.

Lieutenant-Colonel William Welman, newly arrived commanding officer of the 99th, was soon called upon to exert his authority over his men. A party of his regiment were on fatigue duty at the pont, unloading barrels of the rum ration, and moving them up to a store about 200 yards from the river. The sergeant in charge became suspicious when a number of the men came to him and asked to be excused for a few minutes. Following up his suspicions he found a group of his men, out of sight down by the river, sampling the contents of one of the barrels. Welman was alerted to the situation, and collected together a group of officers and other ranks from the camp. He advised Pearson of the situation and requested that no men of other units should be sent down to help, since this would almost certainly lead to a fight, and then set off down to the river. In the meantime the drinking party had crossed over on the pont and continued their binge at Smith's Hotel. Welman's party crossed after them; those who were still able to run tried to escape, but they were all rounded up, while those who were by now incapable were carried back to the camp. Those found guilty of the escapade were sentenced to guard the lines of communication for the duration of the war.

Work parties continued throughout 16 January, ferrying across wagons and oxen, while men of 'The Buffs' and 99th took turns under the supervision of the Royal Engineers to construct the fort on the Zulu bank. This position was to be named Fort Tenedos in honour of the men from that ship who would be left to garrison it. Sadly for her crew the *Tenedos* herself was no longer to be seen riding at anchor at the mouth of the Thukela, since the previous night she had run aground on some unknown rocks, and had seriously damaged her keel and disabled her screw. She had been forced to depart for repairs. Later that day the garrison received the first news of fighting in Zululand. Four days earlier men of

No. 3 Column had attacked the homestead of the important border *induna*, Sihayo kaXongo, opposite Rorke's Drift; this was the same man whose sons had featured in the ultimatum demands. The attack had proved successful and Sihayo's men were dispersed after a short, sharp fight. Chelmsford, who was accompanying No. 3 Column in person, had also had a meeting with Colonel Wood inside Zulu territory to confer on the progress to date. So far, despite Pearson's delay, everything appeared to be going to plan.

By the evening of 16 January, Pearson was at last in a position to plan his first forward movement. During that afternoon he had finally received confirmation that all the wagons, stores, oxen and men that he required for the initial advance were safely across the river. Having dealt with the irritating enquiries of the Press, whom he informed would not be permitted to accompany his advance unless they agreed to submit all their reports to his Staff for censorship, Pearson settled down to consider his final order of march.

Pearson now had an interestingly mixed, but impressive, force at his disposal. A full eight companies of his old regiment, the 2nd Battalion 3rd Regiment 'The Buffs', under Lieutenant-Colonel Parnell; six companies of 99th (Duke of Edinburgh's) Regiment, under Lieutenant-Colonel Welman; two Royal Artillery 7-pounders and a rocket trough from No. 11 Battery, 7th Brigade, commanded by Lieutenant Wilford Lloyd; No. 2 Company Royal Engineers led by Captain W. Wynne; a Naval Brigade with two 7-pounders – the 12-pounders were left at Fort Pearson – a Gatling gun and two 24-pounder rocket tubes under the command of Commander Campbell; a mixed group of Mounted Infantry and Natal Volunteers under Major P. Barrow, and two battalions of the 2nd Regiment Natal Native Contingent commanded by Major Shapland Graves of 'The Buffs'. In addition there was No. 2 Company Natal Native Pioneer Corps, the cream of the NNC.

It is always difficult to assess accurately the strength of an army in the field, since even official accounts seldom tally, and often contain errors and omissions. Nevertheless, by comparing a number of sources, it is possible to obtain a reasonable figure for No. 1 Column. It consisted of 4271 combat troops, made up of approximately 749 'Buffs' and 515 of the 99th Regiment, 26 Royal Artillery, 103 Royal Engineers, 290 Naval Brigade from *Active* and *Tenedos*, 312 mounted men, 2152 NNC, 104 Natal Native Pioneers and 20 members of the Staff and Departments. In addition Pearson had 622 wagon conductors, drivers and voorloopers to control his 384 wagons, 24 carts, 3128 oxen, 116 horses and 121 mules, giving him a total strength of 4893 officers and men.

Although Pearson had 3128 oxen to accompany his force these would only be sufficient to pull 195 of his 384 wagons at any one time. Furthermore, no sooner did the march begin than the number of oxen was reduced as overwork and sickness took their toll. The 121 mules attached to the column were mainly assigned to the hospital wagons, water carts, artillery and engineers. To ensure he could fulfil his orders by seizing the buildings at Eshowe as quickly as possible, therefore, Pearson elected to divide his column into two divisions. The first, a 'flying column' which he would command, was to proceed as fast as possible to the deserted mission, taking with it only fifty wagons. The second division was to follow twenty-four hours later, under Welman's command, bringing with it eighty wagons of supplies. It was hoped that by this method the track would have a chance to recover from any damage caused by the passage of the First Division. This division was to be the stronger of the two sections, made up of all eight companies of 'The Buffs', the two 7-pounder guns of the Royal Artillery, the Royal Engineers, part of HMS *Active*'s landing party with its guns and rockets, the Mounted Infantry, Natal Hussars, Victoria and Stanger Mounted Rifles, half a company of the Natal Native Pioneers and seven companies of 1st Battalion, 2nd NNC. The Second Division was allocated B and G companies 99th Regiment, the Durban Mounted Rifles, half a company of Natal Native Pioneers and the full ten companies of 2nd Battalion, 2nd NNC. The strength of the weaker Second Division was to be increased after their first day's march by the attachment of three companies of 'The Buffs' from the First Division.

To ensure that the men's spiritual welfare was not neglected, they were accompanied on the march by no less than two clerics. The Reverend Robert Robertson, a heavily bearded Scot of not quite forty, was an Anglican who had been granted permission to establish a mission in Zululand in 1860. Robertson's path in life had been an uphill one; in 1864 his first wife was crushed to death when a wagon overturned and upset its load on her – she was buried in the cemetery at KwaMondi. He remarried, but his second wife died after a long illness in 1874. Robertson turned increasingly in on himself, drinking and lovemaking with young Zulu girls on his station. When a visiting missionary had found him drunk in 1876, Robertson had faced dismissal, but given one last chance he rallied, and directed his bitterness against Cetshwayo, whose opposition to Christianity he came to blame for all his woes. In the years running up to the war, Robertson had campaigned shamelessly for British intervention. His mission, KwaMagwaza, was a few miles north of Eshowe, and he knew well the area through which Pearson's column would advance. Pearson also came to rely on him for advice on Zulu customs and politics, and one of his officers significantly referred to Robertson as the column's unofficial political agent. Representing the Roman Catholic faith was one Father Walsh, who had served as a military chaplain in the Ninth Cape Frontier War; Walsh was described by one officer as '. . . a big, raw-boned, Irish priest, with a fund of droll stories, the courage of a lion, the tenderness of a woman, and a hearty laugh that was worth its weight in rifles'.

One company of the 99th and the landing party from HMS *Tenedos* were to remain in camp on the Zulu side of the river and garrison the new fort, while the remaining detachment of HMS *Active*, about sixty-five strong, would garrison Fort Pearson. The other three companies of the 99th, C, E and H, under Brevet Lieutenant Colonel Ely, were to remain temporarily at the drift with the Alexandra Mounted Rifles, to await the next convoy of supplies which needed escorting up. Also left at the drift were three companies of 1st Battalion, 2nd NNC who were required to transfer the accumulated stores into the new depot, Fort Tenedos, which was still taking shape.

The work on the fort had taken longer than expected due to the discovery of a layer of rock about 4 feet down during the excavation of the ditch. Captain Wynne, who was required to march with the First Division, left instructions for the completion of the work with a sergeant and five men of his company who were to remain and supervise the erection of the galvanised iron supply shed.

Having spent 17 January finalising the last details Pearson was delighted that everything was now ready. He issued orders to his officers for the next day, advising them that reveille would be at 3.30am; returning to his tent that night he hoped for a continuation of the fine, warm and breezy weather that had been experienced for the last few days.

CHAPTER 3

The Lightning of Heaven

When the men awoke the next morning, any hopes they might have had for the continuation of the fine weather were dashed for the rain had returned during the night, and a clinging mist hung over the river. After a mug of hot coffee they packed away their soaking tents in the wagons and began to find their positions in the column. In the gloomy pre-dawn, there was some confusion while the wagons took up their allotted places, but by the time the sun began to rise, burning off the mist and heralding a fine day, the column was ready to move. First off were a detachment of mounted men followed by part of the Royal Engineers and the half company of Natal Native Pioneers. Behind these marched two companies of 'The Buffs' with their Colours flying and the band playing, the two Royal Artillery guns, another two companies of 'The Buffs', A and B companies of *Active*'s Naval Brigade with their 24-pounder rocket tubes, followed by the rest of the Royal Engineer company. Behind this advance section came the long line of fifty lumbering ox wagons. The rearguard was formed by three companies 1/2nd NNC, the Naval Brigade Gatling gun under the care of Midshipman Coker, the Royal Marine section, and finally another two companies of 'The Buffs'. As the column gained momentum it stretched out to cover about four miles of road, and to protect the vulnerable flanks guards were posted to either side. Each of these consisted of a mounted detachment, two companies 1/2nd NNC and a company of 'The Buffs'.

Around them, the country seemed deserted, apart from the ruins of a few homesteads destroyed by Barrow's patrols; the Zulus were nowhere in sight. Surgeon Norbury of the *Active* was struck by its beauty: ' . . . I looked down on what appeared like a vast green park, gently undulating, thickly studded with mimosas, a flashing stream winding across it, with the distant glittering sea on the one hand, and the lovely blue headland on the other, some twenty miles off, and towering above the Tugela.'

A short rest was ordered after the column had been marching for an hour and twenty minutes, and when it reached the St Andrew's mission at about 7.50am, some three miles from Fort Tenedos, a halt was made for breakfast. Already it proved necessary to make some road repairs, and progress was delayed. The march recommenced at 11.00am in the direction of the Nyoni river which was reached at about 1.30pm. Then began the long process of dragging the wagons through the river, which, although only a small and muddy stream, had steep banks, so that it was necessary to double-span each wagon to pull it across. At

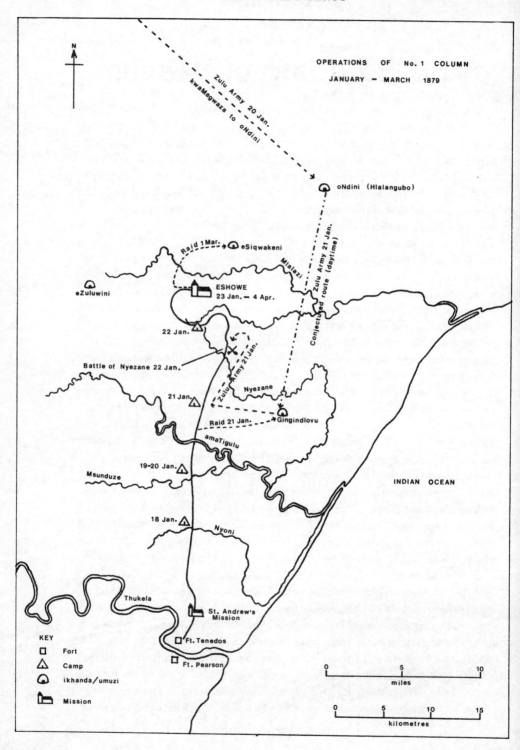

N

OPERATIONS   OF   No. 1   COLUMN

JANUARY — MARCH 1879

Zulu Army 20 Jan.
kwaMagwaza to oNdini

oNdini (Hlalangubo)

Raid 1 Mar.   eSiqwakeni

Mlalazi

eZuluwini

ESHOWE
23 Jan. — 4 Apr.

Conjectured route

Zulu Army 21 Jan. (daytime)

22 Jan.

Battle of Nyezane 22 Jan.

Zulu Army 21 Jan.

Nyezane

21 Jan.

Raid 21 Jan.   Gingindlovu

amaTigulu

19-20 Jan.

INDIAN OCEAN

Msunduze

18 Jan.

Nyoni

Thukela

St. Andrew's
Mission

KEY

☐ Fort

△ Camp

⌂ ikhanda/umuzi

🏠 Mission

Ft. Tenedos

Ft. Pearson

0   5   10
miles

0   5   10   15
kilometres

3.00pm the task was made more miserable by the onset of rain that continued throughout the night. Camp was made about 200 yards beyond the river in the long wet grass that blanketed this part of the country. During the day Barrow had scouted ahead, crossing the mSundusi river and moving on to the ama-Tigulu river, which he reported as being $4\frac{1}{2}$ feet deep. No large groups of Zulus were observed, the country appearing deserted except for a handful of scouts on distant hilltops. The first night in the field was a miserable one for all concerned. Soaked to the skin during the day the soldiers slept in their sodden tents, fully clothed. Norbury noted that the NNC had no more shelter than several parallel lines of branches, which they had cut and fixed in the ground as windbreaks; 'against these their arms were placed, and between them were lines of fires, where they roasted their mealies.' At about 2.00am an NNC picquet raised the alarm, causing everyone to turn out and stand to in the wet grass and cold rain. The picquet insisted that they had seen a group of Zulus, but if so they had melted away again into the darkness.

As day dawned on 19 January Pearson, realising that the weather was turning the road into a quagmire, wisely decided not to push on immediately but to await the arrival of the Second Division. The mud would slow Welman's column to an agonising crawl, and it was unlikely that they would reach the next obstacle – the mSundusi, four miles past the Nyoni – by the end of the day. Pearson therefore decided to make that crossing point the site of the evening's camp. Also, during the morning Pearson had received a report from H.B. Fynney, the Border Agent who had been present at the reading of the ultimatum, which told him that rumours were circulating that Cetshwayo had dispatched a Zulu regiment to attack the column. Considering the weakness of the Second Division, Pearson decided to sit out the morning in the rain at the Nyoni, using his mounted men to scout around for any more information about Zulu movements while the Second Division closed up.

In fact the information that Pearson received was surprisingly accurate and says much for the speed by which the local population could transfer news by word of mouth. Cetshwayo had called the *amabutho* to oNdini after hearing the terms of the ultimatum, and had prepared them for war. He was determined that the war would be waged defensively, since he hoped to gain political advantage in any future negotiations by fighting in defence of his own soil. His regiments would therefore simply have to stop the invading columns. He had insufficient troops to attack all three columns, but decided to direct his main striking arm against Chelmsford's central thrust, and to use smaller forces to harass the flanking columns. Many warriors from various *amabutho* who lived on the coast had therefore mustered at local *amakhanda* – the regimental barracks which served as dissemination points of royal authority – and had been told to remain and hinder the enemy progress in their own area. On 17 January, the day before Pearson began his march, a great Zulu *impi* of about 28,000 warriors had left oNdini, the majority marching west towards No. 3 Column; the following day, however, about 3500 men under Godide kaNdlela, the seventy-year-old chief of the Ntuli clan, were detached from the main body, and turned towards the south. They were to reinforce the local forces in the coastal sector, and try to check Pearson's advance. The force consisted of forty *amaviyo* or companies of the uMxhapho *ibutho*, about 2600 strong and aged in their mid thirties, and fifteen *amaviyo* drawn from the uDlambedlu and izinGulube *amabutho*, a total of about 900 senior men in their mid to late fifties.

Back at the Thukela Welman had his rather thinly defended convoy of eighty wagons ready to move off at 6.00am as planned. Their advance, following the track of the First Division, was a wretched and exhausting one. The mud gripped and pulled at the wagons and the escort was continually obliged to lend a hand freeing those which became bogged down. Pearson's division came into view shortly after 1.00pm on the Nyoni, but if those men who had struggled through the mud and slime all morning thought their exhausting day's work was almost at an end, they were disgusted to see that, in fact, Pearson's section was just about to move off. Welman's men were instructed to cross the Nyoni and advance to the new campsite. Pearson left three companies of 'The Buffs' at the river to bolster Welman's convoy guard, and once again the long task of forcing wagons across the Nyoni began.

Despite the weather the First Division made fairly good progress and reached the mSundusi at about 2.45pm. The heavy rain had had its effect on this river, too, and the mSundusi drift was now about 65 feet wide, and the water almost waist-deep. It took till 6.15pm to get all the wagons and men of Pearson's division across, and camp was established about 300 yards beyond the river. By now, Pearson had only forty-five minutes of daylight left, and the Second Division still had to cross. This proved to be impossible, because although the head of the Second Division had reached the mSundusi, the tail had only just completed its crossing of the Nyoni, and most of the wagons were spread out between the two rivers. Despite the escort's best endeavours, only about thirty of Welman's wagons could be hauled across the mSundusi before nightfall. By then twenty more had reached the river, and the remaining thirty were left to struggle in, unguarded, as best they could. Welman's troops, meanwhile, had been ordered to the new campsite, and only one company of the 99th was left to protect the wagons coming up. Not that those who did cross faced the prospect of a comfortable night; their tents were still in the wagons lagging behind.

The disregard that the British then felt about their Zulu adversaries was most apparent that night. The column was extraordinarily vulnerable, spread out, as darkness fell, over several miles of road, cut in two by a river, and with the troops unevenly distributed; all this, moreover, on a night when intelligence had been received suggesting that a Zulu attack was imminent. Indeed, Barrow's scouts had spotted about fifty Zulus on a distant hilltop watching the evening's proceedings. Lord Chelmsford had been repeatedly advised by Boers experienced in Zulu warfare, and by Natal colonists, to form his wagons into a defensive circle, known as a laager, to prevent a surprise attack; he had, indeed, issued a set of Field Force Regulations which suggested that long-term halts should be laagered. Yet laagers had not been necessary on the Cape Frontier, and even the officers under Chelmsford's immediate command made little serious attempt to implement the procedure. A combination of over-confidence, and the army's inexperience at coping with the very real practical problems posed by wagon transport in South Africa, led to the most elementary precautions being ignored. The Zulus would, within a few days, teach Chelmsford a painful lesson on the folly of such carelessness. Lieutenant Backhouse of 'The Buffs', whose enthusiasm for the campaign was mitigated by the fact that his wife, who had travelled with him as far as Durban, had written to him suggesting she might be pregnant, left a sour impression of his duties about the camp that night: 'Had a lively night of it as I was wet through, and had to patrol in front of the line of sentries during the night, into thick bush, not a wink of sleep.' At least he could console himself that the Zulus did not attack.

Major Barrow had ridden ahead that day to the amaTigulu river to investigate the crossing, and he reported to Pearson that it was so swollen that the drift was impassable. Accordingly, Pearson decided to send forward a work party to prepare a crossing point for the column, and this task devolved on Wynne. He set out at around 8.00am the next morning – the 20th – with half of his company of Engineers, the company of Native Pioneers, two companies of 'The Buffs' and four companies of NNC, and with a detachment from the Natal Volunteers to act as vedettes. Back in camp the troops had a chance to dry their clothes for the first time in forty-eight hours while the rest of the wagons were brought over. The oxen not needed for this task were able to get some urgently needed rest, whilst officers and men alike were able to enjoy the pleasure of a bath in the mSundusi.

About midday there was a sudden scare when a body of black troops were seen approaching the camp, but these turned out to be a group of NNC returning from a patrol, driving before them some oxen that had strayed from the column, and which they had rounded up. More ominously they reported having found some Martini-Henry ammunition in a deserted homestead near by. Later in the day news arrived of the progress of Lord Chelmsford's column; while Pearson's men were delighted to hear how the rest of the war was progressing, it was less reassuring to discover that the general's advance was also delayed by the poor state of the roads. The work party returned to camp from the amaTigulu at about 6.30pm after a hard day's labour. If they were looking forward to a good night's sleep, however, they were to be disappointed for at 10.00pm a picquet of the 99th raised the alarm, and the men rushed to their allotted places. It was, however, another false alarm which the officers of 'The

Buffs' put down to the inexperience of the 99th – it was just 'another 99th scare'.

By 4.30am on 21 January the First Division were formed up and ready to march. It was four miles to the amaTigulu, and the bush on either side of the track became thicker the further they advanced. The Second Division followed immediately in their rear. The head of the column reached the river at 6.45am and found that, with typical contrariness, the water level had dropped sufficiently for the crossing to be made at the original drift. The column spent most of the day hauling the wagons over, and it was only possible to make a limited advance beyond the river. During the morning, Pearson received further information about the Zulu movements which suggested a Zulu force of about 4000 to 5000 warriors strong was concentrating some five miles east of his next proposed campsite at a large *ikhanda* known as KwaGingindlovu. Gingindlovu, which means 'The Swallower of The Elephant', had been established by Cetshwayo in 1856 in honour of his victory over Mbuyazi at 'Ndondakusuka. About midday, Pearson sent a strong detachment, consisting of C and G companies of 'The Buffs', half the Naval Brigade with their two 24-pounder rocket tubes, the Royal Artillery's two 7-pounders, two companies of the NNC and a detachment of mounted men, out towards KwaGingindlovu to test the strength of this rumour. On approaching the *ikhanda*, which was strongly built and surrounded by a palisade of stakes 8 feet high, the British force were disappointed to find the place deserted. Lieutenant Main was with the detachment, and as he rode ahead with two or three other officers, he thought he saw a large porcupine break cover. The officers gave chase, but were taken aback by what they found when they caught up with their quarry:

> We soon ran it down and found, to our surprise, that it was a very old woman, running on all fours . . . who evidently thought her last hour was come. We took her with us, and a 'council of morals' decided that this only female in the column could rest inside or under Mr Robertson's wagon, tho' he got a good deal of chaff accordingly. He kept her as a pet at Ekowe, but she was a vindictive old thing, and had, like the household dog, to be taken out for a run every day.

Robertson was a little more charitable towards his charge and he noted with some interest that she was a half-sister of the famous Mthethwa chief, Dingiswayo, who had been Shaka's patron before the rise of the Zulu kingdom fifty years earlier. 'It was highly amusing,' he wrote, 'to listen to the remarks made upon her: "I wonder how old she is", "I should not like to be as old as that", etc.'

Such a light-hearted conclusion masks the fact that Pearson had once again been over-confident. In an area where the bush grew progressively thicker, a force sent out to discover the presence of an enemy, reported to be up to 5000 men strong, amounted to only about 600 men, over 200 of whom were poorly armed local levies. Had the Zulus indeed been in strength at KwaGingindlovu, the British expedition could have found itself in serious difficulty.

In fact the Zulu force which Pearson was worried about was indeed near by. It had spent the night of the 18th camped near Robertson's deserted mission at KwaMagwaza, and rested the following day. It resumed its march on the 20th, and during the day its numbers were swollen as various local elements joined it. These were local men from a variety of *amabutho*; they totalled about fifty *amaviyo* drawn from the iNsukamngeni, iQwa and uDududu regiments, all men in their mid thirties, and the iNdabakawombe *ibutho*, which seems to have consisted of men in their late fifties. At full strength the *impi* reached close to 6000 warriors. This main body spent the night of the 20th at the old oNdini *ikhanda*, north-east of Eshowe. This homestead had been built by King Mpande in the late 1850s for his son Cetshwayo, but when Cetshwayo became king in 1873 he had built himself a new oNdini in the heart of the kingdom; the old complex still existed, however, and served as an assembly point for the local *amabutho*. It seems likely, however, that part of the advanced guard had pressed on to KwaGingindlovu, and that these were the men whom Pearson's reconnaissance had spotted. They had disappeared by the time the main British expedition had arrived, although a few stragglers had been seen retiring over a hill in the distance.

Having found nothing of interest at the *ikhanda*, the Naval Brigade fired a couple of rockets into the mass of tightly packed thatched huts which immediately burst into flames, and soon spread to the whole complex. With nothing more to be gained, the force turned and retraced its steps, rejoining the main column at the new camp.

The slow advance of the column that day had not just been caused by the river crossing. The bush that was closing in around the track required careful scouting to ensure that it concealed no bodies of the enemy, and about fifteen small homesteads close to the track had been destroyed to deny shelter to any Zulu force which might be tempted to strike at the column's rear. That night's camp was set up about four miles beyond the amaTigulu, on a spot known to the Zulus as kwaSamabela, which was described by one officer as being 'on a rise overlooking a wide and picturesque valley with some beautiful hills lying in the background'.

The British scouting had been successful in that it had denied the bush to their Zulu counterparts, and as a result Godide kaNdlela, the Zulu commander, was not sure of the British column's whereabouts. He had originally intended marching further south towards the Thukela, but after dark on the night of 21 January his force arrived at the smouldering ruins of kwaGingindlovu, and it was immediately apparent that the British were much nearer than he had expected. He pushed on to kwaSamabela, and apparently surrounded Pearson's camp under cover of darkness. The Zulus generally avoided night actions, but preferred to attack 'in the horns of the morning', at that time of day when a beast's horns were first discernible against the dawn. On this occasion, however, Godide was apparently concerned about the difficulties of launching and co-ordinating an attack in unfamiliar terrain at night; and unnerved by the shouting of the British picquets, which convinced him that Pearson was pre-pared for an attack, Godide pulled his men back. He retired to the north, beyond the Nyezane river and into the 'beautiful hills' that lay below Eshowe, to await Pearson's column the next day. There is a story that King Cetshwayo himself had recommended this position to Godide, since he remembered it from the campaign of 1856. If this was an auspicious omen, however, the timing was inappropriate, for the night of the 22/23rd was the night of the new moon, a time when disruptive spiritual forces, known simply as *mnyama* – 'blackness' – were unleashed. In the event, curiously enough, circumstances forced the Zulus to give battle on this day in three separate engagements across the country.

It is not clear whether Pearson's men appreciated the extent of their narrow escape that night. Certainly it seemed to be common knowledge that the Zulus had approached the camp, since a private in 'The Buffs', C.A. Hymas, com-mented perceptively in his journal, ' . . . no attempt was made by the Zulus to attack the camp during the night. I often think they were frightened by the cry of the sentries shouting stand to your arms'. A trooper in the Durban Mounted Rifles, Harry Sparks, recalled years later that

> That night we mounted men had picquet duty. We were posted all round the camp, each man being numbered, and we had to keep in touch with one another by shouting continually to the next man, and reporting whether all was well. The next morning we found from the state of the grass that the Zulus had completely surrounded the camp that night. (Later I learned that they did not attack because, hearing our shouting, they thought that we knew they were there and were waiting for them. If they had rushed the camp they could have blotted out the whole lot of us.)

If this information was passed on to Pearson, however, he did not make much of it, since the advance began the next morning, 22 January, at about 4.00am, with a detachment of mounted men riding out to the front. Along this stretch of the road patches of bush were growing quite close to the road, and Pearson ordered them thoroughly scouted. The men of the First Division had about half an hour to make themselves coffee, to warm themselves in the pre-dawn chill, before the column began to move forward at 4.30. The track was in poor condition, and the Engineers were called on three times during the four-mile march to the Nyezane river to repair the path ahead before the column could proceed. The mounted men crossed the Nyezane, and found themselves on a piece of familiar ground. Some of the Volunteers had been part of the escort which had accompanied a party of Natal officials to King Cetshwayo's coronation six years before, and, as Lieutenant Robarts noted, they had passed up the same track then. There was a fairly open flat patch of ground beyond the river, a 'grassy space almost surrounded by straggling bush', according to Robarts, which gave way to a line of hills rising beyond, and Barrow thought the flat area a suitable point for the column to rest. He placed vedettes around the area, and sent a note back to Pearson advising him of his findings. Pearson rode forward to inspect the proposed site. It was not ideal, and Pearson was wary of the bush, but there had been no water other than the river near the track, and the next stage of the march offered the prospect of a stiff climb. Pearson accepted Barrow's judgement, and ordered the column to close up here for a couple of hours to enable the men and oxen to be fed and rested.

The halt represented a marked change to the gently rolling scenery through which the column had advanced so far. Once across the Nyezane, the track took a sharp turn to the left, and began rising up the first of a series of terraces which lay between the river and Eshowe. The track followed the crest of a spur running up the heights, and was flanked on either side by narrow, bush-choked ravines and, beyond them, higher spurs running parallel to the road. To the right the view was dominated by a dome-shaped hill known to the Zulus as Wombane. A third of the way up the central spur was a small grassy knoll, lying to the right of the track. The sloping ground between the foot of the spurs and the river, where the column was due to halt, was obscured by tall reeds and thick grass.

While the mounted men awaited the arrival of the main column, those Volunteers not required to act as vedettes, the Victoria and Stanger Mounted Rifles, were given permission to fall out and take their breakfast, which consisted of biscuit and tinned beef. Some decided to enjoy the pleasures of a bath in one of the small streams that ran down from the heights. In the meantime the first wagons had begun to arrive at the appointed halt. Major Barrow was in deep discussion with two Volunteer officers, assessing the track ahead, when a vedette rode in with a report that a small party of Zulus had been observed lurking in the hills ahead. The time was just about 8.00am. When Colonel Pearson received this information, he issued orders to the native contingent to advance and drive the Zulus off. Under the personal command of Captain Fitzroy Hart, 31st Regiment, who was Staff Officer to Major Graves and the son of the founder of 'Hart's Army List', a company of 1st Battalion, 2nd NNC began to push up the centre spur.

As the NNC began their climb, the Zulu party – a small group of scouts – appeared briefly on the skyline, melted away into the bush, then reappeared suddenly on the lower slope of Wombane. Undaunted, Hart's men left the track and descended to their right into the valley, before they, too, emerged on

Wombane. Here they paused for a few moments while Hart formed them into some sort of order, and then the command was given to advance uphill, towards the Zulu position. The levies, with their acute hearing and knowledge of Zulu tactics, apparently heard a slight buzzing sound in the grass ahead, an excited hiss or the murmur of concealed men, and they began to suspect a trap. But when they tried to tell their officers and NCOs, they found that none of the whites could understand them, or was prepared to listen. Within a few seconds, however, the position became crystal clear. Suddenly from the long grass ahead there was a shout of 'uSuthu!', the Zulu war-cry, and in front of the NNC appeared not a handful of scouts, but several hundred fully armed warriors. The Zulus fired a volley, then threw down their firearms and rushed forward with their stabbing spears drawn back. H.L. Hall, a civilian wagon conductor with the column, recalled years later that he heard it said that one of the NNC's white officers drew his sword, brandished it in the air and shouted 'Baleka!, thinking it meant 'Charge!' He was not far wrong, but his imperfect under-standing of Zulu cost him his life: 'baleka' means 'run'. The NNC needed no further urging, and fled back down the slope and into the slender cover afforded by the bush at the bottom of the valley.

Some of the European officers and NCOs, stunned by the sudden desertion of their men, rashly tried to hold their ground. They fired a few confused shots before the rushing tide of Zulus overwhelmed them. One of them, Lieutenant J.L. Raines, who had lived in South Africa for two or three years and had recently returned from the goldfields, was shot dead with a bullet through his forehead. With him fell Sergeant Emil Unger, a native of Switzerland who had left his job in the Durban police to enrol in the NNC, Corporal Wilhelm Lieper, Corporal Edward Miller, Corporal Carl Goesch, and three unnamed levies. Quite where Hart himself was at this point is not clear; no one noticed him again until the battle later reached its climax, but presumably he had beaten a hasty retreat. As the Zulus passed over the fallen men, snatching up their Martini-Henry rifles, they stabbed the bodies time and time again. This was a ritual known as *hlomula*, which had its origins in the hunt; when a particularly dangerous animal was killed, all the men in the hunt were entitled to stab the carcass as proof of their participation. It was a macabre gesture of respect towards a fallen foe, though the British were appalled by it. A volunteer in the Stanger Mounted Rifles who later saw the corpses described Lieutenant Raines as being, ' ... so riddled with assegai wounds that it would have been impossible to place your hand anywhere on his body without covering one'.

Nearer the river, the Volunteers were still enjoying their unexpected bath when the first shot sounded, rolling down the hills and echoing from the valleys. Everyone froze. A split second later a rough volley burst out on the hills above and in an instant the men were scrambling for their clothes and horses. As they fell in, a spent bullet struck Trooper Howard of the Stanger Mounted

Rifles in the leg, causing him much pain. Riding back to the track, the Volunteers reached the foot of the hills, where the first wagons were beginning to park, and halted. The Mounted Infantry and Natal Hussars, who had been operating as vedettes, were already in position, dismounted to the right of the path. The rest of the Volunteers were ordered to dismount and form to the left of the track, with their backs to the Mounted Infantry and Hussars who then advanced about fifty yards and opened fire. Their targets were a mass of Zulus who had abandoned their concealed positions, and who were now pouring down from the crest of Wombane. The Victoria and Stanger men then advanced in skirmish order to the left of the track, moving forward to a small rise which gave them a clearer view of the action developing behind them and to their right. From here they could see a disorganised group of black men running towards them, up out of the ravine, and they opened fire before they realised that this was, in fact, the remnant of Hart's party, fleeing the ambush on Wombane. It is not reported whether any members of the NNC were killed in this incident, but it must have been galling for them nonetheless, caught in a crossfire with their enemies behind them, and their friends shooting at them in front. The Volunteers directed their attentions instead to their front, and with good cause, since bodies of Zulus were now appearing on the crest of the spur directly up the road. A member of the Stanger Mounted rifles who was with this group described the anxious moments before the order was given to open fire:

> ... we were not long left in doubt as to where the enemy was, for, looking a little further ahead, every hillside was swarming with them. Down they came, rushing on to us, and defiling as to surround us, disappearing into the bushy ravines below, soon to be seen swarming over the next ridge nearer to us, and preparing to rush down it and close with us. There seemed to be no end of them and exclamations such as 'By Jove! look at them over yonder!', 'Good Heavens! look at them over there!' were heard on every side. It was the lull before the storm, for there was not a shot being fired.

Surgeon Norbury was on the track near the river, discussing arrangements for the halt with a fellow officer when the attack began. Both men were on horseback, which gave them a dangerous vantage-point from which to observe the Zulu attack developing from Wombane:

> As we were conspicuous objects, from being on horseback, we were evidently specially aimed at, bullets whistling by us as we thought in very close proximity. I looked round and saw the Zulus on our right, running like deer, in a long semicircle; this was the [left] horn of their army, trying to surround the first part of the column and cut the line of wagons.

BATTLE OF NYEZANE   Phase One

ZULU ARMY

. 896   650

umuzi

WOMBANE

. 876

Initial contact

650

450

450

Nyezane

stream

stream

E

A

L   C

B

D

F
G
H
I
J
K

Y

651

L

I

1st DIVISION OF
No. 1 COLUMN

A

M   A

N

A

A

O
P
Q
R
A
A

450

450

Heights in feet   Contour interval 100 feet

	0	200	400	600
			yards	
	0	200	400	600
			metres	

Key   A: Company – NNC
       B: Victoria M.R. & Stanger M.R.
       C: Natal Hussars
       D: Mounted Infantry
       E: Vedettes
       F: Company – 'The Buffs' (Jackson)
       G: Company – 'The Buffs' (Martin)
       H: Royal Artillery – two 7-pdrs
       I: A Company – HMS *Active*

       J: B Company – HMS *Active*
       K: Half company – Natal Native Pioneers
       L: Company – Royal Engineers
       M: Company – 'The Buffs' (Harrison)
       N: Company – 'The Buffs' (Wyld)
       O: Royal Marines
       P: Gatling gun
       Q: Company – 'The Buffs' (Forster)
       R: Company – 'The Buffs'

It was immediately clear that a major Zulu attack was developing. In fact, Godide's army had been lying in wait behind the crest of Wombane, presumably hoping to spring the trap as the column struggled up the hill. The NNC had blundered into the concealed Zulu advance guard, and as soon as the firing began the main body advanced rapidly from behind the hill. Pearson was now in a very vulnerable position, since an attack on the march was a circumstance every British commander dreaded. Lord Chelmsford's standing orders specified that, given the choice, his officers should fight with their infantry in extended order, with guns in the centre of the line, and the NNC on either flank. This was a tactic that had been tested on the Cape Frontier, when Chelmsford had achieved his best results by simply lining his men up and blasting away; the amaXhosa had seldom been able to withstand the devastating effect of British firepower. It was to prove a most inappropriate tactic for the Zulu War – indeed, the standing order seems to have been discreetly forgotten in the light of subsequent events – but it is possible that Pearson had it in mind as he struggled to deploy his troops in the face of the Zulu rush.

As soon as the firing had begun, Pearson ordered the Naval Brigade, Lieutenant Lloyd's two Royal Artillery pieces and 'The Buffs' companies under Captain Jackson and Lieutenant Martin, who had arrived with the head of the column, to take up a position on the knoll just to the right of the track. The knoll, although overlooked, was centrally placed and offered an excellent view of the Zulu position. These detachments pushed up the slope at the double, passing between the lines of mounted men and the artillery deployed on the knoll. This movement must have been very rapid, given the speed of the Zulu advance, since the guns were in place – the sailors helping to drag them into position – before the Zulu attack had fully developed. The Zulu left was clearly visible rushing down the slopes of Wombane, and it soon became apparent that the Zulus were adopting their usual encircling attack formation, *izimpondo zankomo*, 'the horns of the beast'; yet the Zulu centre and right were only just coming into view. Lloyd's guns opened fire on the left horn, showering the slopes of Wombane with shrapnel. The two 'Buffs' companies shook themselves into line and also began to fire at the Zulus on Wombane. They were joined by a third company under Captain Forster which had doubled up from the rear of the column, and which formed up below the knoll facing Wombane. One man of 'The Buffs', Lance Corporal Taylor, was so keen not to miss the action that, although sick, he left his bed in a hospital wagon to join his colleagues in the line.

As they reached the foot of Wombane, many of the Zulus on the left horn sought out the cover afforded by the bush that filled the bottom of the ravine. Masked from the British fire, they skirmished swiftly forward, heading towards the wagons that were still stretched out on the track nearer the river. Some of them got to within 100 yards of the Mounted Infantry and Natal Hussars, who had great difficulty picking out their targets in the thick vegetation. The British were much impressed with the Zulu skill at skirmishing, described by Colour Sergeant Burnett of the 99th: 'They came on with an utter disregard of danger. The men that fired did not load the guns. They would fire and run into the bush, and have fresh guns loaded for them, and out again.'

Although the Zulus kept up a heavy fire, much of it flew over the heads of Pearson's men. Lieutenant Knight of 'The Buffs' believed this was due to the close range at which much of the firing was carried out. He wrote:

... their want of skill (in firing) may be attributed in a great measure to a misapprehension as to the use of the sights of their rifles. Knowing that when a white man wants to hit an object a long way off he puts up his back sight, they concluded that the effect of so doing is to cause the rifle to shoot harder, and wishing to develop the full powers of their arms at all times, they invariably used their rifles with the back-sight up, a misconception to which many a British soldier owes his life.

Captain Wynne's Engineers had been working hard at the drift when the battle began:

When I got my company together at the Inyezane I was just about to give them a short rest and some water, when suddenly we heard shots in the distance. I at once pushed forward along the road and saw the troops hotly engaged on the hill. The heights seemed swarming with Zulus, who were also showing signs of working round the right flank so as to get at the wagons. I therefore determined to leave the road, and turned off to the right, and having reached a low narrow ridge, where I found the Mounted Infantry posted (on foot), I extended my company in skirmishing order from their (Mounted Infantry) right. We no sooner showed ourselves on the further slope of this ridge than the Zulus, who were concealed in bush 150 to 250 yards off, began firing at us, bullets whizzing close by, right and left. We returned it in good earnest and I selected places of cover behind trunks of trees, etc, for my men.

Up at the knoll, Pearson was directing events. Both the artillery and 'The Buffs' companies were now fully engaged – 'The Buffs' had uncased their Colours, which were being carried by Lieutenants Gordon and Lewis – and they were supported by the Natal Native Pioneers, who had found themselves in this exposed position through being at the head of the column. Lieutenant Main, who was with them, was not impressed by his first sight of the Pioneers in action; they were clearly very anxious, and '... commenced a rapid fire at nothing, and nearly did for me'. Main forced the men to lie down by threatening to shoot them, and there they remained, 'sweating profusely'. Having thus dealt with his charges, Main was asked by Lieutenant Lloyd of the RA to temporarily take charge of one of the guns while he moved the position of the other. It was a testing moment:

> ... I found myself suddenly an active officer of RA. I must say I didn't like the look of things – Nothing seemed to stop the Zulus. They slithered through the long grass and although they suffered severely, they came nearer, and got nearer. I saw the RE sergt. who had to be left in charge of our wagons in the column come sneaking up. He had (rightly!) deserted his charge, but I took away his rifle and 24 rounds and felt happier at once. Lloyd came along and I gave him back his gun which was splattered with bullets, though with no casualties. I went down over the side of the hill and there I found two old soldiers of the Buffs (officers' servants I think), one of whom, I remember, was firing away and smoking a short black pipe ...
>
> I took charge of this small party and agreed with them that we should combine in firing only at distinct figures, and then all at the same one. As the Zulus were now not 200 yards away I feel sure we did much damage, as I fired away my 24 rounds and at that range one could not well miss one's target. Some of the Zulus got within 100 yards of our position, but could not get home ...

While the battle was raging on the slopes, the remainder of the column was still crossing the Nyezane, and as the wagons came up they were parked on the flat to the left of the road. This shortened the length of the column considerably, freeing some of the troops who had been guarding it, and Pearson sent to Captains Harrison and Wyld of 'The Buffs', to order them to deploy to their right, below Wynne's Engineers. The British position was gradually shuffling into an extended line, facing Wombane, with its left flank curled to refuse it to the Zulu centre and right.

At first, Wyld and Harrison were supported by Lieutenant Dowding with the Royal Marines, and Midshipman Coker's Gatling gun. As the Gatling was manoeuvred into position, Coker's driver clumsily broke the limber pole, much to his commander's annoyance, and it had to be hastily repaired. The naval party advanced a few yards into the bush, but could see little enough of the enemy, and decided instead to return to the track and push on up towards the knoll. One company of 'The Buffs' was left to guard the parked wagons of the First Division with some NNC support.

Supports were hurrying up, too, from the rear. Further down the track, Welman, in command of the Second Division, heard the outbreak of firing, and ordered two half companies, one from the 99th and one from 'The Buffs', to double up to the front while he brought on his wagons as quickly as possible. When he reached the rear of the First Division's column, he ordered the remaining one and a half companies of 'The Buffs' and a half company of the

BATTLE OF NYEZANE   Phase Two

896

650

umuzi

WOMBANE
876

650

450

450

stream

Nyezane

stream

E

450

B

A   A   A

R

A

A   A   A

651

P

O

S
T

PART OF
2nd DIVISION

450

U

V

W

F

K   H

G

Q   C

D

L

M

N

O

450

Heights in feet   Contour interval 100 feet

0	200	400	600		

yards

0	200	400	600		

metres

Key

A: Company - NNC
B: Victoria M.R. & Stanger M.R.
C: Natal Hussars
D: Mounted Infantry
E: Vedettes
F: Company - The Buffs' (Jackson)
G: Company - The Buffs' (Martin)
H: Royal Artillery - two 7-pdrs
I: A Company - HMS *Active*
J: B Company - HMS *Active*
K: Half company - Natal Native Pioneers
L: Company - Royal Engineers

M: Company - The Buffs' (Harrison)
N: Company - The Buffs' (Wyld)
O: Royal Marines
P: Gatling gun
Q: Company - The Buffs' (Forster)
R: Company - The Buffs'
S: Half company - The Buffs'
T: Half company - 99th Regt.
U: Company - The Buffs'
V: Half company - The Buffs'
W: Half company - 99th Regt

99th into the bush on the right, although by the time they arrived the fighting was largely over. A company of the 99th, the Durban Mounted Rifles and NNC were left to guard the 2nd Division's wagons.

Back at the knoll the battle had been at its hottest. The infantry and artillery had been keeping up a heavy fire all around the position, forcing the Zulus to seek cover wherever possible. They were, however, fully exposed in the open, and shots from the Zulus on Wombane struck down among them with some effect. Pearson's horse was wounded – it had to be put out of its misery – and one Zulu marksman in particular caused some concern by his steady and accurate firing. He drew the return fire from a number of men, who carefully and deliberately aimed at the base of a tree behind which he was thought to be hiding. A good deal of ammunition was wasted before a chance shot struck the Zulu, who had in fact been hiding up in the branches. Whenever a number of Zulus were seen to concentrate, the artillery and rockets would shower them with shells. The artillery had one 9-pounder rocket trough, but the Naval Brigade had two heavy 24-pounder rocket tubes, commanded by Boatswain Cotter. Rockets were unpredictable at the best of times, since they were little more than a giant firework, with no fins to stabilise them in flight, and no detonator to ensure that the charge exploded on impact. They were acutely vulnerable to cross-winds and obstruction; on the Cape Frontier Main had found himself temporarily in charge of a rocket trough, and the rockets had displayed a disconcerting tendency to explode as they left the apparatus – on one occasion a fragment had severed the ear of the lanyard man. They were terrifying objects in flight, however, spewing out sparks and smoke and giving vent to a nerve-stretching screech. It was widely thought that they would terrify unsophisticated enemies, and the Zulus certainly regarded them with suspicion; they called them 'paraffin', after that combustible material white traders had introduced them to, or, more poetically, 'lightning from heaven'. Whatever they thought of them, however, the Zulus did not allow the rockets to deter their attack in the slightest.

About 300 yards to the left front of the position on the knoll, near the top of the spur, elements from the Zulu 'chest', the centre, had begun to collect in an *umuzi* (homestead). From here they opened a troublesome fire on the knoll, which effectively threatened Pearson in the flank. Cotter directed his rocket section at this, and at the first attempt he sent a rocket straight through the circle of huts, which immediately burst into flames, driving the Zulus out. Coker, meanwhile, had arrived at the knoll at the head of his panting and breathless Gatling crew and their charge, and the gun was brought into action against a body of Zulus forming up on Wombane. The Zulus were in a patch of thick bush, and were firing heavily at the knoll. The Gatling was not a particularly efficient weapon – when it became heated, the wrench of the retractor arm was such that it often tore the ends off soft brass cartridges, leaving the rest fouled in the breech – but when it was working it could spew out rounds at the noisy rate of 300 a minute. Coker directed a minute's burst into the bush opposite, suppressing the Zulu fire, and forcing the surviving warriors out of their cover. Coker's detachment took to their rifles to pick off the individual targets.

About 200 yards to the left of the knoll the men of the Victoria and Stanger Mounted Rifles had been firing at a line of Zulus who had collected at the *umuzi*, and were then trying to deploy into the horn formation, extending towards the spur running parallel to the road on the British left. This was a line of advance that would have carried them straight into the Volunteers. The Zulus here appeared to be less inclined, however, to expose themselves to the full weight of British fire than their comrades on Wombane. Those who did try to press forward found that they had to cross a patch of open ground before they reached the spur, and this drew a heavy fire from the Volunteers. Lieutenant Robarts of the Victoria Mounted Rifles witnessed the moment and noted:

> They were evidently intending to come down upon us. Our men behaved capitally, at first there was little excitement but no sign of fear, in fact, it seemed a pleasant sensation of excitement. They fired steadily, took aim carefully, and in a few minutes they had cleared the ridge of kafirs, who went down over the hill and towards a ravine on our left as fast as they could.

Unfortunately, this movement, too, was blocked, for as they emerged from the ravine the Zulus found themselves within 100 yards of a small party of Natal Hussars – Sergeant Preller and three men – and four Mounted Infantry. These men had been acting as vedettes and had been left in position since the onset of the action. The fire these eight men unleashed killed several Zulus, and forced the others to retire. It was too much for the right horn, who stayed out of sight throughout the rest of the battle.

Opposite the knoll, meanwhile, the Zulus on Wombane at last seemed to be retiring. Many were coming out of the bush on the lower slopes, and retreating back up over the crest and out of sight. Commander Campbell of the Naval Brigade now suggested to Pearson that the Zulus still lingering near the burning *umuzi* at the top of the spur should be driven off. Pearson agreed, and ordered Captain Forster's company of 'The Buffs' to support the move. Campbell ordered half of the *Active*'s B Company to guard the rockets, and left his Marine detachment with the Gatling. The rest of B Company, and the whole of A Company, he formed into skirmish order, and began to advance them up the slope. It was undoubtedly a stirring moment, even if Campbell's idea of 'skirmish order' differed markedly from that understood by Lloyd of the artillery:

The Jack Tars seemed mad for blood, for they charged up the hill in any formation banging away right and left, driving the Zulus before them. The
company of 'The Buffs' did their best to keep up with the sailors, but were not
equal to the occasion, as they had been 'doubled' up from the rear in order to
take part in the attack.

A body of NNC, under Captain Fitzroy Hart, conspicuous by the twisted red
and blue puggeree he wore around his helmet, moved up the hills to the left of
the road in support of the advance.

The attack slowed as it reached the top of the spur, for the Zulus, who were
in a secure position, refused to give way. The sailors were exposed not only to
the fire of the men in front of them, but also from parties of warriors still
lingering on the high ground on either side. Seven men were hit; two of them
were blacks recruited into the navy in West Africa, and known as Kroomen,
and another, Ordinary Seaman Doran, was dangerously wounded in the left
thigh. Another man was temporarily stunned when a bullet passed through his
helmet. Lieutenant Colonel Parnell now came up with Captain Forster's
company of 'The Buffs', and the attack regained its momentum. Commander
Campbell was out in front, and he had been joined by Fitzroy Hart who had
detached himself from his own command to join the fray, supporting Main's
judgement that Hart was 'a brave but somewhat eccentric leader'. The attack
reached a position about 100 yards from the Zulus before it stalled again. Two
members of 'The Buffs' were killed, and two more severely wounded, one of
them, Private Dunne, mortally. Parnell had his horse shot from under him.
Interestingly enough, when the bullet which killed it was later extracted, it was
found to be from a Martini-Henry. Since the likelihood of the Zulus having
many Martinis is extremely slim, the possibility exists that Parnell was unseated
by a stray shot from his own men.

Campbell sent his adjutant, Lieutenant Craigie, back to the knoll to collect
the rest of B Company, and to order Lieutenant Dowding to bring up the Royal
Marines. Before these men could come up, however, Campbell had led his
detachment forward once more, and this time the Zulus collapsed. Lieutenant
Hamilton's A Company reached the Zulus first, and the first man into their
position was Ordinary Seaman Thomas Harding. A prisoner taken in this action
later told Lieutenant Lloyd that the Zulus had considered they were getting the
best of the action until 'those horrible men in the white trousers (the sailors)
rushed up and showered lead on them'. Hart's NNC, advancing on the left and
without their commanding officer, drove the last warriors out of the burning
umuzi.

Campbell's foray broke the Zulu resistance, and the warriors were now
streaming away all across the battlefield, trying to mask themselves from the
British fire by slipping beyond the skyline of Wombane. The Naval Brigade

and the company of 'The Buffs' on the ridge pushed on as soon as the men had regained their breath, clearing the hill ahead and the northern shoulder of Wombane itself. Some of the Zulus here were so exhausted that they threw their shields and weapons aside and simply fled.

Below the hills the Mounted Infantry and Natal Hussars were ordered to advance through the bush, and the Victoria and Stanger Mounted Rifles, who no longer had any Zulus to their front, were wheeled about and sent to join them. The Victoria and Stanger men advanced over the Zulu position, littered with dead and dying men, but by the time they reached their colleagues, the battle was over. It had lasted just an hour and a half, and the Zulus were in full retreat.

For the Zulus it had been a horrendous introduction to the effects of con- centrated firepower. Bodies were lying thick on the ground, some in large groups where a shell had burst among them. Pearson reported, 'The dead were lying about in heaps of seven or eight, and in one place ten bodies were found close together. At another thirty-five were counted in a very small space'. One survivor, Chief Zimema of the uMxhapho *ibutho*, who had been among the men of the left horn, recounted his experiences many years later:

> We were told to advance and, grasping our arms . . . we went forward packed close together like a lot of bees . . . we were still far away from them when the white men began to throw their bullets at us, but we could not shoot at them because our rifles would not shoot so far. . . . When we were near them we opened fire, hitting a number of them. . . . After that they brought out their 'by- and-by' [a Zulu term for artillery] and we heard what we thought was a long pipe coming toward us. As we advanced we had our rifles under our arms and had our assegais in our right hands ready to throw them, but they were not much good for we never got near enough to use them. We never got nearer than 50 paces to the English, and although we tried to climb over our fallen brothers we could not get very far ahead because the white men were firing heavily close to the ground into our front ranks while the 'by-and-by' was firing over our heads into the regiments behind us. . . . The battle was so fierce that we had to wipe the blood and brains of the killed and wounded from our heads, faces, arms, legs and shields after the fighting.

Another survivor of the same regiment, Sihlaha, agreed:

> We fought hard but we could not beat the whites, they shot us down in numbers, in some places our dead and wounded covered the ground, we lost heavily, especially from the small guns [rifles], many of our men were drowned in the Nyezane river, in attempting to cross at a part of the river where it was too deep for any but a swimmer, in the rush made for the river several men were

forced over trees and dongas, and killed that way, the 'Itumlu' [rockets] killed people but the small guns are the worst.

After the battle Lieutenant Main, who escaped injury despite the fact that a bullet had cut the sole of his boot, decided to seek out the Reverend Robertson. Having located the Reverend's wagon drawn up below the hill Main found him unhurt, but disillusioned at the apparently negative effect of nearly twenty years of preaching the Christian gospel:

I found him inside, with a rifle across his knees, reading the Bible, a faint specimen of the Church Militant. He told me that he now considered he had never really made a Zulu a true Christian. His faithful driver (a zealous Convert) he said had just come in, covered with blood and had stated that he found his own brother among the wounded Zulus and so killed him. Scarcely a Christian act!

Robertson himself admitted that the battle had been a sobering experience:

A battle is all very well to read about at a distance; it is another thing to be in one, to hear the bullets whistling past, to see the dead and wounded carried in, and to know that you may, at any moment, be in eternity. There may be those who feel utterly indifferent at such a moment, but I know that on the 22nd of January, at Nyezane, very many did feel the awefulness of the moment, and vowed that if God preserved them they would live more to him than they had done . . .

With the battle now over the Volunteers retraced their steps through the bush back towards the track, and took a closer look at their fallen enemies. One Volunteer recalled that, '. . . men carried up water in their helmets to give the poor wretches a drink, or dragged the maimed and writhing bodies out of the broiling sun into some cooler spot'. Lieutenant Robarts left a graphic description of the scene:

We then had leisure to look at the wounded men, and very pitiful it was to see the poor fellows lying with fearful wounds. They were very quiet, and seemed to bear pain well, no groaning or crying out. We could not do anything for them except give them water to drink. Some of them were very anxious to be taken by us, and to remain and work. Of course it was impossible . . .

The vedettes found a great many dead and wounded up on the ridge – one of them had crawled at least a quarter of a mile with a broken leg. One poor fellow was in an antbear hole about 70 yards from the vedettes in front of them, and they did not see him for a long time until he called out – asking them to find him. He also wanted to be taken but of course it was impossible.

It is a fearful thing to see a wounded man uncared for . . . The excitement is all right enough while it is on – but I do not like to think of those poor fellows left. The rockets scorch whoever they go near – we saw several bodies with burn marks on them.

The compassion and lack of bitterness apparent after Nyezane would not always characterise the fighting in Zululand; after a string of Zulu victories, it all too often gave way to a desire for revenge, often vented on wounded and prisoners alike. The Zulus, of course, took no prisoners, and the bodies of the NNC officers and NCOs presented a terrible and pathetic spectacle: 'One poor fellow, an Englishman, was literally riddled with assegai wounds. The writer of this has a copy of "Sacred songs and solos, sung by Ira D. Sankey," taken from his pocket. It is saturated with his blood, and has been pierced by an assegai in two places.'

There was a good deal of curiosity about the performance of the rockets, whose terrible howl and fiery trail in flight had been noted by most of the troops present. Lieutenant Lloyd, RA, who had the 9-pounder trough under his command, clearly felt a professional disappointment, and wrote:

The rockets, as I expected proved of little value; so much has been said of their moral effect on savages, but, to my mind, the Zulus displayed the utmost contempt for them. The enormous 24-pounder Hale's war rocket fired from tubes by the Naval Brigade seemed to cause as much anxiety to our own men as to the enemy.

Yet the wounds caused by rockets, when they struck home, could be terrible. Norbury noted that on the top of the ridge lay several Zulu corpses 'some of which were terribly burned.' At one of the later Zulu War battles, a warrior on the receiving end commented 'the paraffin that was shot at us made a great noise and burnt natives so badly they couldn't recognise who they were.' Captain W.R. Ludlow, who travelled in Zululand a couple of years later, described one such victim who had survived: 'I remember . . . a man who had been struck by a rocket, which, catching him on the breast, had literally melted the flesh off his chest, then taking a course down his side and leg, had cut a deep furrow down his thigh and calf, making the leg four inches shorter than the other.'

If the Zulus had not been daunted by such weapons, it speaks volumes for their extraordinary courage. Certainly the British troops had been impressed. Colour-Sergeant Burnett of the 99th summed up the mood among Pearson's men when he wrote home to a friend in England: 'I tell you what it is: our "school" at Chatham, over one hot whiskey, used to laugh about these niggers, but I assure you that fighting with them is terribly earnest work, and not child's play.'

For a while, the British toyed with the name Victory Hill to describe the battle. Someone in the camp explained that this was the name by which the Zulus themselves knew Wombane, and suggested that they had won previous battles on the spot. If so, there was a pleasant irony in the name, although in fact there seems to be nothing to substantiate the story. It may have been a mistranslation of the name Wombane itself; 'wombe' is the name for a clash of arms, which in itself is suggestive, but there is no firm evidence that a previous battle had ever taken place there, either during King Shaka's time, or during the more recent Zulu civil war. Perhaps the mysterious expert in the column simply mistook Wombane for 'Ndondakusuka, nearer the Thukela. In any case, the British opted for the name Nyezane, after the river; the Zulus called the battle Wombane.

The battlefield needed tidying. The Native Contingent were ordered to dig a pit for the bodies of the British troops who had been killed. Pearson had lost a total of twelve men killed and twenty wounded. Two of the wounded were to die later at Eshowe. The pit was dug under the shade of a tree by the left of the road and a simple inscription cut into a makeshift wooden cross placed upon it. Some of the Zulus were apparently collected on the slopes of Wombane, but the rest were left where they fell. Calculations of the number of Zulu dead were difficult to make, since their bodies were spread over a wide area and Pearson did not have time to locate them. Many of the wounded had been evacuated by their comrades as they withdrew, and some of those left on the field would have crawled away, only to die some miles away from shock or infection. Pearson's initial estimate of the Zulu loss was 'upwards of 300' but the actual figure was probably much higher. Later official estimates put the dead at over 400 with hundreds more wounded.

A large number of firearms were taken from the Zulu dead, and a contemporary newspaper report suggests the extent to which the gun trade had short-changed its Zulu customers. All of the weapons were obsolete types:

There were all sorts of guns. From Potsdam, from Danzig, Mutzig, and Tulle, from 'Manchester, NH, United States', &c. The majority, however, were Tower muskets. The foreign weapons are very ancient indeed; some of them being manufactured in 1835. As far as I could make out by the inscriptions, the continental weapons were condemned army ones. The sights were most extraordinary contrivances.

'Our fellows found several guns on the field', wrote Robarts. 'I have fitted out Gingwayo [his servant] with an enfield rifle, 6 bullets, a powder horn and caps – so he feels himself every inch a soldier – and is very proud.'

Only one Zulu prisoner was taken, a man of the senior uThulwana *ibutho*, wounded in the leg. He was questioned about the Zulu plans and the com-

position of their forces, but when asked why he fought at all, he answered with
a dignity which impressed Norbury, 'And what would you think of a people
which would desert their king?' His wounds were dressed and he was taken
along with the column.

Despite their losses, the Zulu retreat had for the most part been orderly. A
large number of Zulu civilians from the local homesteads had turned out on
hilltops some way off to watch the fight, and were shocked to see the army
beaten. Large crowds of warriors and civilians drifted away in all directions;
some of them could be seen from the top of the ridge,

> ... to the right and to the left, in one endless file, all making for a certain kraal,
> far in advance, and commanding a view of our column. The dusky warriors
> seemed to be very dignified as they stalked along, one after the other – no
> running or shuffling. They were, however, at very safe distance. Gradually,
> beyond one or two scouts, they all disappeared.

Some at least made an attempt to rally a few miles off. Trooper Harry Sparks
saw them later that day,

> ... collecting about four miles away from where we bivouacked that night, and
> congregated on the top of a flat-topped hill. We saw them scaling up the sides of
> the hill in dense files along different routes, looking for all the world like so many
> black snakes wriggling up to the top. They started shouting, 'ghiering' and
> dancing, and even where we were we fancied we could feel the vibration caused
> by the stamping of their feet.

There were bitter recriminations, afterwards, among the Zulus who had
taken part in the battle. The younger warriors of the uMxhapho *ibutho*, who had
attacked down the Wombane spur, accused the older uDlambedlu and izin-
Gulube *amabutho* of not pressing forward with the right horn. A report reached
the Natal authorities from an informant that 'Cetshwayo was very angry with
Godide, who was commanding the older regiments ... for not taking a more
active part in the fight. It's said that they merely looked on, and took no part at
all'.

The British, in contrast, were very pleased with their performance. In his
official dispatch, Pearson wrote: 'All the commanding officers speak highly of
the behaviour of their men during the engagement, and of the coolness of the
officers and the pains taken by them to control the expenditure of ammunition.
This I can personally vouch for. . . .' There was some debate as to whether the
Native Contingent had performed well or badly in its first engagement, but the
general view, as one eye-witness succinctly put it, was that 'the native contingent were true to their reputation, and behaved badly at first, but well, when

once a good lead was given.' The Natal Volunteers, many of whom had also been in action for the first time, were also pleased with themselves. One anonymous participant declared to the *Natal Mercury* that 'the mounted volunteers kept up the credit of the colony'. 'You may wonder, I dare say,' Robarts wrote to his wife, 'what my feelings were while in action. My only sensation was that of pleasurable excitement.'

When the adrenalin wore off, the men succumbed to thirst and fatigue. Pearson allowed them to rest for two hours on the battlefield, and then ordered them to fall in and resume the march. The sun was now at its hottest, but Pearson was keen to move the column on; he did not want to give the Zulus any reason to think that their attack had checked him in the slightest. He was also aware that some warriors were still lingering in the vicinity, and he wished to be clear of the bush country as soon as possible. The suffocating heat was also beginning to affect the Zulu corpses which lay all around.

The column resumed its march at midday. Progress was still painfully slow as the 130 wagons were dragged up the hill. About four miles further on Pearson had selected the site for that night's bivouac, on a narrow winding ridge-top. The tail of the lumbering convoy did not reach the camping ground until well after dark. Limited space was available on the ridge so the order was given for no tents to be erected. As each element of the column was allocated its position the men eagerly cooked their meals, which for many was the first food they had taken in 24 hours, other than a mug of coffee in camp that morning. The men of the Victoria and Stanger Mounted Rifles, who had started the day earliest of all, as advance guard, had been made rearguard on the last stage from Nyezane and did not eat until 9.00pm. According to Lieutenant Robarts, having finished the meal, 'We laid down with our saddles for pillows, wrapped in a macintosh ... each man was opposite to his horse and to speak for myself I never slept so well and enjoyed a night's rest so much in my life'.

CHAPTER 4

A Garden Spoilt

The next morning, 23 January, the order 'Stand To' was given at 3.00am. This had become standard procedure, to ensure that the men were prepared should the Zulus attempt to launch an early morning attack. At 3.45am reveille would sound, and the men would have time to snatch some coffee and breakfast before the start of another exhausting day. The whole column paraded at 5.00am and began to march off shortly after, with the Durban Mounted Rifles acting as advance guard. Eshowe was only about five miles ahead, but progress was still painfully slow; four times the column was forced to halt while the Engineers repaired the track ahead. The Zulu presence of the evening before had disappeared, and there was no sign of life apart from a few lurking dogs, and a young calf found wandering near the track. Any deserted *imizi* along the line of march were put to the torch. When the column arrived within about two miles of the mission, Pearson and his staff, accompanied by Wynne and a mounted escort, rode ahead to inspect the site. The head of the column lumbered into the deserted mission station at Eshowe at about 10.00am, but it was not until after 3.00pm that the last wagons were dragged, pushed and cursed in. The sight that greeted them came as a surprise to many in the column, and a correspondent serving with the Durban Mounted Rifles wrote of:

> ... the peculiar impression it gave one when we came in view of a church, houses, and gardens containing fruit trees of all descriptions. Fancy in the heart of Zululand, on the day after a battle ... riding through a garden – laid out grounds, containing splendidly grown orange trees, at least ten or twelve years old, peaches, limes, etc, finely grown blue gum trees, clumps of bamboos, granadillas, etc, etc.

Gunner Carroll of the Royal Marine Artillery commented that he '... had no idea of seeing the marks of civilisation so far advanced in this wild country'.

To everyone's delight, the buildings in which so much hope had been placed were still intact. They consisted of a church built of plastered sun-dried bricks with a corrugated iron roof, and three other buildings of similar construction but with thatched roofs. These buildings had provided a home with veranda, a school and a store room/workshop. The mission land, which covered an area of 120 yards by 80 yards, sloped from west to east with the church situated on the higher, western ground. The house was lower down, surrounded by a garden and a fine grove of orange trees. Oftebro had been particularly proud of this orchard, which was considered by some to be one of the finest in South Africa. Before the war began, he had asked Pearson to spare the orange trees, and Pearson had been happy to agree, although circumstances would force him back on his word. Beyond the orange grove ran a bubbling stream, overhung by thick bush. The stream ran in a south-easterly direction and was joined by a smaller one on the south side of the mission. On the far side of the junction, two further houses had been built, while a third stood about 250 yards to the south-west of the mission. Wynne, the senior Engineer, cast a professional eye over the post, and his first impression was not a favourable one. His main concern was that although the mission was on high ground, it was commanded by rises 20 or 30 feet higher between 400 and 1200 yards away. Moreover, about 70 yards west from the mission church the ground fell away into a deep ravine, choked with bush, through which an enemy could approach largely unseen. However, Wynne had little option; he had no building materials with him, and there was a lack of suitable timber growing in the vicinity. The existing buildings would have to serve as stores. Since the wagons would not be available to be used as a defence either – they would be sent back to the Thukela to fetch up more supplies – Wynne would have to make the best of a poor site.

As soon as the column began to arrive the men were allocated positions for their encampments on the ridges that overlooked the ravine, to the north-west and south-west of the church. Some sort of garrison would have to be left to protect the post, but most of them expected to remain in these positions for no more than ten to fourteen days. The Royal Engineers camped on the mission site, and Pearson set up his headquarters in the garden of the mission house. As soon as the tents were erected and the men had eaten, orders were given to start clearing the bush that grew from the ravine adjacent to the camps, to ensure a clear field of fire.

While all this activity had been going on Pearson gave some thought to the safety of Lieutenant Colonel Ely's convoy which was coming up from behind. Ely's escort, which consisted of just three companies – 300 men – of his own regiment, the 99th, and a handful of mounted men from the Alexandra Mounted Rifles, had originally been intended to protect sixty wagons, but at the last minute twenty more wagons had been added, overstretching the escort. The convoy had started up from the Thukela on the 22nd, and Pearson was worried that it was too vulnerable. He sent an order for it to wait at the mSundusi river until reinforcements were sent down from Eshowe to fetch it. To this end Pearson detailed two companies, C and E, of 'The Buffs', two companies of the NNC and ten Mounted Infantrymen to be ready to march to their relief first thing in the morning. Just before retiring for the night, a messenger arrived with a note from Captain Cherry, 32nd Foot, who was commanding the 3rd Battalion of Durnford's 1st Regiment NNC at Kranzkop, further up the Thukela. Cherry had received information that a Zulu force was in Pearson's area, and was preparing to oppose his advance. It was old news to Pearson; he had already defeated the *impi* at Nyezane.

Early the next morning, the force assembled to fetch Ely's convoy marched out of the mission and retraced their steps down the winding road up which they had struggled with so much effort the day before. Pearson did not believe that, after Nyezane, the Zulus would be in a position to launch a major attack, but he was concerned that they might 'be tempted to meddle with our communications'.

At the mission, work continued to improve the site throughout that day. An attempt to burn out the bush proved unsuccessful, so there was no choice but to clear it by hand, a task that became most uncomfortable in the heat of the day. Wynne planned to surround the buildings with an entrenchment, and when the Engineers traced it out, it was found to have a perimeter of 450 yards. This was considered too large for the proposed permanent garrison of 400 men and two artillery pieces, but it was impossible to include all the buildings within a line any smaller. Even then, the position failed to provide a field of fire that reached into the ravine to the west, while the valley of the stream on the north side also remained dead ground. Whereas Pearson had intended to honour his promise to Oftebro, Wynne advised that the risk of the orchard providing cover to an attacking enemy was too great, so the fruit trees, too, fell under the axes of the working parties. Only two, which stood within the line of the Engineers' trace, were spared. Even Wynne admitted that 'it has been heart-breaking to be compelled to make a wilderness of this spot which was so beautiful before.'

While this back-breaking work was continuing, Pearson considered his column's next moves, and also the supporting role of Durnford's No. 2 Column. It had certainly been Lord Chelmsford's intention that as the general advance of his columns progressed, all would be supplied eventually directly from the Thukela/Eshowe line that Pearson was establishing. Following the completion of the entrenched depot at Eshowe, Pearson was to move on to another deserted mission, either St Paul's or KwaMagwaza, both about twenty-five miles away. Pearson wrote to Chelmsford on 24 January – all communications were carried by black messengers – urging him to advance No. 3 Column so that it would be close enough to support Pearson's move through the Mhlatuze valley ahead. He stressed that if this support was not possible he would only be able to advance with small convoys; he could thereby move more quickly, and reduce the risk of an attack on the road, but it would delay his ability to build up the stockpile of supplies necessary to feed the other columns. On the same day, Pearson also wrote to Durnford. The original plan of campaign had called for Durnford's column to cross the Thukela at the Middle Drift once Pearson had established himself at Eshowe, and then move across country to the mission at eNtumeni, about twelve miles west of Eshowe. In light of his experiences Pearson now suggested to Durnford that he should follow the longer but safer route, and bring his NNC battalions from the Middle Drift to the Lower Drift of the Thukela before crossing into Zululand and marching up to his new position. Pearson also suggested to Durnford that he should leave one battalion of the NNC at Thring's Post, between the Middle and Lower Drifts, until he was established at eNtumeni. In fact, unknown to Pearson, Lord Chelmsford had already reassigned Durnford's men to other tasks, and they were no longer supporting his advance; Cherry's 3rd Battalion alone remained near the Middle Drift.

Although he knew virtually nothing of the movements of the other columns, Pearson could feel pleased with his own performance. His advance had been slow, but this had been due entirely to the difficulty of the ground, and at the end of his first full day at Eshowe he could have no complaints. He was in his appointed position, he had fought off a determined attack by the enemy in an exposed position, work on the entrenched depot had begun, and the next wagon convoy was on its way up. If Pearson could rest easily in his bed, however, some of his men were clearly not so relaxed; at 8.30pm a picquet sounded the alarm. The men tumbled from their tents and took up their positions, but there was no sign of the enemy. According to Norbury, a solitary Zulu who had surrendered when the column arrived had been allowed to go; he returned that night, and a sentry had mistaken him for a war-party. The curse of the false alarm continued.

At dawn on 25 January a convoy of forty-eight wagons was assembled and dispatched to the Lower Drift to collect more supplies. Accompanying the convoy were B and H companies of 'The Buffs', B and G companies of the 99th, two companies of the NNC and ten Mounted Infantry, all under the command of Brevet Lieutenant-Colonel C. Coates, 99th Regiment. With these wagons out of the way, work continued on the entrenchment. Some parties began digging out the ditch on the south side, piling up the earth to provide ramparts which the Engineers then shaped. Others were cutting down trees and clearing away more bush and undergrowth. It was a long, hard day.

Coates's convoy travelled for about seven miles before halting for breakfast. Resuming its march, the convoy found itself approaching the battlefield of Nyezane. Lieutenant Backhouse of 'The Buffs' was present with H Company, and wrote in his diary:

> ... there was an awful stench, and the unburied Zulus were something awful to see. On our way to the place, we picked up a wounded Zulu, who had his arm and leg smashed by a shell, poor wretch he had been lying there for three days without food or drink, and was starving, we gave him some biscuits, and took him on the wagons with us; I believe we heard two others calling out in the bush, but they were too far off and we had to leave them to their fate.

The convoy made further contact later when black figures were sighted about a mile off. The escort opened fire but there were no casualties. Backhouse nonchalantly commented, '. . . luckily we did not hit any of them, as they proved to be messengers returning from the Drift'. The convoy pushed on and made camp for the night on the ground it had occupied on 21 January, having advanced about seventeen miles that day with its unladen wagons. Because they were being driven down empty there were no tents for the escort, and the heavy thunderstorm that broke that evening spelt a wretched night for all. At Eshowe that night things were little better; another false alarm meant that no one in No. 1 Column enjoyed a restful night.

Coates's convoy moved off at 9.00am the next morning, but after only a mile it met Ely's convoy on the way up, and was forced to halt by a stream for most of the day to allow it to pass. While the column was halted the condition of the wounded Zulu who had been picked up the day before worsened to such an extent that it was decided to amputate his arm and leg. The operation was carried out but there is no record of whether it was successful or not. During the day, a curious rumour reached Coates's men that Durnford's column had been involved in a battle with the Zulus, and had been defeated.

At Eshowe, meanwhile, work had begun later than usual because it was a Sunday, and a church parade had been held. Fatigue parties were set to work digging out the ditch along the northern side of the entrenchment, while others began adding revetments, made from tree branches formed into hurdles, to secure the earth walls of the southern ditch. During the day a runner had arrived with a message for Pearson from Sir Bartle Frere, the High Commissioner for Southern Africa. The note, hurriedly dispatched from Pietermaritzburg, vaguely informed Pearson that Durnford had been killed and his column of black troops had been defeated by the Zulus, but went on to add that Chelmsford had also been in action and gained a victory over the Zulus. All of this had taken place on 22 January, the same day that Pearson had been attacked at Nyezane. The note gave no hint as to where the action had taken place. This was disturbing, since the last Pearson had heard was that Durnford was stationed at the Middle Drift. If he had been overrun, then the Zulus had presumably driven a wedge on Pearson's left, cutting him off from Chelmsford's column further north. Indeed, the victorious Zulus would probably be in a position to threaten Pearson's own base at the Lower Drift. The news that Chelmsford had somehow been victorious was reassuring, however, despite a confusing series of messages that were then brought into the camp by runner. One was from Chelmsford himself, and had been written at his camp at Isandlwana on 21 January. This merely informed Pearson of the general's intended movements. The next note was from Senior Lieutenant Kingscote of HMS *Tenedos*, who had been left in command at the Lower Drift, and it informed Pearson that an attack had taken place the previous night at Fort

Tenedos. The alarm had been sounded at 9.40pm, and the garrison turned out and opened a heavy fire on an unseen enemy thought to be lurking in the darkness. The 12-pounder guns across the river at Fort Pearson also lobbed several shells into the night. There were no British casualties, and, more significantly, patrols sent out the next morning found no Zulu bodies. It seems that the nervous garrison had over-reacted, since a correspondent to the *Natal Mercury* suggested that the Zulu attack had amounted to '... only a few straggling shots' aimed at the fort.

Whatever the truth of the incident at the Thukela, it was clear that Nos 2 and 3 Columns had all been engaged. Rumours had already reached the men, since Trooper Harry Sparks of the Durban Mounted Rifles had been on picquet duty that morning and claimed to have heard Zulus shouting from one hilltop to another that they had won a victory. Sparks noted, however, that none of his officers appeared to take the news seriously, and indeed Pearson himself saw no reason to be unduly worried about the safety of his own command. He determined to stick to his orders, but that night, at 10.30pm, there was another false alarm at Eshowe, and the men stood to for more than an hour and a half. It seemed that an air of general unease was permeating the camp.

First thing the next morning, 27 January, Pearson passed on the news he had heard the previous evening to his men. The situation as understood by those who heard it, according to Lieutenant Robarts of the Victoria Mounted Rifles, was:

> ... that Colonel Glyn's Column with the General [Chelmsford] have had an encounter with a large force of Zulus on the same day as ours and that they utterly routed them ... there is no doubt that two such reverses as they suffered with this column will tend to discourage the enemy. The news of Colonel Durnford's death is very sad.

The parade over, the men returned to their normal duties. Major Barrow took all the mounted men off to the north on a reconnaissance to the Mlalazi, a stream six miles away, which promised to be the next obstacle when the column moved on again. About forty Zulus were sighted on the hilltops some distance off, but no attempt was made to intercept them. The infantry, sailors and NNC left at Eshowe returned to their digging, revetting and clearing away the remaining bush. The south ditch was almost finished and the revetting of the north ditch was begun during the day. At the south-east corner, between two large gum trees, construction of a stockade, 17 feet high, had begun; this would allow two tiers of musketry to be directed into a valley on the south side. The two small buildings to the east of the entrenchment were blown up, and wagons, lined with tarpaulins, were placed within the growing ramparts. They were filled with water to act as an emergency reserve. However, this practice was soon done away with as the oil in the tarpaulins tainted the water.

Coates's convoy, meanwhile, left the mSundusi about 9.00am, and eventually rolled into camp at Fort Tenedos just after 5.00pm. Here they learned the shocking truth behind the rumours that had reached them the previous day.

Work at Eshowe began as usual the next day, 28 January. At about 8.00am the mounted troops departed on another reconnaissance, westwards towards eNtumeni. Their patrol was interrupted by a message from Pearson, however, to return at once to Eshowe. They arrived back at about noon to find a scene of great confusion and excitement. Pearson had, at last, received a telegram from Lord Chelmsford, brought up to the mission by runner; if it had been intended to clarify the situation, however, it was not a success. It had been sent from Pietermaritzburg on 27 January. Baldly, it ordered Pearson to:

> Consider all my instructions as cancelled and act in whatever manner you think most desirable in the interests of the column under your command. Should you consider the garrison of Ekowe too far advanced to be fed with safety, you can withdraw it.
>
> Hold however, if possible, the post on the Zulu side of Lower Thukela. You must be prepared to have the whole Zulu force down upon you. Do away with tents, and let the men take shelter under the wagons, which will then be in position for defence, and hold so many more supplies.

Pearson immediately called together all his staff and company officers to discuss the situation. The general consensus of opinion was that the Zulus who had defeated Durnford at Middle Drift must have burst through into Natal and attacked civilian settlements, thereby forcing Chelmsford to withdraw his column to check them. With nothing else to go on, Pearson was unsure what to make of the situation, and the meeting became a council of war. He asked all the officers present to give their opinion on whether the column should stay at Eshowe, or withdraw into Natal.

The council of war was an unusual option in Victorian military convention, but it was not without precedent. Hitherto, all of Pearson's actions had been undertaken in accordance with Lord Chelmsford's grand strategic plan. Now, whatever else was clear, it was at least obvious that that plan had been abandoned, and Pearson was anxious to hear what his officers had to say. It was a difficult decision to make; if Pearson withdrew to the Thukela he would lose all the ground that had taken so much time to gain. A withdrawal could be dangerous too, potentially exposing the column to an attack by – as Chelmsford himself put it – 'the whole Zulu force'. That force, furthermore, must presumably be buoyed up by a recent victory and confident of success. Any withdrawal would also have a very negative effect on both the black and white civilian populations of Natal. If, on the other hand, the column stayed in Zululand, it might, for all Pearson knew, be the only British force still inside the country, and it would therefore be equally likely to be attacked. It would, however, tie down a large part of the Zulu army, who would be wary of raiding into Natal with a large enemy force in their rear, and it would demonstrate to King Cetshwayo that the British were not entirely defeated.

Having considered all the arguments put forward by his officers Pearson felt inclined to retreat to the Thukela. He believed that until reinforcements could be sent for from Britain every man would be needed to defend Natal from Zulu raids. Just as the decision appeared final, however, Captain Wynne arrived late at the meeting:

> I found it had been pretty well determined to retreat at once, leaving all [defences] standing. The fort being in a tolerable advanced state, I could not concur with this decision, looking upon such a retreat as hazardous in itself, and the moral effect of it to be greatly deprecated. I therefore was in favour of remaining and strengthening our position to the utmost. It was, however, a question of provisions and ammunition, and about the sufficiency of these holding out for any length of time there was some uncertainty. At this point Colonel Walker, AAG, and Capt. MacGregor, AQMG, came in, and being decidedly of the same opinion as myself, the question was again opened, and after a short discussion it was determined to remain . . .

The decision was finally confirmed when later that day Ely's convoy was observed some seven miles off, bringing with it the fresh supplies the isolated garrison would require if it was to hold the position.

The whole encampment was now galvanised into action, and work began again on the defences with a new urgency. This was the scene that greeted Barrow's mounted men when they returned from their reconnaissance. Pearson promptly told Barrow of the decision to stay but added that it had been decided that both the NNC and Barrow's command were to return at once to the Thukela. There was no room for either within the confines of the entrenchment, and by reducing the garrison in this way the supplies would last much longer. Such was the confusion in the camp that the Volunteers were not permitted to collect their personal belongings, a fact which would be much appreciated by the garrison in the weeks to come. At the last minute Barrow's Staff Officer, Lieutenant Courtenay of the 20th Hussars, offered to carry down letters from the garrison, and several officers hurriedly scribbled notes for home. At 2.15pm the mounted men, leaving only those on the sick list behind, and accompanied by the black auxiliaries, left the mission station to begin their journey back to the Thukela. Barrow passed Colonel Ely about three miles out and, as ordered, informed him of developments and advised him to make all speed to Eshowe, abandoning any wagons that could not keep up the pace. Barrow also handed over a number of spans of oxen, which he had brought down for the purpose, to assist Ely over the last few miles.

At the mission station orders were flying fast. All tents were to be struck, and from now all outside camps would be abandoned, and the men would move into the entrenchment. While work was pushed on to try to complete the trenches that day, it was decided to drive the loaded wagons within the entrenchment. These were to be placed in a line about ten yards behind the parapets all around, to act as traverses to protect the defenders manning the ramparts from enemy fire from the rear. About seventy were disposed of in this way. The remainder were parked on a west/east line roughly across the centre of the entrenchment. By this time a certain nervousness was apparent in the garrison, and many of the wagons were so badly driven in the confusion that much of the earthwork defence was damaged. To ensure some level of all-round protection this damage was temporarily repaired as quickly as possible by using any containers that came to hand: tents, blankets, sacks, provision boxes, even the men's valises, which were filled with earth and piled up to the required height. Gunner Carroll mentioned in his diary that '... everyone was employed during the afternoon in making the fortifications more secure. Officers as well as men handling the pick and shovel, everyone was more aware that his own safety depended on such a course being taken.'

Wynne and the other Engineer officers attempted to supervise the defensive measures but found it virtually impossible to maintain control in the confusion. Orders were given for the church to be prepared for use as a hospital, and made defensible with loopholes driven through the walls about a foot below the eaves, and galleries added for its defenders to stand upon. All the windows were blocked up, but holes were knocked through here and there near ground level, to increase the ventilation. 'The Church tower,' remembered Norbury, 'from which a very extensive general view could be obtained, was used as a "lookout", and one of our signalmen, with his telescope, was stationed therein.' A party of picked-shots from 'The Buffs' was told off to guard the church, under Captain and Paymaster A.W.H. Gelston. Firing platforms were also constructed around the post for the garrison's artillery, four 7-pounders and the Gatling.

Much to everyone's relief, the head of Colonel Ely's convoy arrived at about 6.30pm, although its tail was not in until about midnight. Following Pearson's orders Ely had found it necessary to abandon eight wagons on the road; his oxen were exhausted, and several of the vehicles had been damaged on the way up, and were in need of repairs he had not had time to perform. Seven of the abandoned wagons contained food supplies – flour, biscuit, lime juice, coffee and sugar – and the other forage. By the time the whole of Ely's force had arrived there were an additional seventy-two wagons to find space for. Those that could not fit inside the entrenchment were formed in a large V-shaped laager, with the legs resting against the southern face of the defences. Most of the transport oxen were placed into this laager, while the rest were contained in the ditch.

The concerns and worries of the day continued into the night. Without tents, the men were required to sleep at their posts on the ramparts ready for action at a moment's notice. If the garrison had been jittery at night before, it was even more so now, and that night there was another alarm. Captain Wynne, who had turned in after a long and trying day, was woken again at 11.30pm:

> ... the church tower being on fire, which had been caused by one of the Sappers having endeavoured to smoke out a nest of bees there during the afternoon and left some smouldering straw. Sent two Sappers up and had buckets of water hauled up from inside the church by them. The fire was put out before midnight – no damage of consequence.

Barrow, meanwhile, was back at the Thukela. When he had passed Ely's convoy, he had relieved him of all but five of his mounted escort, the rest joining the retreat. Barrow was only too aware that his men were in a very exposed position, and he pushed them forward as quickly as possible. The NNC, confused by this sudden movement, and feeling abandoned, were unable to keep up, and soon lost their discipline and cohesion. They broke up into small groups, and found their own way back to the border. Barrow's men arrived at the camp at the Lower Drift at about 11.00pm, and bivouacked for the night on the ground outside Fort Tenedos; the disordered NNC arrived throughout the night and next morning. Barrow carried a note from Pearson to be forwarded to Chelmsford which summarised Pearson's plans; its tone was deeply revealing of Pearson's state of mind: 'I trust I am doing right, but I feel responsibility deeply ... We are still in the dark as to what has happened'. That night, Lieutenant Backhouse of 'The Buffs', who had arrived the day before with Coates's convoy, confided the prevailing view to his diary: 'I hope to goodness they won't send the wagons we brought down, up again without more troops coming to join us, for very few of us will see Natal again if we go alone'.

On 29 January, still with no firm news from Natal, Pearson analysed his position. He ordered his officers to provide him with an inventory of all supplies and ammunition, and on the strength of this he initially calculated that he had foodstuffs for about three weeks, although this estimate was later revised upwards. Ammunition was plentiful; he had approximately 1200 rifles in the garrison with 332 rounds for each gun. In addition there were 127,000 rounds of Gatling ammunition, 37 naval rockets (24-pounder shot) and 46 Royal Artillery rockets (9-pounder shell). The four 7-pounder artillery pieces had a total of 200 rounds of shrapnel, 254 common shell, 20 double shell and 33 case shots. Nevertheless, the NNC had left behind a store of black powder, intended for their antiquated firearms, and Lloyd's men put some of it to good effect making spare case-shot using old jam tins; they tested it on dummies set up around the post.

It is difficult to be precise about the exact strength of the garrison, since Pearson himself prepared three separate listings during his stay at Eshowe, which did not always tally. He also generally omitted to include the black wagon drivers and leaders who had remained at the fort. However, by comparing them with figures published in an article in *Blackwood's Magazine* later in 1879 – believed to have been compiled by Captain Pelly Clarke, 103rd Foot, who was serving as Pearson's senior transport officer – it is possible to arrive at a reasonable estimate:

UNIT	OFFICERS	NCOs & MEN
Staff	4	3
Naval Brigade	8	158
11/7 Battery, Royal Artillery	1	25
No. 2 Company RE	4	92
2/3rd Foot 'The Buffs'*	19	590
99th Foot**	11	368***
2nd Squadron Mntd Inf.	1	22
Commissariat Dept. & Transport Dept.	4	9
Army Hospital Corps	5	15
Natal Volunteers****	0	11
Natal Native Pioneers	4 (White)	98 (Black)
Natal Native Contingent	4 (White)	12 (White)
" " "	0	26 (Black)
Wagon Conductors	–	15 (White)
Drivers and Leaders	–	270 (Black)
Servants	–	20 (Black)
TOTAL GARRISON	65	1734
Combat Troops	56	1405
Non-Combat Troops	9	329

*   Six Companies and Regimental Band.
**   Three Companies and Regimental Band.
***   Four of these men later transferred into the Mounted Infantry.
**** Five Alexandra Mounted Rifles, three Durban Mounted Rifles, two Victoria Mounted Rifles, one Natal Hussar.

At about midday on the 29th a large body of Zulus was observed moving past the mission some miles off. As the alarm sounded the men rushed into the entrenchment, badly damaging parts of the rampart as they scrambled all over it. The Zulus, however, seemed oblivious of the garrison, and continued on their way. Once they had gone, Wynne resignedly set men to work repairing the ramparts again.

That night, about ninety slaughter oxen had clambered up out of the ditch and disappeared, to be captured later by the Zulus. The cattle, indeed, were beginning to be a problem since it was difficult to contain them and to provide grazing, and Pearson decided to ease the situation by sending some of them back to the Thukela. He was aware of the danger that they might be captured, but he felt the only other alternative – killing them – was impractical, since the carcasses would have to be buried to prevent them spreading disease, and he could not spare the men. If they were captured, he might at least be able to recapture them at a later date. Therefore during the 30th about 1000 oxen and 28 mules were driven from Eshowe by some of the wagon drivers and leaders. The mules were captured less than a mile from the mission; the Zulus drove off the guard, mounted the mules, and rode them away. One, however, made good its escape and returned to the entrenchment. It was later discovered that the other mules were killed, presumably because the Zulus could not decide what to use them for. The oxen managed to get a little further before some of their drivers, frightened by large numbers of Zulus gathering on the track ahead, turned back and returned with about 500 of the beasts. The other drivers simply disappeared into the bush, and the remaining 500 oxen were lost to the Zulus.

Throughout the afternoon, several large bodies of Zulus were spotted in the distance, forcing Wynne to abandon work on the entrenchments as everyone rushed to man the ramparts. Indeed, the strain under which he had been working was beginning to tell on Wynne; in the oppressive heat he felt ill, and was forced to lie up for most of the day. Even so, he managed to select a spot, west of the post, for a new cattle laager. To add to the general nervousness that night, the men were forced to sleep under the wagons, and there was another inevitable alarm at about 11.30pm. This time a volley was fired into the darkness before order was restored and it was realised that there were no Zulus nearby.

Although still feeling weak, Wynne was back on his feet the next morning, supervising the clearing of the ravine for the cattle laager. He also ordered a gateway to be made in the west face of the entrenchment, and a drain constructed through the east rampart. Work parties were employed to deepen the ditch, which by now fully surrounded the site, and to prevent any further fouling of the central area by the officers' horses arrangements were made for them to be 'stabled' each night in the north-west section of the ditch. The livestock quartered in the ditches at night continued to cause concern, for both cattle and horses sometimes broke loose, and someone would have to venture into the darkness to sort them out. Such forays could easily provoke a false alarm, and Norbury recalled the shouts that announced them: 'Sentry, there's a man gone out to look after the 'orses.' It was nonetheless an uncomfortable task, with a more than average chance of being shot by one's own side, as an anonymous participant recalled: 'I was turned out three times last night to get cattle into the Ditches which had got out. To go sneaking about the country after stray cattle, with revolvers cocked, on a pitch dark night, is not pleasant.'

Life was no more comfortable at the Thukela than at Eshowe. All through their first night at Fort Tenedos, Barrow's men suffered the attentions of clouds of mosquitoes, brought out by the day's hot weather. When dawn broke, the mosquitoes gave way to flies. During the day the mounted men found themselves in the way at Fort Tenedos, and crossed over to the Natal bank. From here communications with the rest of Natal were quite open, and the men, who had left all of their belongings at Eshowe, began to write to friends and family to ask them to send whatever comforts they could. They had no idea of what would become of them, but by this time the news of Durnford's defeat was common knowledge among them. Lieutenant Robarts wrote to his wife with an open-mindedness rare in the British camp: 'A retribution must overtake the Zulus which will destroy them as a nation. However we must not forget that they are fighting fair, and in a just cause, though opposed to us. They are fighting for their own country, as we are indirectly fighting for ours.'

In the early hours of the morning of 31 January, word came to Fort Pearson that the Zulus were crossing the Thukela into Natal upriver in the Thring's Post area. Accordingly all the Volunteer units, except the Durban Mounted Rifles, were ordered upstream to investigate. It proved a false alarm but the Volunteers remained at Thring's Post, and kept open communications between the two points.

The return of the NNC had produced a confused situation at the river. Many of them had decamped immediately to their homes presuming their job was done. Others returned to their families to regale them with stories of their brave deeds, and the rest were just pleased to be out of Zululand. Nevertheless, a few did retain their discipline and awaited orders. Unsure what to do with them, their commander, Major Graves, telegraphed for advice. In reply Graves was informed by Deputy Adjutant and Quartermaster-General W. Bellairs of Chelmsford's staff that the NNC should be given one month's pay, told to keep their blankets, and allowed to disperse in batches. They were also to be made to understand that they would be required to turn out for the defence of Natal if it should prove necessary. Those men who had remained, delighted with this arrangement, assured Graves that they would respond when called, and happily went on their way.

The rains returned on the night of the 31st, and from Thring's Post to Fort Pearson and on to Eshowe, complaints continued. At Thring's Post Captain Arbuthnot, commander of the Alexandra Mounted Rifles, wrote in his diary, 'We had no tents that night and as it looked like rain we took possession of the veranda of the commissariat store and packed in as thick as we could stick.' At the river Lieutenant Backhouse of 'The Buffs' had a miserable time, too; not only was the rain bad, but he had been suffering from diarrhoea for a few days – a common enough problem – and had been forced to venture out into the elements four times during the night. At Eshowe Gunner Carroll was one of the sentries on duty; he wrote, '. . . everyone feeling very miserable having no tents or shelter, but had to remain on their posts on the parapets getting a thorough good drenching'. One sentry, a man of 'The Buffs', unable to suffer the rain any more, abandoned his post and took shelter. For this dereliction of duty he later received fifty lashes.

The rain continued into the early morning of 1 February, and at Eshowe the endless work continued. Wynne ensured that his projects were pursued with the maximum effort by all concerned; as sacks and boxes of stores were unloaded from the wagons and packed into the buildings, the empty containers were returned to the Engineers, filled with earth, and stacked back on to the wagons, which were then used as traverses, internal barricades to prevent cross-fire. The new cattle laager in the ravine was to be constructed in the form of a trapezium, with its longest face parallel with the western face of the entrenchment.

Vedettes watching the approaches to Eshowe observed a number of Zulus during the day, and a few shots were exchanged. The vedettes claimed to have seen several Zulus fall, but it was impossible to confirm this. Lieutenant Lloyd, RA, mentions in his account of his time at Eshowe that in the early days the artillery would occasionally fire a shell when groups of Zulus were spotted in the distance. This invariably proved ineffective, however, because '. . . as soon as they saw the smoke from the gun they would either lie flat down, or, bending themselves nearly double, would run like madmen.'

The lack of medicines at Eshowe had worried Pearson since the beginning. To eke out the limited supplies, he had authorised a search to be made of the private possessions of the Volunteers who had left with Barrow on 28 January. To the garrison's delight, this produced not only a useful range of medicines – Eno's Fruit-Salt, Lamplough's Pyretic Saline and vast quantities of Cockle's Anti-Billious Pills which were recommended in the advertising material of the day to those suffering from bile, liver, headache, heartburn and indigestion – but also an unsuspected quantity of luxury goods.

Even so, despite every effort, disease began to make its mark at Eshowe, and on 1 February Private A. Kingston of 'The Buffs' succumbed to fever and became the first man to die from its effects. Two men had already died at

Eshowe – Sergeant Hydenburg of the NNC and Private Dunne of 'The Buffs', both of who had been mortally wounded at Nyezane, and who had been buried close to the church. It was now felt necessary, however, to create a new cemetery, a spot high on the south side of the ravine, overlooking the site of the new cattle laager. Here the body of Private Kingston was wrapped in flannel and lowered into the ground with full military honours, which included a volley fired as a salute over his grave.

Pearson was also growing more concerned with the lack of information from Natal. He still did not know the true story of the fate that had befallen Durnford, or of the part played in it by Lord Chelmsford, but he knew there were large bodies of Zulus moving freely in his area, and that these were seriously interfering with his communications. As the rain returned again that night he wrote a letter to Chelmsford, hoping the bad weather would enable the runner to pass through to the Drift unobserved. In his letter Pearson updated Chelmsford on his failed attempt to send the cattle down and in desperation added, 'We can obtain no news of you whatever. Our messengers keep coming back and say they cannot get through the Zulus who are now all around us, large bodies often seen at times coming in different directions chiefly towards Natal.'

Having dispatched the letter Pearson issued orders to the commissariat; from now on the men were to be placed on three-quarter rations to preserve supplies. The garrison at Eshowe was under siege.

CHAPTER 5

'We Will Drink Your Coffee Tomorrow!'

The rain that had returned on the evening of 1 February continued throughout the night. As the troops awoke the next morning, the 2nd, and began to go about their duties, the interior of the entrenchment soon turned into a quagmire of slimy, oozing mud. Just as the day's work began two black runners, cold, wet and exhausted, splashed into Eshowe. With them they brought the full story of the disaster that the garrison had hitherto only known as 'Durnford's Defeat'. It was far worse than anyone had suspected: Pearson assembled his officers and they listened to the tale with horror and disbelief. The battle had not occurred on the Middle Drift, since Durnford had been ordered north to support Chelmsford's own Centre Column operating from Rorke's Drift. Chelmsford had split his force, and while he was out on reconnaissance a Zulu army 20,000 strong had swept down and overwhelmed the camp at Isandlwana. Durnford was indeed dead, but most of the casualties were from the 24th Regiment. 'The Buffs' had served with the 24th on the Cape Frontier, and many of the officers in the garrison at Eshowe had friends among them. The report did not list all the names of the fallen officers, and the Eshowe men were left to ponder the fate of their friends. Lieutenant Hamilton of HMS *Active* summed up the feelings of many when he wrote home:

> We all knew the 24th Regt. so well, they were quartered at Cape Town when we first came out here, and we were with them all through the campaign in the Transkei; there is a universal feeling of grief and horror at the loss of so many officers and men, of one of the finest regiments in the army.

Lieutenant Main, RE, pondered his own good fortune as he had originally been assigned to the Centre Column, but had exchanged appointments with Lieutenant Macdowel: Macdowel had been killed. Pearson intended to pass on the news of the disaster to the men at church parade that day, but the weather was so bad that the parade was postponed, and it was not until 3 February that most of the garrison heard the truth of the matter. They reacted to the news with anger and a burning desire to exact revenge.

It is indicative of Pearson's communications difficulties that he had received the full news of Isandlwana only nine days before it reached London. Immediately upon receipt, Pearson wrote a further letter to Chelmsford, asking for the two companies of 'The Buffs' and five companies of the 99th – three currently at the Lower Drift, and two in Stanger – to be sent up to him. Although aware of the difficulty in supplying such a large addition to his garrison, he wanted to bring his infantry battalions as close to full strength as possible. The news had convinced him that it would be a fatal mistake to abandon his post. 'If we retired to the Thukela, we should most likely have all the Zulu army at our backs, and be obliged either to destroy all our ammunition and stores before we left Eshowe, or abandon them on the march if attacked, as in all probability we should be by overwhelming numbers.' Two days later – not a bad response time – Pearson received a reply from the Deputy Adjutant-General advising him that all troops in Natal were required for the defence of the colony, and that in any case it was impossible to send up supplies for so many more men. In response, Pearson wrote again on the 6th asking Chelmsford to send him a supply convoy of twenty wagons as soon as a battalion-sized escort could be found to protect them. He asked that they bring mainly food, but also some artillery and rocket ammunition, which – if it was captured on the way – would be of little use to the Zulus. He also asked that the two companies of 'The Buffs' be part of the escort, and he proposed that these should stay at Eshowe, while the returning convoy should take with it three companies of the 99th, half the Royal Engineers, the Natal Pioneers, and the odds and ends from the Volunteers, NNC, wagon-drivers and conductors. He also wanted to send back the sick and wounded and some of the oxen, provided the way seemed clear. His idea was to keep the number of fighting men roughly the same, but to reduce the overall number of mouths to feed. It may be that he shared his old battalion's unease about the 99th; it was, however, an axiom of the time that battalions should serve together where possible, and it is not unnatural that Pearson wanted his old regiment under him.

It was at this point, however, that the communication system faltered. Firstly, Pearson's letter crossed with one of Chelmsford's. Besides containing more information on Isandlwana, including a list of all officers killed, and full details of the defence of Rorke's Drift, this letter went on to issue a change of orders for Pearson. Chelmsford wanted the Naval Brigade to strengthen the garrisons of the forts at the Lower Drift, and he felt that Pearson should also be there with his staff. Arrangements were to be made for a smaller garrison to defend a reduced entrenchment at Eshowe under the command of Pearson's best field officers. On receiving Pearson's letter of 6 February, Chelmsford replied on the 8th, reiterating these instructions. He stated that it was essential for Pearson to move to the Lower Drift, and for the garrison at Eshowe to be reduced to a minimum. He felt he would not have a force available to march up to Eshowe with a convoy for at least six weeks, but a garrison of 500 or 600 men left there could provide him with a useful flying column, provided the entrenchments were reduced accordingly. Having received intelligence that the Zulus intended to raid into Natal, Chelmsford felt it necessary to concentrate a column at the Lower Drift which could respond to these threatened incursions, and he wanted Pearson to command it. When Pearson received this letter on 11 February, he called his second Council of War to discuss its contents.

The Council, at which only senior officers were present, carefully considered Chelmsford's orders in the light of their own predicament. Many Zulus had been seen in the past few days, watching the garrison, and it was generally felt that there were a large number of the enemy in position between Eshowe and the Thukela. The possibility of pushing through to the river with 500 or 600 men was keenly debated, but fears of another Isandlwana were uppermost in their minds. Chelmsford's instructions to reduce the size of the entrenchment at Eshowe were also discussed, but Wynne was adamant that this was not practicable, and that a new defensive position would have to be constructed elsewhere. The Council therefore agreed that it was impractical to follow Chelmsford's instructions but, unwilling to disobey orders, Pearson and his officers made secret arrangements to march out should Chelmsford insist on the move. To clarify his position Pearson replied to Chelmsford's letter the same day, 11 February, pointing out his concerns but stating that if Chelmsford wrote back confirming his orders then he would march out as instructed, on Sunday 16 February. There was to be no reply; the Zulus were now in the bush in increasing numbers, and had cut all communications. The garrison at Eshowe stood alone.

Once this became clear, Pearson felt that his principal duty was to look after the well-being of his men, and to protect the cattle. The indefatigable Captain Wynne, who had already been working flat out on the defences, set to again with a will. What had started merely as an earth entrenchment to protect a supply depot was taking on the appearance of a fully fledged fort, featuring all the latest thinking in fortification construction. By Sunday 9 February most of the heavy work had been completed. The whole position was now surrounded by a ditch 7 feet deep and 10–13 feet wide. The average height of the defences was 6 feet, but at one point on the northern side the height reached 8 feet 6 inches. A drawbridge, designed by Lieutenant Main, was almost completed and fixed into place at the main West Gate, and a smaller drawbridge was being constructed for the Water Gate at the north-east corner of the fort. This gate was used by those on fatigue duty collecting water from the stream about sixty yards away. The firing platforms for the two Royal Artillery 7-pounders, in the north-west and south-west angles, had been protected with blindages of sandbags, as had the two Naval Brigade 7-pounders on the north-east rampart and the Gatling gun on the south side. Work had commenced on a caponnier in the south face of the fort to allow the defenders a line of fire along the ditches, as well as one in the west face which would also operate as a sally-port, serving the defenders of the cattle laager in the ravine. Those parts of the ditch which could not be covered by fire from the caponniers had stakes sunk in the bottom as an additional defence. Beyond the eastern ditch work commenced on a series of *trous-de-loup* – wolf pits – obstacles made by digging holes 3 feet square and 2 feet deep, and placing a sharpened stake upright at the bottom. They were designed to break the impetus of any charge, and slow the enemy down at a range where rifle fire was most effective. Attempts to sink a well had so far failed to yield any positive results, but a water spout was placed under the eaves of the church to catch rain-water running off the roof and direct it into a wagon as an emergency reserve. The church bell was removed from the tower and positioned in the centre of the fort where it was rung to sound the alarm. Next to the bell a small magazine was constructed to house what remained of the NNC's gunpowder, to prevent any accidental explosions. All of these efforts began to take their toll on Wynne, who admitted in a letter to his wife dated 7 February, 'I feel the responsibility of the work very much, and occasionally have small trials of temper from contrarieties of those I work with or superintend.'

The weather throughout these early days at Eshowe had been changeable; some days warm and sunny, others cold, wet and misty. Inevitably, when it did rain it was during the night and early morning, which made the hours of darkness long and unpleasant. While a few of the officers were allowed tents inside the fort, the majority of the garrison had to accept the makeshift shelter offered beneath the wagons. Over these were spread wagon sails and tarpaulins, propped up by tent-poles. Lieutenant Knight of 'The Buffs' generally enjoyed this arrangement: '. . . underneath a wagon is by no means a bad shelter, especially in wet weather, and with tarpaulin let down on the windward side it forms a cosy quarter, preferable to a tent'. However, there were disadvantages, too, according to Lieutenant Lloyd, RA:

> It took some time before one became accustomed to sleeping under these wagons without doing damage to one's head, for on the command going round at night to 'stand to your arms' one naturally jumped up imagining oneself in a tent, but the real situation was promptly suggested to one by a violent contact of head and wagon.

To preserve the health of his men, cramped together in the fort each night, Pearson took great care over the sanitary arrangements of the garrison. It was particularly important to ensure that the water supply from the stream to the north of the fort remained pure. Each day between reveille and retreat an infantry picquet and mounted patrol was assigned to ensure the water was not fouled in any way. According to Lieutenant Knight of 'The Buffs' the contamination of water supplies by the auxiliaries and teamsters was one of the great difficulties of South African warfare. In an article he wrote for the *United Services Magazine* about his time at Eshowe he stated:

The entrance to the fort at the northern angle.

The fort during the siege, based on a sketch by Surgeon Norbury. Note the *trous-de-loup* obstacles in the foreground.

The native has a rooted and superstitious objection to the use of anything like an organised latrine, and affects the immediate neighbourhood of running water. The nearer the source the better ... the utmost vigilance, accompanied by the severest punishments for any infraction of the regulations, was the only way of checking it in the slightest.

This protected portion of the stream provided the drinking and cooking water for the garrison, although no cooking was allowed on the north side of the fort. Further downstream Quartermaster Bateman of the 99th Regiment constructed two bathing places, one for the officers and one for the men. The horses and cattle were watered in a separate stream. Latrines were dug outside the fort for use during the day, and wooden boxes lined with tin were sunk into the ditch for use at night. Urine barrels were also provided each night for the garrison. In the morning these would be carried out by fatigue parties and emptied into trenches dug the night before. Great care was taken to sprinkle ashes from the cooking fires over the area where the barrels had stood overnight. The ashes were then removed and fresh sand added to the spot. All dirt and litter was collected and removed to offal pits away from the fort. These efforts seemed to prove effective as by 9 February there had still been only the one death through disease, although Pearson reported that there were thirty-seven men on the sick list. Most of them were suffering from diarrhoea, which he was concerned could develop into dysentery. To ensure that patients in the hospital received as much fresh air as possible, those who were fit enough were removed to a rise near the fort each day, where they rested beneath a shelter erected from tree branches. It was Pearson's orders that everyone, except those working on the defences, should be outside the fort each day. To ensure that no Zulu spies infiltrated the fort when the troops returned in the evening, the black members of the garrison were issued with patches of blue cloth to be sewn on to their coats if they had them, or, if not, to be worn on a string around the neck, so as to identify themselves. Even so, after all these precautions, with the proximity of so many men and livestock the fort was a horrendous place to be each night. Captain Pelly Clarke mentioned that 'the stench at times ... was quite sickening' while Lieutenant Lloyd added that the smell '... at night may be easier imagined than described'.

Other than completing the defences of the fort at Eshowe, the main task for the men was guarding the large number of cattle attached to No. 1 Column. The cattle had to be protected at all times, since not only did they provide the means of transportation for the garrison if and when it moved, but they were also a major source of food. The cattle laager in the ravine was now ready, and the trek oxen were driven into it each night. The slaughter oxen were kept in a separate circular laager close by. Pearson, in his letter to Chelmsford on 6 February, noted that '... the cattle are a constant source of anxiety to me, as

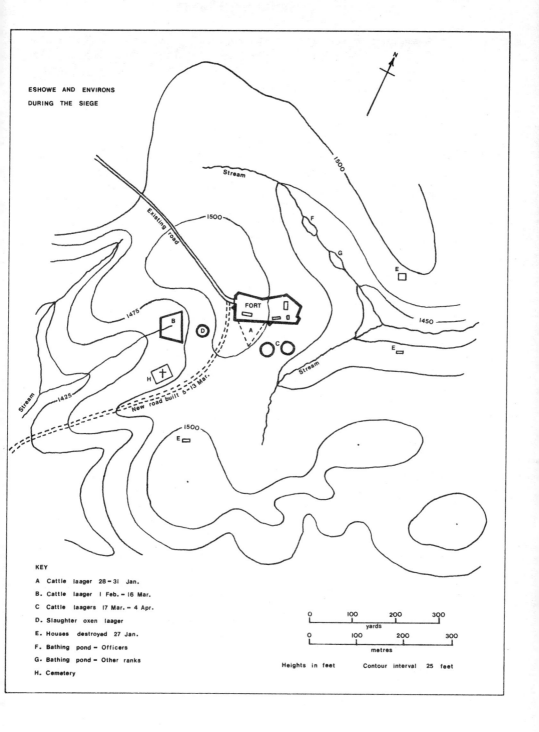

ESHOWE AND ENVIRONS
DURING THE SIEGE

N

Stream

1500

Existing road

1500

1475

FORT

B

D

A

C

H

1450

E

E

Stream

1425

New road built 5–13 Mar.

Stream

1500

E

F

G

E

KEY

A Cattle laager 28 – 31 Jan.

B. Cattle laager 1 Feb. – 16 Mar.

C Cattle laagers 17 Mar. – 4 Apr.

D. Slaughter oxen laager

E. Houses destroyed 27 Jan.

F. Bathing pond – Officers

G. Bathing pond – Other ranks

H. Cemetery

0   100   200   300
        yards

0   100   200   300
        metres

Heights in feet   Contour interval   25 feet

they might be taken away during a dark night, if the Zulus should be enter-prising'. While the main construction work continued, Pearson felt it necessary to keep the cattle close to the fort, within the line of vedettes which had been posted to warn of the approach of the enemy. In a very short time, however, all the grass in this area had been eaten; furthermore, Pearson ordered the cattle to be driven in whenever there were any Zulus about, which lost them further grazing time. On the night of 3/4 February forty-four oxen in the main laager collapsed through weakness brought on by hunger, and the following morning they were discovered, crushed to death by the others, at the bottom angle of the laager. Efforts were made to redesign the laager but it was always regarded as a cattle-trap by the wagon conductors.

With the departure of the mounted men at the end of January, Pearson had lost the eyes of his column. However, just before Major Barrow had left, Lieutenant Rowden and a group of men from the 99th Regiment had volun-teered to join the Mounted Infantry. There had been no time for any formal training before Barrow was ordered away, and a number of the men had never ridden before, but they were joined by the eleven Natal Volunteers who had been left behind, and under Captain Charles Shervinton of the Native Con-tingent an efficient body of mounted irregulars was created. Shervinton was something of an adventurer, one of three brothers who would all serve during the Zulu War; his brother Tom was a Lieutenant in the NNC, currently lan-guishing sick at Fort Pearson. Using officers' horses and those sick mounts left behind by Barrow, this enterprising group, operating under a collective sobriquet, the 'Uhlans', soon earned the respect of all at Eshowe. Every day groups of three riders would occupy the four vedette posts, each about 2000 yards from the corners of the fort, in advance of the infantry picquets, to give an early warning of any Zulu activity.

Despite the great progress made on the defences of the fort there was still a feeling of anxiety among the garrison which intensified each evening as dark-ness closed in. During the night of 2/3 February, after the first detailed news of Isandlwana had been received, seven men of the Native Contingent deserted. About three miles from the fort they were attacked by Zulus who opened fire and threw assegais at them. Three were killed while the other four made good their escape and returned to Eshowe, reporting that the country was full of armed scouts. Throughout 3 February large numbers of Zulus, in groups as large as 200, were observed moving southwards past Eshowe. Pearson hoped the Zulus would attack the fort as he believed that 'he (Cetshwayo) will find it a very hard nut to crack indeed'.

On Sunday 9 February Captain Shervinton was out on a patrol with a party of the 'Uhlans' in the morning when they came under fire from a group of Zulus on top of a hill a mile to the south-east of the fort. Although no one was hit, the riders returned with a message that the Zulus had shouted to

1. The commander of No. 1 Column, Colonel Charles Knight Pearson, late of 'The Buffs', photographed in Natal in 1879. *(S.B. Bourquin)*

2. 'The Bulldog of Eshowe': Colonel Pearson, looking confident, probably photographed in December 1879 at about the time of his presentation to Queen Victoria. *(Tim Day)*

3. Officers of 'The Buffs', photographed in 1876, just before their departure for South Africa. About half of these men fought in the Zulu War, the majority in the Eshowe campaign. They are *(back row, left to right)*, Second Lieutenant Upton, Lieutenant Addison, Captain Lefroy, Lieutenant Backhouse, Quartermaster Cleary, Second Lieutenant Newnham-Davis, Second Lieutenant Gordon, Lieutenant Martin, Captain Gelston; and *(front row, left to right)*, Colonel Pearson, Captain Jackson, Surgeon Walker, Captain Alexander, Captain Hamilton, Colonel Parnell. *(Buffs Museum, Canterbury)*

4. The start of it all: a historic photograph of John Shepstone's delegation reading the British ultimatum to King Cetshwayo's representatives beneath the 'ultimatum tree' at the Lower Thukela Drift, 11 December 1878. *(S.B. Bourquin)*

5. The photograph that embarrassed the Zulu deputation; Vumandaba kaNtati and his colleagues, 11 December 1878. *(S.B. Bourquin)*

6. Off to War: the 2nd Battalion, 3rd Regiment ('The Buffs'), on parade at Mullingar, Ireland, in April 1876, prior to its departure for South Africa. These are the men who fought at Nyezane and endured the siege at Eshowe; Colonel Pearson stands in front to the left, with Colonel Parnell on the extreme left. The Colours are visible in the centre, carried here by Lieutenant Lewis *(left)*, who carried one at Nyezane, and was wounded at Eshowe, and Lieutenant Knight *(right)*, who was Pearson's ADC throughout the campaign. Captain Gelston is third from the right among the officers. *(Bryan Maggs collection)*

7. 'An enterprising photographer named Lloyd from Natal ... took a photo of the Brigade': the Naval Brigade from HMS *Active*, Lower Thukela, 12 December 1878. The Marines are in the centre, and the Gatling in front of the sailors, right. On the extreme left are a group of black sailors, recruited in West Africa, and known as Kroomen. *(Local History Museum, Durban)*

8. Commander Campbell and Naval Brigade officers from HMS *Active*, January 1879. Lieutenant Dowding, commanding the detachment's Marines, is on the left in the back row; Midshipman Coker sits front row, second from the left. *(S.B. Bourquin)*

9. Fort Pearson, the impressive earthwork built on a knoll overlooking the Lower Thukela Drift, the base of operations for Pearson's column. *(Bryan Maggs Collection)*

10. Sailors on the top of Fort Pearson. This photograph probably shows men from HMS *Active* and dates from the beginning of the campaign: note the Gatling, left, and the 24-pounder rocket tube, centre right background. *(Killie Campbell Africana Library)*

11. The troublesome anchor of HMS *Tenedos*, which served to secure the pont to the Zulu bank, and now stands outside the Museum of Zululand in Eshowe.

12. Major Percy Barrow, 19th Hussars, who commanded No. 1 Column's mounted men throughout the advance to Eshowe and the relief expedition. *(S.B. Bourquin)*

13. Invasion: a company of the 99th is ferried across the Lower Drift in the pont, 12 January 1879. *(Bryan Maggs Collection)*

14. The camp complex at Fort Pearson, photographed from the middle of the Thukela. Smith's Hotel is on the left, and tents stand on the slopes below Fort Pearson, right. *(S.B. Bourquin)*

15. Pearson's first camp in Zululand, photographed from across the Thukela on 14 January 1879. *(Local History Museum, Durban)*

16. Fort Tenedos, the impressive earthwork built by Captain Richard Wynne's Engineers on the Zulu bank of the Thukela; the Fort Pearson complex is on the bluffs on the Natal side beyond. *(S.B. Bourquin)*

17. Captain Warren Wynne RE, Pearson's senior Engineer, who masterminded the defences at Eshowe.

18. 'Gingwayo', the servant of Lieutenant W. Robarts of the Victoria Mounted Rifles, with a percussion rifle taken from a dead Zulu at the battle of Nyezane. The rifle was still a treasured possession when this photo was taken several years later. *(Mr W. Robarts, Empangeni)*

19. Natal Volunteers: officers of the Victoria Mounted Rifles and Stanger Mounted Rifles, two of the local units which accompanied Pearson's advance. *(Natal Archives Depot)*

20. A drawing by Second Lieutenant George Evelyn of 'The Buffs', depicting the height of the battle of Nyezane. The viewpoint is from the foot of the spur, where some of the wagons have parked; Pearson's position on the knoll is just beyond, marked by Lloyd's guns and the Colours of 'The Buffs'. Note the Naval Brigade rocket tubes in action. The hill in the centre is Wombane, the burning homestead is in the left distance. *(Buffs Museum, Canterbury)*

21. The same artist's view of the closing stages of the battle at the top of the ridge. The NNC clear the burning homestead *(left)*, while sailors and men of 'The Buffs' drive the Zulus over the crest of Wombane *(right)*. *(Buffs Museum, Canterbury)*

22. A somewhat romanticised – but otherwise accurate enough – rendition of Midshipman Coker directing the *Active*'s Gatling gun at Nyezane. *(Rai England Collection)*

23. The Bluejackets' finest hour: Commander Campbell's advance against the Zulu centre at Nyezane is depicted in stirring style in this contemporary illustration. *(S.B. Bourquin)*

24. Paymaster Gelston's cross on the graves of the British dead at Nyezane. *(S.B. Bourquin)*

EKowe. Church, Head Quarter Tents, Amunition & Quarter Masters Stores. The bell is the one now in the Mess

25. A sketch by Lieutenant Knight of 'The Buffs' of the interior of Pearson's fort at Eshowe: the mission church is in the centre, with the Headquarters tents outside; the bell *(centre)*, was used to raise the alarm. *(Buffs Museum, Canterbury)*

26. A general view of the ruins of the fort at Eshowe, photographed from beyond the stream to the north-east, in *c*. June 1879. *(S.B. Bourquin)*

27. The remains of one of the trenches, *c*. June 1879, showing the *caponnier*, or covered way which provided enfilading fire into the trenches. Note the loopholes on the wooden supports *(left)*. *(S.B. Bourquin)*

29. Unsuspecting warriors trigger the booby-trapped 'torpedo', left by Pearson's road party on 11 March.

28. Naval Brigade troops rush to man the ramparts during one of the many scares that took place throughout the siege. (*Rai England Collection*)

30. A skirmishing at Eshowe: a Zulu patrol is engaged while supports rush up from the rear. The hut in the centre of the picture is typical of the temporary shelters built by the men watching the immediate vicinity of the fort.

31. The remarkable escape of Lance-Corporal Carson of the Mounted Infantry, who was ambushed on picquet duty outside the fort on 7 March. *(S.B. Bourquin)*

32. Mbombotshana, the hill to the south-west of the fort, from where the Zulus fired on British vedettes on 9, 10 and 11 February; they were driven off on the 12th by Shervinton's 'Uhlans'. Pearson later established his signal station on this vantage-point. *(S.B. Bourquin)*

33. Charles St Leger Shervinton, photographed in 1877; Shervinton was a captain in the 2nd Regt, NNC, and proved a dashing leader of the 'Uhlans' throughout the siege. He was the only man of the garrison considered for the award of the Victoria Cross.

34. Lieutenant and Adjutant Arthur Davison of the 99th, who died of disease at Eshowe on 27 March.

them, 'We shall meet tomorrow'. Throughout the day numbers of Zulus were observed lurking about the fort, and a patrol came in later and reported that they had seen a group of about 1000 Zulus some two miles off. That night the nervous sentries peered out into the dark, expecting at any moment to see a great army descending upon the fort. Suddenly, at about 9.00pm, a single alarm shot rang out from a sentry of 'The Buffs', who had seen a Zulu moving south-west of the fort, and this was followed by two or three more shots. The whole garrison, who slept fully clothed, were at their posts in seconds, and five or six more shots rang out from 'The Buffs'' parapet. Lloyd's artillerymen broke out the case-shot and were about to open up when the order was given to cease fire, as no further enemy movement could be discerned in the dark. The next morning, when a patrol went out to see if any Zulus had been killed, they returned with a pair of sailor's white trousers and a grey shirt, both riddled with bullet holes, which they had found drying on a small bush. Apparently a freshening breeze that had blown up in the night had revived a small cooking fire which had been inefficiently extinguished before retreat. The glowing embers had faintly illuminated the clothes as they fluttered in the breeze; these were the sentry's Zulus.

Captain Wynne was still hard at work on the fort through the second week of February. The digging of *trous-de-loup* continued to the east of the defences, and work continued on the construction of the caponniers and sally port. One of the naval guns' battery positions was relocated further down the east rampart, and the drain was improved at that end of the fort, to try to relieve a build-up of rain-water in the ditches. The muddied main entrance was suffering badly from the constant traffic in and out of the fort, so a paved roadway was begun, using bricks collected from the ruined outhouses. In the same week Wynne also laid out range markers all around the fort at distances from 300 to 700 yards. He planned at a later date to add a rather flamboyant touch, cutting the range distance numbers out of the turf and filling them with white clay, so that everyone could plainly see them and adjust their sights accordingly. However, this was never carried out. In addition to these works, Wynne organised the construction of a series of wire entanglements, with wire taken from the trek tows of the oxen and stretched between stakes in the grass on the east and north-east faces of the fort.

The hill from which the Zulus fired on Captain Shervinton's party on 9 February, known locally as mBombotshane, was again used to attack the vedettes on the following two days. On Monday the 10th this desultory fire was kept up for two hours. Due to the Zulus' careful use of cover the vedettes found it impossible to inflict any casualties on the snipers. Uncertain as to how many Zulus were ensconced on the top of the hill, the 'Uhlans' felt unable to attack it on their own, and appealed to Pearson for assistance. Unwilling to expose his men to any unnecessary risks, Pearson, however, refused to order any infantry

PLAN OF FORT AT ETSHOWE: ZULULAND.

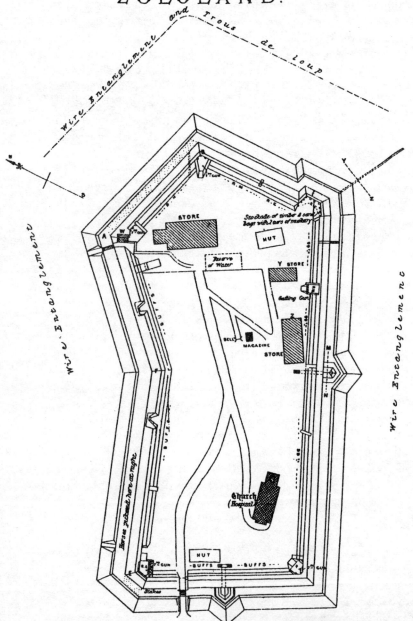

Traced from plans drawn
by Lieuts Main & Willoch R.E.

FORT AT ETSHOWE.

General Profile.

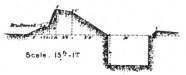

Scale. 15ft = 1in.

Section through Drawbridge

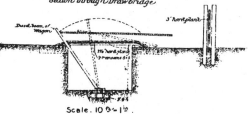

Scale. 10ft = 1in.

Profile of Faces A.F. – F.E. at Point near F.

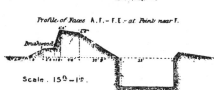

Scale. 15ft = 1in.

Section at A. shewing Gun Blindage

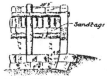

Scale. 10ft = 1in.

Sectional Elevn of Drawbridge.

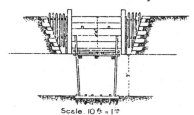

Scale. 10ft = 1in.

Section & Elevn of Drain at Y.Z

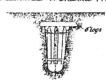

Scale. 10ft = 1in.

Section at M.N.

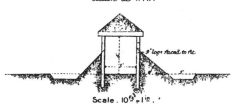

Scale. 10ft = 1in.

Sectional Elevn of Stockade

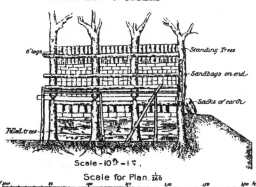

Scale – 10ft = 1in.

Scale for Plan. 1/120

support to such an enterprise. Undaunted and determined to remove this threat, Captain Shervinton called for volunteers from the 'Uhlans' and six men stepped forward; Corporal Adams, Native Contingent, Privates Higley, Keys, Robson and Whale of the 99th Regiment and Trooper Garland, Victoria Mounted Rifles. Under cover of darkness, they left the fort on foot, climbed the hill, and lay in wait behind some rocks near the summit. Shortly after first light a group of Zulus were duly spied climbing up towards Shervinton's party, and on the word of command from their leader the 'Uhlans' opened a sudden and rapid fire which caught the Zulus by surprise and wounded three of them. The rest fled back down the hill and out of sight. The Zulus never again troubled the vedettes from this hill.

Away from rigours of work, boredom soon became a problem. On Wednesday 5 February the band of 'The Buffs' played its first concert in the afternoon, and this became a daily routine, alternated with the band of the 99th. Reading material was rare and much sought after, no matter what the subject. Lieutenant Davison, Adjutant of the 99th, was happy enough with what he acquired, a two-month-old copy of *The World* containing an article on Kew Gardens which, as a keen botanist, greatly appealed to him. His other reading matter in the first week of February comprised a review of *The History of Merchant Shipping* and a piece on the Queen's Regulations. By the end of the second week of February, he had returned to the Bible as his sole reading matter. As an amateur botanist, Davison also enjoyed walks in the locality of the fort where he could study the flora of the area, and he amused himself by planting cuttings of eucalyptus trees close to one of the streams. As adjutant, he sat on two courts martial in this first week of February, both for men of the 99th Regiment. Three more followed in the second week, and as two men were ordered to be flogged at the same time on 11 February, Davison had to borrow a 'cat-o'-nine-tails' from the adjutant of 'The Buffs', Lieutenant Somerset, to ensure the sentence could be carried out.

The changeable weather of the previous week continued, heavy rain and mist followed by baking sunshine, which did little to aid the recovery of those patients suffering in the hospital. Although Norbury and his team gave them all possible attention, the shortage of medicines was apparent, and three men died that week. Norbury was a conscientious officer, worried about the health of the garrison, but his theories on the cause of the insidious sickness reveal how limited was medical knowledge, even in the 1870s:

The soil in Ekowe was of an unhealthy nature ... the upper portion, about two feet thick, consisted of black mould, formed by the consecutive decay of many generations of grasses, and large quantities of other vegetable matter; beneath this was a stratum of sand some four inches in thickness, also containing organic matter; and then came several feet of soft clay, in which water could easily be obtained by digging ... a soil consisting almost entirely of vegetable matter placed over a watery subsoil in so hot a climate could not be healthy.

It resulted, he was convinced, in 'malarious emanations from the ground', which mingled with 'exhalations from the bodies of men, so closely packed together, produced a poisonous atmosphere.' Nearer the mark, he also deplored and tried to discourage the habit of some men of filling their water-bottles at the stream in the ravine, which drained off the slope where the newly dead were buried. The toll continued; on 11 February Artificer J. Moore (Gunner Carroll knew him as Charles Moore), who had been shoemaker for the crew of HMS *Active*, died of dysentery after many days' suffering. Two days later Private W. McLeod of 'The Buffs' also succumbed to the same disease. On 15 February they were joined in the new cemetery by another soldier of 'The Buffs', Private E. Oakley. Oakley had originally been admitted to the hospital suffering from fever but later developed diarrhoea from which he died. All these men were accorded full military honours at their funerals, but due to the increasing regularity of these events Pearson – concerned for his ammunition supplies – ordered that in future the volley firing would no longer take place.

Pearson, who had written to Chelmsford on 11 February asking for confirmation of the order to march out with part of his garrison, watched and waited anxiously for the arrival of a runner from the Lower Drift. He had said he would be ready to march on Sunday 16 February, but as each day passed with no word from Chelmsford, he became confused as to what action to take. Although the decision to march out was supposed to be a secret known only to a few senior officers, rumours soon started to circulate in the cramped conditions of the fort. Davison heard them from Lieutenant Rowden of the Mounted Infantry, and by the time they had reached Gunner Carroll it was said that half the garrison were to go, travelling light with no wagons or carts, and anyone who was wounded on the way down was to be killed to prevent him falling into the Zulus' hands and being tortured. Sunday arrived, but still no news. Church parade was held as usual at 10.00am; it was the practice for Reverend Robertson and Father Walsh to alternate services, and a favourite hymn, appropriately enough, was 'Hold The Fort'. As the morning passed with no word from Chelmsford, Pearson, who as a civilian wagon conductor observed with unintentional irony, was '... one of the last men to run us into any unnecessary danger', happily cancelled the move to Thukela. In the afternoon a typical summer wind blew up, reaching almost hurricane force, and carrying with it heavy rain. Pearson remarked 'It was the worst night we have had since we left Maritzburg'. Had the column marched at midnight as planned it would undoubtedly have been seriously disrupted and would have presented a very tempting target for any Zulus lurking in the bush. As it was, the garrison's only discomfort was a severe flood in the fort.

The bad weather continued into the next day, Monday 17 February, and prevented any work parties being assembled from the infantry units. But poor weather or not, Captain Wynne and the Engineers enjoyed no easing of their schedule and continued working throughout the day. Indeed, there was no respite for the Engineers for the next two weeks as Wynne's various projects continued. Although each infantry company provided work parties by rota the Engineers were engaged in these strenuous physical duties every day. By the end of February work to secure additional lines of fire along the ditches had been carried out, efforts had been made to ensure the buildings within the fort were both bullet-proof and fire-proof, and the construction of the caponniers was completed. Additional traverses had sprung up all over the interior of the fort, a large oven had been built, and a road was laid on the approaches to the fort using more stone and brick collected from the remains of the buildings to the east of the position. This road was then continued along the centre of the fort itself to prevent the soldiers having to struggle endlessly through a sea of oozing slime every time it rained. Towards the end of February Pearson informed Wynne that he would like to replace the wagons with a continuous line of huts designed to serve the same dual purpose of shelter and barricade. The first of these, commenced on 26 February, was laid out in the south-east corner and covered an area 33 feet by 20 feet. The lack of suitable timber made progress very slow and almost thwarted the scheme, although a second hut of a simpler design was added later, situated close to the main gate.

Each day eyes scanned the surrounding countryside for a sight of any approaching runner from the Lower Drift with a response to Pearson's letter of 11 February. With none forthcoming, Pearson sent off another letter on 18 February, containing much the same information as the previous one. Needless to say, there was now a certain reluctance on the part of the Native Contingent men to act as runners, until a fee of one sovereign was agreed upon, the equivalent of a month's pay. In this letter Pearson also confirmed the results of a detailed analysis of the state of his food supplies which had been compiled by Assistant Commissary Heygate and Sergeant-Major Wishart of the 90th Light Infantry, who was attached to the Commissariat Department. This report stated that as of 11 February the present garrison had the following supplies:

200 slaughter oxen
6 weeks breadstuffs, exclusive of whole mealies
2 months coffee
1 month tea
6 weeks sugar
3 months salt
1 month pepper
6 weeks lime juice
1 month preserved vegetables

Pearson concluded his letter by adding that the mealies growing in nearby fields belonging to the Zulu civilian population would soon be ripe so he intended to start raiding to boost his larder.

If Pearson had been over-cautious since the news of Isandlwana reached him, his confidence now began to return. As yet, he had been largely untroubled by the Zulus; although he was well aware of their presence in the area, they had not attempted to make any attack on the fort. Therefore on 19 February he personally rode out for the first time, with his staff and Captain Wynne, on a reconnaissance towards the Mlalazi river, while another party, protected by a company of the 99th, raided the local Zulu gardens. This was to be the first of many such forays. The party returned with a wagon full of mealies as well as a number of pumpkins, which the Zulus habitually grew together. Often these raiding parties would come into contact with Zulus intent on the same purpose. In his reminiscences Lieutenant Knight of 'The Buffs' wrote of one of these raids:

> One morning a couple of European transport riders fired at a group of natives standing near a kraal, into which they promptly bolted, reappearing, however, in a few minutes carrying a huge, bell-mouthed blunderbuss, which they loaded amidst great excitement. It went off with a report like a young cannon, sending the Zulus flying in all directions, but without doing any damage.

Generally, there were no casualties on either side during these encounters.

With the grass now exhausted within a mile of the fort, it became necessary to send the cattle further afield for grazing. On 21 February they were sent about a mile and a quarter to the north, where the grass was as yet untouched. To ensure that they would not be troubled, Pearson himself set out with the black transport drivers and leaders, and a company of infantry, to scour the bush around the grazing area. There were no signs of the enemy, and at the end of the day the cattle were brought back safely to the fort. During the day, however, a curious incident emphasised the sense of isolation felt by the garrison. The sound of distant gunfire carried across the wind from the south. The black wagon drivers, with their acute sense of hearing, suggested that the firing was coming from the direction of Fort Buckingham, close to the Middle Drift. In fact, the firing probably came from an insignificant skirmish which took place near John Dunn's home at Mangethe, nearer the Lower Drift, but the truth remained a mystery to the garrison, and served only to remind them how powerless they were to intervene in the struggles of the outside world.

The following day the cattle were again driven out, but this time the Zulus were expecting them. As the cattle drivers arrived with their charges, they came under fire from between thirty and eighty snipers hidden in the bush. Word was immediately sent back to the fort, and two companies of 'The Buffs' were dispatched to their assistance. These men were joined by twelve of the 'Uhlans', who arrived to find the Zulus retiring, and who pursued them for some distance. The 'Uhlans' passed through a ravine and up the far side before contact was lost. They then set fire to an *umuzi* (homestead) they found nearby, and retired to the cattle guard. None of the mounted men were hit, but one or two Zulus were said to have fallen in the skirmish. After this, it was felt necessary to allocate two or three infantry companies each day to the tedious duty of cattle guard. That same day a party, consisting of thirty men from the Naval Brigade and a company of the 99th, went out to burn another Zulu homestead. Lieutenant Hamilton accompanied them, unofficially, and reported that '... we saw about 200 Zulus, but all a long way off, and out of range. We burnt a kraal and captured a fowl, the latter very precious in these hard times'.

At 9.00am on 24 February Colonel Pearson himself rode out on one of these raids. The target was an *umuzi* a short distance from the fort. The homestead was positioned down in a valley, so the task of looting it was entrusted to the Native Pioneers and wagon drivers, supported by H Company of the 99th Regiment. A short distance off, a body of about 200 Zulus watched them collecting mealies, but made no attempt to interfere. But as the raiders set fire to the homestead and began to move off with the spoils, a Zulu shouted out menacingly, 'You are eating our mealies today, but we will drink your coffee tomorrow'. Pearson, whose confidence was fully restored, greeted this in belligerent mood: 'They will get no quarter with us. "Remember No. 3 column" will be our war cry, and I long for nothing better than to see the country laid to waste and the ground strewn with black carcasses'.

Food, by now, had become the main preoccupation for those besieged in Eshowe. Their ration had been reduced, and the daily allowance was now one and a quarter pounds of tough beef, 6 ounces of mealie meal, a half of an ounce of preserved vegetables, one and a quarter ounces of sugar, a third of an ounce of coffee, a sixth of an ounce of tea, a ninth of an ounce of pepper, and a quarter of an ounce of salt. Wynne summed up the monotony of the diet: 'How one longs for butter, milk, and fresh vegetables, and good bread. Biscuits (sometimes very musty), and the heaviest of doughy flat cakes or loaves, without any lubrication, are not a good substitute for home bread and butter.'

A few days later Wynne returned to the subject of food, describing the messing arrangements of the Engineer officers:

Lieut. Main, of ours, and I grub together, i.e. join rations, but we all four, i.e. Courtney and Willock as well, sit at one table for meals under a pleasant shady tree, which we monopolised from the first. There we chew the generally very tough, much stewed ox, with as a rule, about a tablespoon of preserved carrots, sometimes some large haricot beans. These, and either biscuit, or a kind of 'fudge' manufactured by my servant, out of Boer's meal, a sort of oatmeal, is our daily food at breakfast, lunch and dinner; in fact every meal the same except that we have coffee at breakfast and tea at dinner. I really do not mind it, but most fellows get very tired of it, and complain of insufficiency.

Lieutenant Lloyd's catering arrangements were quite similar to Wynne's:

The two excellent officers of 'The Buffs' (my messmates) and I divided our rations as follows. At breakfast toasted biscuit and tea, at mid-day meal the same, and at dinner our meat and anything our soldier-cook could make out of the flour. At first his cakes were indigestible, as we had no baking powder, but he improved as time went on. Occasionally, when our troops made a raid on the Zulu mealie fields, a large supply was brought into camp, we then had an entree of roast mealies.

These raiding parties also brought back pumpkins and this variation to the diet was greatly appreciated by all. Captain Pelly Clarke was most enthusiastic as to their versatility: 'Boiled as a vegetable or put into stews! frittered pumpkins! pumpkin-pie! (just like a good apple-tart) pumpkin squash! – there is no end to the variety of dishes you can make with it. Its tops make a nice green vegetable too.'

For these men haunted by their unvarying diet Sunday 23 February became a day firmly entrenched in their memories for years to come. On this day Colonel Pearson decided to hold an auction of foodstuffs recovered from the baggage of the Volunteers, which they had left behind on their hasty departure over four weeks previously. No account of the siege fails to describe in great detail the excitement of the sale, and the exorbitant prices, for the time, that each item raised; men were determined to acquire for themselves items they had only dreamt of for weeks. The prices attained were as follows:

Tin of sardines	5s
Tin of lobster	18s
Tin of salmon	15s
Tin of preserved herrings	13s
12 pound ham	£6 5s
Bottle of curry powder	20s/27s
Pot of jam	24s
Tin of condensed milk	17s/26s
Tin of cocoa	7s 6d/11s 6d
Bottle of pickles	25s
Bottle of ketchup	20s
Bottle of Worcester sauce	25s
Matches	5s/6s
Tobacco	20s/30s
Two wooden pipes	25s
Tin of boot dubbing	9s 6d

Wynne refused to have anything to do with these high prices, but Lieutenant Davison successfully bid for a tin of milk and a tin of salmon. A private soldier who bought a tin of salmon and one of lobster, walked straight outside the fort, sat down, and ate the lot. He claimed that he 'wasn't going to waste it on friends'. Pearson estimated that about £7 worth of goods were sold for over £100.

With the passing of the excitement generated by the auction, life returned to normal in the fort. The bands continued to play, but their limited selection of music was becoming trying. Reverend Robertson organised a couple of lectures on the history of Zululand which were very well received and his Bible classes were also well attended. 'You would have been astonished to find,' he wrote, 'how little all of them knew of the people against whom they were fighting, or why they were fighting.' Some cricket equipment had been found in the Volunteer baggage along with a tennis ball, and the more sportingly minded members of the garrison found a rewarding way of spending their leisure time. Captain Gelston of 'The Buffs' evidently had a fondness for working wood, for, together with a civilian surgeon, Dr Giles, he fashioned a wooden cross, engraved with the names of the dead at Nyezane, which he intended to place on their grave as soon as he could. He also devoted a lot of attention to the cemetery, making some of the crosses, as well as a neat fence around it, and improvised furniture for the sick. Lieutenant Davison, who was kept busy with three more courts martial and two floggings, kept up his botanical walks, collecting some unusual ferns and mosses and planting more eucalyptus cuttings. Towards the end of February, however, he was a little disturbed by a bout of diarrhoea which, according to Pearson, generally manifested itself among the garrison when the wet weather returned.

Indeed, the weather had been extremely changeable for some time, alternately hot and sunny then cool and breezy, with the inevitable downpours of rain in between. On the night of 22/23 February the rain returned with a vengeance. The thunderstorm that broke over the fort poured such a deluge of water into the position that as it flowed down to the lower, eastern, end it gained such force that the men of the Naval Brigade were washed out from under their wagons and the weight of water destroyed much of the parapet and drains at that end. Gunner Carroll recalled that he and his comrades spent the rest of the night standing up, huddled under a wagon sail. Many an envious glance had previously been cast in the direction of the Naval Brigade quarters, but overnight these ceased. It rained almost continuously for the next three days.

Since the death of Private Oakley on 15 February the health of the garrison had remained static until 21 February, when three deaths were recorded on one day. The first of these was Lance Corporal T. Taylor of 'The Buffs', who died of dysentery. Taylor was the man who had left his berth in the hospital wagon at

Nyezane to join the fighting. After the battle he had returned to the wagon, and was placed in the hospital as soon as one was established at Eshowe. He stayed there until his death. That same day Private J. Shields of the 99th Regiment also died of the same disease. In the evening a patient in the hospital, Private W. Knee of the 99th, who had been ill for some time and become unstable, left the hospital and managed to talk his way past all the sentries and walked outside the perimeter. He was found drowned in the stream the next morning. His death was considered suicide.

Pearson's new confidence further manifested itself on 28 February when he announced his intention to make a large-scale raid the following day to attack an *ikhanda* controlled by Prince Dabulamanzi kaMpande, the king's brother. The *ikhanda*, eSiqwakeni, was about seven miles north-east of Eshowe along a circuitous route which the mounted patrols had discovered. One of Dabulamanzi's personal homesteads lay a couple of miles beyond eSiqwakeni, and this Pearson had also targeted. Another of Dabulamanzi's *imizi*, eZulwini, 'In the Heavens', lay west of Eshowe, on the slopes of eNtumeni hill, and it was from these three homesteads that Dabulamanzi had been instrumental in organising the Zulu investment of Pearson's position.

Although the garrison had been able to discover little of the Zulu intentions, these were nonetheless quite specific. Dabulamanzi was a young, aggressive man in his thirties, and he had commanded the unsuccessful Zulu attack on Rorke's Drift on 22 January. In the lull following the first great wave of battles, King Cetshwayo had been irritated by his brother's foray across the border, and Dabulamanzi had returned to his home on the coastal belt. Here, probably in conjunction with Mavumengwana kaNdlela – Chief Godide's brother – he orchestrated the Zulu response to Pearson. The king was infuriated that Pearson had apparently settled down inside Zululand as if the country was already defeated, but he refused to allow his army to make a direct assault upon it. Rorke's Drift had already suggested that such attacks were costly and inevitably unsuccessful; as he told his men later, 'If you put your face into the lair of a wild beast, you are sure to get clawed.' Instead, the Zulu policy had been to cut off communications between Pearson and the Thukela, sever his supply route, and attempt to force him into the open. Then the Zulus believed he would be vulnerable to attack. It was certainly an effective strategy, and one which almost worked on a number of occasions. A force of up to 5000 Zulus was maintained in the area, drawn from the *amabutho* based in the coastal region, and strengthened by local irregulars. They were based in a number of *amakhanda* in a loose ring around Eshowe, of which eSiqwakeni was one, and in civilian *imizi*. A cordon of 500 men, operating from temporary grass huts, surrounded the garrison each day. The frequent skirmishes with the cattle guards and raiding parties were part of a deliberate policy of antagonising the garrison while avoiding a serious confrontation. They would taunt the cattle guards, who knew their language, on a regular basis, attempting to highlight the vulnerability of their position. It was a deadly game of cat and mouse, with the main body ready to pounce whenever the garrison were provoked, but, as Lieutenant Lloyd's comments suggest, Pearson's men never quite realised the danger they were in:

> The impertinence of the Zulus was becoming laughable. They would shout out 'Come out of that hole you old women; we always thought the English would fight, and not burrow under the ground!' Having in the meantime looted the wagons of the convoy abandoned by Colonel Ely, they frequently informed us that our coffee and sugar etc was excellent, and that they hoped to come and share ours with us!

Captain Pelly Clarke also experienced some of these exchanges:

> The Zulus used to shout across ravines, and chaff our herd-boys on the thin state of the oxen they were herding, and our deserted state, saying, 'Pray that the sun shines a long time today, for you look on it for the last time. We are coming to take coffee with you tomorrow morning'. And another time; 'Why don't you take more care of Cetshwayo's cattle and get them fatter? He will want them soon'.

Pearson planned his sortie to raise the moral of the garrison, and to put the Zulus on the defensive. The raiding party was due to muster at midnight on Saturday 1 March, and was ready to march at 2.00am. The force, which assembled in order of march, consisted of thirty 'Uhlans', the Royal Engineer company under Wynne (sixty men), one Royal Artillery 7-pounder and crew commanded by Lloyd, about 40 Royal Marines, four weak companies of 'The Buffs' and their bandsmen, the Natal Native Pioneers and one company of the 99th Regiment. In action, it was the duty of bandsmen to act as stretcher-bearers, and the men of 'The Buffs' band were sent out for this purpose; some of the Pioneers were detailed to assist them. The total strength of the force was about 500 men. Shortly after 2.00am the column marched off with the mounted men scouting to the fore.

It was a very clear night and the black guides soon found a path which led through grassy country, fringed with bush. Lieutenant Lloyd described the advance as 'the most silent march I ever took part in, and will be long remembered. All orders were given in whispers, we seemed to glide along, and yet the gun-wheels creaked outrageously, or one seemed to imagine so'. The march was not quick, however, as halts were continuously called to overcome obstacles or to allow the guides to check the path ahead.

The head of the column reached a high point overlooking eSiqwakeni, about three-quarters of a mile away, without being spotted. It was about 4.30am, and day was just beginning to break. Lieutenant Main, with the Engineers in the advance guard, peered down into the lifting gloom and considered that an attack should have been launched at once. 'We looked down on the kraal in a hollow and apparently all the Zulus were asleep in the huts, but Pearson would not let us rush it, and insisted on waiting for the solitary gun to come up which took ten minutes'. As Pearson waited while the artillery and Marines struggled to haul the gun up the incline, a lone Zulu emerged from a small *umuzi* on a hill about 500 yards off to the left of the British position. Initially he had his back to Pearson's men but on turning around he saw their full force arrayed before him, preparing to attack. Lloyd wrote that he 'fled like a hare', and four mounted men sent after him failed to cut him off before he reached the *ikhanda* unscathed. Aware that his men had been discovered, Pearson immediately ordered the Royal Engineers to form a skirmish line and inspect a bush-filled ravine to the right of the line of advance. Lieutenant Main felt it strange that the Engineers should be acting as advance guard and was amused by the action of his comrades: 'I laughed to see dear old Courtney stalking through the long grass, with big spectacles on and his revolver at full cock'. Having declared the ravine clear of Zulus, Wynne was ordered to take the Engineers to the left front of the column and, in skirmish order, advance over a hill covered with long wet grass, and down towards eSiqwakeni. The Zulus were now emerging from the *ikhanda* and flying in all directions, carrying their possessions and driving their cattle before them. Lloyd attempted to speed them on their way with a shell from the 7-pounder which was aimed at the circle of huts. Wynne now found himself about 800 yards from the *ikhanda* and about 200 yards ahead of the main column, which had tentatively begun to move forward behind him. Fifteen of the mounted men then rode ahead and began to burn down the sixty-two huts, now deserted, that were eSiqwakeni. The Zulus who had fled were observed moving up a hill about 1500 yards off; Dabulamanzi's own *umuzi* lay just below it. Unlimbering his gun again Lloyd fired two or three rounds of shrapnel into them, killing or wounding, he estimated, about ten of them. Colonel Pearson now sent forward some of the Natal Pioneers and 'Uhlans' to attempt to bring back one of the wounded for interrogation. Approaching the foot of this hill the party came under a heavy fire from the Zulus above, prompting Pearson to sound the 'retire' and forcing him to abandon any hopes he had of burning the second homestead as well. As soon as these men turned and began to retrace their steps, the Zulus, emboldened by their retreat, moved down the hill again and opened fire on them.

Pearson's main force had been uninvolved in these operations, and now, at about 6.45am, he ordered them to march back to Eshowe. The Engineers were instructed to return across the hill down which they had advanced, in order to cover the right of the column. When they reached the crest, a sentry of the

99th, who had been left to protect the rear, told Wynne that a body of about fifty Zulus had now occupied the ravine the Engineers had cleared earlier. Wynne took his men over to investigate, and as they approached the edge a couple of shots rang out, and Wynne, who was mounted, noted that one 'whizzed past pretty close':

> We saw two or three black fellows making away, and as it was useless to descend into this deep kloof one section was ordered to fire a volley into the suspected part of it, but without effect that we could see. Some were seen on a ridge to the right and fired at by a few of our skirmishers, and we would have advanced in their direction and attacked a kraal a short distance off, but that the column had by this time begun to retire, and we were somewhat left behind.

At this point an order came to Wynne directing him to retire, which was probably very wise, considering that a large gap had now opened between the column and the rearguard. The Zulus who had come down from the hill were now observed working their way around the flanks of the column, firing off the occasional long-range shot. The way back lay through bush country, and Pearson, not wishing to expose his command to the possibility of ambush, took advice from his scouts who recommended a longer but more open route back. As the march continued three more *imizi* were burnt. The pursuing Zulus maintained a respectful distance, but occupied every hill as soon as the British vacated it, and took advantage of every patch of bush from where they could open fire. To keep the Zulus from closing in too much, the mounted men were divided into two sections, one to clear the front, and the other the rear of the column. The artillery fired a few more rounds of shrapnel during the return march to discourage the Zulus, and skirmishing parties were sent out on either flank to drive off groups who appeared to be getting too close. On one occasion the Engineers furnished one of these flanking parties. Lieutenant Main, who was with them, described a bizarre incident which then took place:

> At one of the few anxious moments of the retirement, when it looked as though the Zulus might push between us and the column, and when our men were lying very low and firing, a hare jumped up and bolted away. A sergeant RE grew so excited at this that, regardless of the enemy, he rose, and seizing his rifle by the muzzle, hurled it after the hare. The rifle was badly damaged and the Sergeant got into trouble.

Whether the sergeant was unable to resist the temptation of adding the hare to the garrison's pot, or whether he was simply carried away by surprise in the tension of the moment, is not recorded.

The work certainly kept the men on their toes. Lieutenant Dowding of the Royal Marines described another of these flanking moves:

When I arrived at the top (of the hill) nothing was to be seen, but all at once a volley from at least ten guns was fired at us from less than 300 yards off, making no end of a whistle over our heads – we laid down pretty quick – I luckily had detected two puffs of smoke from a tree just below us but across a deep ravine. I told off six of the best shots at once to the spot, and the volley brought down two of the gentlemen.

Lieutenant Lloyd had been much impressed with the Zulu tactics:

It was really a pleasure to watch the manner in which these Zulus skirmished. No crowding, no delay, as soon as they were driven from one cover they would hasten rapidly to the next awkward bit of country through which our column would have to pass. Luckily for us their shooting was inferior or we should have suffered severely.

The Zulus called off their pursuit about two miles from the fort, much to the relief of those in the column. Safely back in camp at about 10.00am, the men sought what shade they could from a very hot sun and swapped stories of their exploits. Pearson had been lucky: although effectively pursued all the way back, his command had suffered no casualties. Some of his officers, however, were less than impressed with the morning's work. Lieutenant Lloyd described it as a 'most unsatisfactory expedition' while Lieutenant Main summed up the feelings of many with the comment that 'we got back safely to Eshowe, to grumble over a badly organized outing'. It was difficult to avoid the conclusion that the Zulus had got the better of the affair.

After his exploits of the previous day, Captain Wynne did not feel at all well on Sunday 2 March. He had been affected by diarrhoea during the night and felt 'weak and headachy' in the day. He was very upset to have to miss church parade, but comforted himself by reading the day's service. After the service the men were all dismissed as no work was scheduled for the day, apart from those assigned as cattle guards and vedettes.

One of these vedettes was patrolling to the south of the fort when, at about 3.00pm, he noticed a persistent flicker of light from the distant hills towards the Thukela. He reported it to the Fort, and a group of officers rode out to investigate. Despite the fact that the country fell away in front of them and was laid out like a map, the Thukela was too far away to distinguish details, even with the aid of field-glasses, but the light itself was still clearly visible. What did it mean? Opinions varied; a Zulu homestead, set alight by the Thukela garrison, perhaps, or even a natural grass fire? The light was too bright and the flash too regular; besides, there was no sign of smoke. The sun glinting on a piece of glass somewhere? Possibly, but why was the flash so systematic? Suddenly the truth dawned, and someone realised that the distant flickering represented an attempt by the Thukela garrison to open communications with Eshowe. It was the first sign of friendly life outside the fort for nineteen days, and its significance was not lost on the beleaguered garrison; for the first time in five weeks there was a chance that messages might again be regularly exchanged with the rest of Chelmsford's army. If nothing else, it proved that the garrison in Natal had not been entirely overrun by the Zulus, and news of friends and family would surely follow. Best of all, it offered the hope that Chelmsford's men were aware of Pearson's plight, and that relief might therefore be at hand.

The news spread like wildfire through the garrison. The air buzzed with excitement, and men crowded out of the fort to look. There was no obvious means of reply, but everyone who could lay their hands on a mirror or a piece of shiny metal pushed to the front to try to flash back a response. In fact, the distant flicker was so faint and broken it was impossible to make anything of this first message, and the amateurish attempts to respond were hopeless from the start. More practically, someone suggested that rockets fired into the sky might be visible at the Thukela, and would at least confirm that the efforts of the men there had been seen. Two rockets were sent up, without any clear result; in the air of sudden euphoria that had swept the fort, however, that failure did not matter. Morale had soared, and even the sick seemed to take fresh heart. Pelly Clarke was one of those gripped by the excitement of the moment: 'Great was our joy! Faces that had for long borne an anxious and desponding look, assumed a more hopeful aspect; new energy, new life, seemed to be instilled in us, as we found all was not over. Natal had not been destroyed, and we had friends still at the Tugela who would come to our aid.'

CHAPTER 6

Listening for the Guns

The next day, Monday 3 March, broke wet and misty. This was a bitter disappointment to the garrison, who were eagerly awaiting the renewal of the signals from the Thukela. The garrison's own signalling equipment was nonexistent; although the British army had adopted the heliograph by that time, a relatively sophisticated apparatus which reflected sunlight and flashed messages by Morse code that could be read at considerable distance, there were none with Pearson's column. Nor, indeed, were there any at the Lower Drift, since Chelmsford's army seems to have embarked on the Zulu campaign without any thought to signalling procedure. This may have been a consequence of the lack of home government support, but it condemned his troops in the field to test their ingenuity improvising signalling equipment without any appropriate materials.

Wynne responded to the challenge with his usual determination. That morning he began work on a hot-air balloon. He made the canopy from tracing paper, and with typical originality he fashioned a burner from a small paraffin lamp slung below. His idea was that, if he launched it on a day when the wind was blowing evenly towards the Thukela, the balloon might just drift far enough to carry a message through. His work was interrupted at 11am, however, when the sky cleared, and the distant thud of a gun drew the garrison's attention once more towards the Thukela.

The signalling had started afresh. To most of the eager watchers at Eshowe, the flashes were incomprehensible, but a sergeant who had been on a signalling course began to note down a few letters, and, to everyone's delight, a fragment of a message began to emerge.

'Look out for....', it read, and 'meet me at ...', and 'soon as you are aware of my presence'. To the garrison's exasperation, that was all that could be understood. What did it mean? Clearly something was in the offing, and once again everyone with access to a pocket mirror tried desperately to flash back a reply, most of them without the first idea of the principles of either the heliograph or of Morse code. If any of these attempts had been seen by the troops on the Thukela, one wonders what they would have made of them.

Nothing further could be made of the message that Monday, but little by little over the next few days, whenever the clouds allowed, more of it was revealed. It was not until Thursday 6 March that the whole thing was deciphered; it was a message from Lieutenant-Colonel F.T.A. Law, RA, whom

Two incidents from the siege. Much of the fighting around the fort consisted of small skirmishes between British and Zulu patrols – here a British outpost overpowers a solitary Zulu scout. Wynne's hot air balloon was an ingenious attempt to send messages to the outside world, but was thwarted by the vagaries of the weather.

Chelmsford had recently placed in command at the Lower Thukela, and it advised Pearson that a column of 1000 men, supported by black auxiliaries, would set off from the border towards Eshowe on the 13th. Pearson was instructed to watch for this column's approach, and to sally out to meet it at the Nyezane with his surplus garrison. This was news indeed.

The garrison were naturally desperate to find a means of sending messages back, and Wynne started work on a second plan. A large black tarpaulin, 12 feet by 10 feet, was stretched on a frame with a horizontal pivot. Wynne hoped that by swinging the screen up and down for long or short 'flashes' he could transfer messages by Morse code. The balloon had been ready for launch at 4.30pm on 4 March, but just as it was about to be released, the sky darkened as heavy thunderclouds rolled in, and the attempt was abandoned. The screen was completed on the 6th but bad weather delayed its erection on a hill to the south of the fort. When it was finally fixed into position, it was caught by a gale-force wind on the afternoon of 8 March and wrecked, much to Wynne's disappointment.

Meanwhile other officers were doing their best to open communications with Natal. A search organised to find a larger mirror failed to produce results until a servant of Pearson's Principal Staff Officer, Brevet Colonel Forestier Walker of the Scots Guards, discovered one packed away in the officer's baggage. The mirror, measuring 18 inches by 12 inches, was handed over to another of Pearson's staff officers, Captain G. Macgregor of the 29th Regt, who established a signalling post on mBombotshane, the hill south of the fort. This was a superb vantage point, since the ground fell away below the crest for several hundred feet, and rolled away in an undulating carpet to the Thukela, which was just visible twenty miles away. Nevertheless, the first attempts were a failure. A length of old gaspipe, which had been found in the church, was pressed into service as a means of directing the mirror's flashes towards Fort Pearson, but when the pipe was correctly aligned it was necessary for a man to look down the other end to check that the sun's rays were travelling the entire length. Lieutenant Main, who was with the signalling party, remarked casually in his journal that, 'It took about ten minutes to get the ray through and then the man looking down the pipe was almost blinded and the ray was gone again'. That idea was abandoned when someone suggested that by covering each end of the tube with paper, it would be apparent to the operators that the ray was travelling cleanly through the pipe when both pieces of paper were illuminated. Once the light was properly aligned on the Thukela, the letters of the Morse alphabet could be made by interrupting the ray with a board strapped to the operator's hand. While this method saved the eyes of the unfortunate man whose unpleasant duty it had been to line up the beam, it proved to be a very time-consuming operation. Lieutenant Knight's description suggests something of its frustrations:

The sun was for the greater part of the day behind the signallers, thus making it very difficult to work with a single mirror. In fact, in the afternoon when the sun got low the mirror had to be laid almost horizontal, and the flash travelled so quickly off the sights that the apparatus had to be readjusted after almost every word.

Whilst the signallers struggled to perfect their improvised heliograph, Wynne constructed a second signalling screen. The new screen was in position by 10 March, and was brought into operation for two or three hours that day; unfortunately, the distance seems to have been too great, and it was invisible to the party at the Thukela end. However, much to the garrison's delight, communications were again received from the Thukela on 14 March. Captain Beddoes of the Natal Native Pioneers streamlined the laborious process at the Eshowe end by making a pivot for the mirror, which was then fixed to a barrel, and by perfecting a sighting system using wire directing rods. From that day on, so long as the sun shone, Eshowe had a means of communicating with the outside world.

As soon as he received Law's message, Pearson began to prepare for the possibility of sallying out of the fort with part of his garrison. Although the received message was clearly incomplete, it was obvious that a column would be starting up from the Thukela very shortly. The road up to Eshowe was long and dangerous, because it wound through thick bush here and there where the Zulus could assemble for an attack unseen. Pearson asked Wynne to try to find a shorter route, which would cut off a particularly difficult stretch near Eshowe itself. At 1.00pm on the 14th Wynne, Courtney, Main and Willock, the four Engineer officers, assembled with an infantry escort, a company of the 99th and two companies of 'The Buffs' under Lieutenant-Colonel Ely of the 99th. Lieutenant Main left a fascinating and amusing account of the reconnaissance that followed:

> We duly paraded and waited for the infantry to push out and cover our pro-
> ceedings and were a little surprised when Colonel Ely said 'If you Engineer
> Officers will start on, we will back you up' and it required a little courage to
> point out to him that it would be better for the infantry to open the ball.
> However eventually he agreed to that and we had quite a lively afternoon with
> small parties of Zulus. But Colonel Ely was anything but a leader of men and
> just when it seemed that we might teach the Zulus a lesson, his courage failed
> him and he shouted to Captain Wayman (99th) who was spoiling for a fight to
> withdraw at once or he would place him under arrest. Wayman had suddenly
> become conveniently deaf, so Ely added 'I heard a dog bark and that means there
> are Zulus about'. This I regret to say caused much laughter among the men, and
> ever afterwards when Ely went out in command of a party the wags used to
> imitate a dog's bark, and even in the fort itself.

A romanticised, but otherwise accurate, rendition of one of Pearson's sorties from the fort. Here the attempt to signal from the church tower rather optimistically resembles a searchlight. *(Rai England Collection)*

Despite Ely's reluctance to push on, the Engineer officers felt that it would be possible to cut a new road down a spur south of the ravine, intercepting the old road further down, and thereby shorten the route by about five miles and avoid much of the thick bush. Wynne reported back to Pearson who approved the plan, and ordered him to begin construction without delay. Unfortunately the rain was so heavy the next day, 7 March, that it restricted the work parties to just three hours' effort before a storm drove them back to the fort.

This new enterprise of the British soon attracted the attention of the watchful Zulu cordon. The rain plagued the project for the next couple of days, and no sooner had the sun come out on the 9th, and the fatigue parties set to work, than a group of Zulus appeared some distance off and opened fire on them. The work party returned their fire, but no casualties were caused on either side. This, however, had not been the only confrontation between outposts in the first week of March. Two days earlier a far more serious incident had taken place.

On the morning of Friday 7 March Corporal Carson of the 99th, attached to the Mounted Infantry, rode out to take up his position at No. 4 vedette post. As he approached his allotted position, a group of twelve or fifteen Zulus burst from the long grass and rushed toward him. Carson's horse reared up in fright and the first warrior up grabbed at its mane. Carson, who was holding on for dear life, managed to retain his seat and put spurs to his horse, which leapt forward and away from its attackers. One of the Zulus thrust forward with a spear and plunged it into the rump of the terrified animal as it galloped away, while the rest fired a ragged volley to bring Carson down. Several shots struck him; one passed through the front of his right thigh and continued on through the pommel of his saddle before coming to rest in his left thigh, while another smashed into his right hand, almost severing two fingers, and leaving them attached by no more than a thread of skin. A final bullet, aimed for the very centre of his back, failed to find its target only because it struck the lock of the Swinburn-Henry carbine which – contrary to orders – was slung across his body. Carson managed to reach his fellow vedettes, and the Zulus abandoned the pursuit. Carson rode back to the fort in such a calm manner that it was a few moments before anyone realised the seriousness of his wounds. He was immediately taken to the hospital where his two damaged fingers were amputated. Carson recovered well and was promoted to sergeant, his calm handling of this traumatic experience being noted by all. As a postscript to this incident, at the conclusion of the war Carson was invalided home and had to retire from the army due to his wounds. Some time later he appeared before a brother of Lieutenant Lloyd, who was a Resident Magistrate in Ireland, charged with assault. Carson had apparently assaulted an old man and stolen his hat, and in the words of Lieutenant Lloyd '. . . for which joke the Ekowe hero, I am sorry to say, paid the penalty'.

The bad weather which had caused such problems for the signalling parties and road builders also made life difficult at the fort itself. In the heavy rain of Saturday 8 March part of the caponnier in the south ditch collapsed. Gunner Carroll complained that the strong winds sweeping across the heights at Eshowe were also making it extremely difficult to cook. This was already a difficult enough task which was stretching the ingenuity of the garrison to the full. It was generally bemoaned that the last of the slaughter oxen was eaten on 8 March, after which the garrison had to resort to the very tough trek oxen that had hauled the wagons up from the border. Because the quality was so poor, Pearson authorised an additional meat allowance, which increased from one and a quarter pounds a day to one and a half pounds. Captain Pelly Clarke grumbled that since there was no fat on the meat, 'our "pound of flesh" would not fry without it'. Attempts to improvise were both unappetising and unsuccessful; boot-dubbing did not work, nor did wagon-grease which contained too much tar! According to Lieutenant Lloyd, 'Hard was no name for the meat; it was simply impossible to get one's teeth through it unless it was stewed down to ribbons'. Lieutenant Knight cast an envious eye towards the Naval Brigade encampment at times, remarking that

> the resource and handiness of the blue jackets was a considerable cause of amusement and wonder to the rest of the garrison. No matter how short the supply of food, nor the time of day, Jack always seemed to have something to cook, and small parties of men were preparing little snacks of some dainty-smelling dish at all hours.

Perhaps one or two envious glances were also cast in the direction of the Engineer officers' mess on 6 March when it celebrated no less than two birthdays – Lieutenant Main was twenty-nine, and Lieutenant Willock twenty-five. While on the road reconnaissance the day before they had captured a 'fine old rooster' which they now served up with a pumpkin acquired from a nearby Zulu garden by some of the Natal Pioneers, at great personal risk to themselves.

The first full week of March saw no let-up in the solemn processions to the cemetery. On the 4th Private Paul of the 99th Regiment succumbed to the effects of sunstroke. Two days later Drummer Mortimer of 'The Buffs' lost his battle against dysentery; so did Leading Seaman Radford of the *Active* on 8 March. That same day Private Barber of the Army Hospital Corps died of enteric fever, and on Sunday the 9th Private Stack of 'The Buffs' was buried. His death had been caused by an obstruction in his intestines. Commander Campbell wrote an official dispatch on 9 March in which he mentioned that about twenty of the Naval Brigade were ill in hospital, including Midshipman Coker, who had been in command of the Gatling gun at Nyezane. Coke had dysentery but according to Campbell was showing some improvement. Lieutenant Hamilton of HMS *Active* was concerned about the increasing sickness; in a letter to his father at the end of the week he wrote, 'We have had four days of incessant rain, which is very trying for everyone. I am well, I am thankful to say, but there are a number of officers laid up – six on the list this morning'. Lieutenant Davison went on one of his regular walks that Sunday afternoon after the rain had cleared, but on his return he, too, complained of feeling very sick.

At about 7.00am on the morning of 10 March great cheers echoed through the fort as a runner arrived bearing a letter for Pearson from Law, written fourteen days before. When questioned, the runner claimed that he had been hunted through the bush for the last two weeks, but had fired off all his ammunition and managed to evade his pursuers. The garrison were not convinced. The man wore a greatcoat marked for the 24th Regiment which bore no tears or rips, suggesting that it had been looted rather than issued to him, and his feet showed no signs of having been in the bush for any period of time. Furthermore his body had been recently oiled in the Zulu fashion. These were not the signs of a man who had been living on his wits, alone in the bush for two weeks. It was suspected that in fact he was a Zulu spy who had probably killed the real messenger, and taken his place. After much questioning, he was clapped in irons and handed over to a RE guard with whom he remained a prisoner. Lieutenant Lloyd wrote, 'What became of the wretched man I know not. When with us he was continually informed that his fate would be the gallows'. However, it seems that the poor man was in fact who he claimed to be, and was quite innocent of any duplicity. On 19 March a flashed message was received at Eshowe from Law which enquired blandly, 'What has happened to my messenger of 24 February? He is Mr Fynney's groom. Have you hung him?'. The garrison responded simply, 'He is still a prisoner'. The truth of the prisoner's story was finally confirmed on 23 March when Law sent a further message to the effect that 'the name given to you by the messenger who is a prisoner with you is the name of Fynney's groom whom I sent'. However, Pearson was unwilling to take any chances, and refused to have the man released; it seems he remained under penalty of death until the end of the siege, when he was presumably set free. The whole incident suggests just how nervous Pearson and his officers had become; even had the man been a spy, it is difficult to imagine what he could have told the Zulus that might have made an attack on the post any easier. Most of its defences were only too apparent, after all, to the scouts who watched it every day.

That Monday also promised good weather, and Wynne was keen to make progress on the road which would be needed in a few days. Setting out at 6.00am, the working parties were no sooner in position than several groups of Zulus appeared on the surrounding hilltops. The Zulus opened an ineffective long-range fire, and the work party's escort replied. The British fire was equally ineffective, however, and this encouraged the Zulus to try to work around the flanks of the force. There was no one in overall command of the British party, and more and more men were withdrawn from the road to add their fire to the futile exchange. Back in the fort Pearson could hear the sound of gunfire, and was told that the Zulus were threatening both the road party and the cattle, which were also out in that direction. Having lost a little of his confidence after the attack on eSiqwakeni, Pearson, rather than sending out reinforcements, sounded the retreat and ordered one of the Royal Marine Artillery 7-pounders out to cover it. Delighted by their success the Zulus kept up a heavy fire on the soldiers as they retired. Gunner Carroll, who was with the 7-pounder, fired a few rounds of shrapnel at the Zulus and studied their reaction with interest:

> I observed them several times looking around wondering where the bullets came from, which they could not understand, the shrapnel bursting fifty yards from them and the bullets flying about their ears, it is no wonder they were startled, for to see a volley sent in their very midst and not knowing where it came from was enough to startle the bravest of them.

When the firing died down the Zulus inspected the road party's efforts and set about disrupting it where they could, removing marking lines, pulling up road posts and generally taking steps to hinder the progress of the new track. In the afternoon Pearson agreed to allow another work party, this time solely consisting of the Natal Pioneers, to return to the road, with a covering party of about 700 men – which far outnumbered the work party. The RMA gun also accompanied the expedition. Although the covering party scoured the surrounding hills, they found no sign of the Zulus, who had wisely melted away. Because the work party was so small, little enough was achieved that day, and in the evening the Zulus returned and once again destroyed what they could. Back at the fort Captain Wynne, who described the afternoon's efforts as a fiasco, was angry at Pearson's over-caution, and 'found it necessary to speak strongly and earnestly on the subject to [him] in the evening, saying that I could not be responsible for the completion of the road unless the most vigorous measures were taken on the remaining days.'

That night Wynne suffered a recurrence of the diarrhoea which had plagued him earlier in the siege, and the following morning he felt weak. Nevertheless, he was determined to work on the road again the next morning. Pearson had taken notice of his criticism, and the day's fatigue party was a strong one, protected again by about 700 men, under Ely, and with the two RA guns. Following the pattern of the previous day, the Zulus appeared on the surrounding hills and opened a long-range fire on the soldiers below, which made the work a nerve-wracking experience but failed to cause any casualties or hinder progress. The worst moment came when a chance shot struck Lieutenant

D.F. Lewis of 'The Buffs'. Lewis, who had been with the Colour party at Nyezane, had been directing his company's covering fire when a home-made bullet hit the peak of his helmet. It clipped his left temple, then passed across his forehead. Lieutenant Lloyd saw him fall and ran over to him, and Lewis '... was instantly picked up by two of his men. On arriving on the spot, I saw his face covered with blood', but miraculously it proved to be no more than a flesh wound. Apart from a severe headache which lasted for two days, a pair of black eyes and an impressive scar, he was uninjured.

At the completion of the day's work the road party determined to put an end to the Zulus' interference with their progress, and so, under the direction of Captain Beddoes of the Natal Native Pioneers, they improvised a booby-trap. The device, a landmine made from dynamite with a friction tube as detonator, was tied to a wooden stake planted in the ground. The dynamite was covered by some planks of wood. To ensure that no unwary soldier tampered with it, a board was attached to the top on which was painted the word TORPEDO. Even before the work party reached the fort they heard a tremendous explosion behind them as the mine detonated. The Zulus had pulled up the stake and set off the charge; some must inevitably have been killed, and the rest could be seen fleeing in terror in all directions. It was the last time the Zulus attempted to interfere with the road party's works.

Earlier the same day No. 4 vedette post was again the scene of an ambush attempt. Captain Shervinton of the 'Uhlans' was about to post three vedettes when

> ... about 30 Zulus jumped up out of the long grass and fired a volley into us. Two of the men's horses took fright, turned straight round and bolted, the third man, Pte. Brooks 99th, was thrown from his horse and his foot caught in the stirrup. The Zulus who had fired into us had retired immediately afterwards but another party on a hill across a kloof about 300 yds distant shouted out there is a man down. About 12 men immediately returned to assegai Pte. Brooks who could not yet get his foot free. I had been sitting on my horse which was very fidgety waiting for Pte. Brooks to mount when I saw these men return, they were then only a few yards (5 or 6) from him (it being impossible to see them before owing to the length of the grass). When I charged in among them and drove them back, I put Pte. Brooks on my horse as he was a good deal shaken by being dragged about. After placing him under cover I returned and picked up his rifle and helmet, and shortly afterwards more mounted men coming up the party of Zulus on the hilltop ceased firing and retired.

This incident was to lead to a campaign after the war to secure for Shervinton the award of the Victoria Cross – the only one recommended for the entire Eshowe campaign.

Unknown to the garrison there were other narrow escapes for the vedettes and sentries guarding the fort. Bertram Mitford, a traveller and writer who visited Zululand in 1882, only three years after the war, delighted in talking to Zulus about the conflict. One had a convincing story of the siege:

> This bold warrior ... in the company with seven other congenial spirits, were amusing themselves one day stalking a couple of men on picket duty, who sat quite unconcernedly while their deadly foes were advancing nearer and nearer upon them. 'While they were talking,' said my informant, 'we crept on; when they were silent we lay still as if dead. We got within fifty yards of them, when others came from the fort; we did not like the look of these, so we were obliged to go away again'. I venture to say that those two will never know what an escape they had.

The second week of March, indeed, suggested to the garrison that the Zulus were stepping up their activity around the fort. Not only was the work party constantly harassed, while smaller Zulu bands menaced the vedettes, but on the 11th and 12th large numbers were observed skirting the fort and moving down towards the Nyezane. Gunner Carroll claimed to have seen one group which he estimated at being 3000 strong, moving past on the 12th. It became obvious to the garrison that the Zulus were aware that the relief force was about to march, and that they intended obstructing its progress. Captain Pelly Clark left a fascinating description of these Zulu movements:

> A tiny speck would appear on the top of a hill, it would soon after grow bigger in circumference, till it attained that of a huge circle. The 'speck' was the 'lookout' man of a regiment, which, when he had reported 'all correct', would gradually come up the hill and form round him in a circle. . . . After a short consultation – squatting the while – the circle would slowly unwind itself, and move till again only the 'speck' would be left; he would wait till joined by the 'lookout' man of the next regiment, when he would hasten on to join his own corps.

The night of 11/12 March was another bad one for both Captain Wynne and Lieutenant Davison. Wynne's hard work on the road had not helped his poor health and Davison was still feeling very sick. Nevertheless Wynne rose early on the morning of the 12th, and marched out with the road party, but he soon realised he was not fit enough for work and reported to the hospital. He was joined on the sick list that same day by Davison, who had handed his responsibilities as adjutant of the 99th to Second Lieutenant Johnson a week before. Curiously, Davison seems to have resigned his post after an argument with Colonel Welman over a court martial on the 3rd; a prisoner had been acquitted, 'at which Col. was angry and said I was not fit for my post.' When the court reconvened the next day, however, it confirmed the original findings; what the charge was, and why Welman was so angry, Davison did not say.

Sadly, as Wynne and Davison were reporting sick, the first death of an officer in the garrison occurred. Captain H.J.M. Williams of 'The Buffs' was a robust forty-year-old, who was something of a seasoned traveller; he had served abroad with the army, and had enjoyed numerous exotic shooting trips. Nevertheless, this did not save him from exposure, which sapped his constitution, and laid him open to a fatal attack of fever and diarrhoea.

The road party continued its work under the supervision of Lieutenant Courtney of the Engineers. Surgeon Norbury recorded that the weather was sometimes so hot that several of the fatigue party collapsed with heat-stroke; nevertheless, the project was completed by the deadline of 13 March. On the 12th, Pearson had issued his orders to the party who were to march out to meet the relief expedition on its way up. It was to consist of the three companies of the 99th, the Naval Brigade, thirty Royal Engineers and fifty Natal Native Pioneers, a total of about 600 men. They were to take with them the Gatling gun and two mule wagons, which were to carry fifteen rockets and their tubes, three days' basic foodstuffs, one day's preserved meat, and the camp-kettles. In addition six oxen were to be taken along for slaughter and eight pack-oxen were supplied for the officers' effects. Each man was to carry his greatcoat, one day's cooked rations, one day's biscuit and one hundred rounds of ammunition. There were those who felt this force, so encumbered and weakened by the long sojourn at Eshowe, would be hard pushed to fight off the Zulus if they chose to attack.

On the morning of 13 March this column duly packed its baggage and was formed up by 9.00am, waiting for the order to march. The morning had started cloudy, but at about 9.00am the sun broke through, and signals could be seen flickering at the Thukela. The first message, however, cast a pall of gloom over the garrison as the words were spelt out, 'Relief postponed till the 1 April'. In addition, it went on to inform the garrison that the relief column would now consist of 4000 white troops and 2000 black, and that the whole garrison was to be relieved. They would be replaced by the 60th Rifles, who had just arrived from England. Eshowe was further informed that fifteen transport ships were plying their way across the ocean towards Natal, bringing with them an extra 8000 men as reinforcements.

The news received a mixed reaction; those who had been concerned for the safety of the column were relieved, as, indeed, were some of those who had been selected to remain in what would have been a much more vulnerable garrison. However, the majority of the men shared Lieutenant Lloyd's emotions:

Our hopes, buoyed up for the past ten days, were now dashed to the ground; we were to return to monotony and imprisonment. It was heart-breaking to be forced to impart this news to the sick, some of whom had, seemingly, taken a new lease of life at the idea of relief being so close at hand.

The rest of the week was an anti-climax for the garrison, the only excitement being the success of the signallers in establishing two-way communications between Eshowe and the Thukela on 14 March. Crowds of men congregated around the signallers as they worked their improvised heliograph, trying to guess the meaning of messages as the letters were received. Sometimes their enthusiasm got the better of them, and they would surge forward and obscure the apparatus completely, prematurely bringing communications to a close. At the end of each day all the messages that had been received would be posted on a notice board so that the garrison, for so long starved of news, could gather round and savour every snippet.

The garrison, however, was starved not merely of news. By this stage many of the men were feeling weak through weight loss; most had lost over a stone, and some two. The monotonous diet continued, sapping morale and adding to a feeling of melancholy which prevailed at the post. It had become general knowledge that the biscuit supply was now going mouldy and was infested by weevils. The weevils had also got into the remains of the mealie meal. Captain Pelly Clarke, at least, appears to have retained his sense of humour through it all, and he remarked that 'the biscuit when baked is quite good, even if full of weevils; and some mealie meal that had got full of them, was pronounced by some as all the better for the little animals'. Gunner Carroll, who was not so enthusiastic about the 'little animals' in his food also complained that the men were still sleeping fully accoutred under the wagons each night, as they had done since the siege began. When it had rained during the day, the men would inevitably get wet, and spent the night shivering in damp uniforms. The sickness that was prevalent in the fort had found the perfect breeding ground. One officer wrote that 'there was a great amount of sickness among both officers and men, from which, too, no one who was once seized appeared to rally'. Lieutenant Lloyd commented on the deficiency of medicines and the ceaseless efforts of the medical staff to alleviate the suffering of the patients, 'the majority of whom suffered from fever, which in most cases turned to delirium. The moaning of these poor men throughout the night was painful to hear'. Another common complaint was 'Natal Sores'. These sores, which were extremely painful and difficult to heal, were believed to be caused by the exposure of a cut or scratch to the sun. The treatment was basic; Pelly Clarke, described the appearance of those so afflicted: 'There were few in the fort that did not appear with a piece of rag round one of their fingers, or their noses enveloped in cotton wool, with some white powder on it, giving them a most unearthly appearance.'

Tough as life was at Eshowe, the men greatly lamented the shortage of one commodity in particular. Tobacco, that great luxury and comfort of troops in the field, was so much in demand that the little which remained in the fort changed hands at hugely inflated prices. At the beginning of March an ounce of tobacco sold for three or four shillings; by the middle of the month it fetched ten shillings and sixpence, on the 17th an ounce changed hands for eighteen shillings and sixpence, and on the 22nd one sold for twenty-two shillings and sixpence. Those soldiers unable to afford these prices tried smoking dried leaves and herbs, which they found growing near the fort, while many settled for tea-leaves. According to Private Hymas of 'The Buffs' this produced a 'peculiar smoke'.

A short period of relatively fair weather ended on Sunday 16 March with a terrific thunderstorm that ushered in three days of heavy rain. With the rain came death for some of those ailing in the hospital. Private Tubb of the 99th died from sunstroke, and Marine Stagg of HMS *Active* lost his fight against pneumonia. These two were followed by perhaps the one death that affected the garrison more than any other, that of Midshipman Lewis Coker, also of the *Active*. Coker, who had been in command of the Gatling gun at Nyezane, was still only eighteen, and had become ill through choosing to sleep in the open each night, close to his charge. Coker was a popular lad among the garrison, and his youthful enthusiasm and devotion to duty held the promise of a successful career. Stricken by dysentery, he had clung on to life for some time in the hospital, where he was regularly visited by his shipmates. He had appeared to rally, but on that Sunday morning he suffered a relapse and never recovered. He died at about 10.00pm that evening. At his funeral Lieutenant Lloyd noted that there were 'very few dry eyes'. Davison and Wynne who were both on the sick list were also showing signs of improvement. Davison wrote sparingly in his diary that he was suffering from 'bad headache no appetite several internal pains'. Wynne, who was regularly visited by Pearson, 'felt nausea and was feverish'.

The intelligence network of the Zulu army, meanwhile, was obviously working very well. The large concentrations which had been seen making their way down towards the Nyezane earlier in the week were now seen making their way back again on the 15th; they were clearly aware that the advance had been postponed. Estimates of the number of Zulus were as high as 20,000, moving north-west of the fort. This figure is unlikely, but it may be that many of them were in fact heading inland towards the king's capital, oNdini, where a general muster had been called.

The following morning, Monday 17 March, the ever-present dangers of vedette duty were brought home to the garrison once again. The notorious No. 4 vedette post was the scene of another ambush. At about 8.00am Private Kent of the 99th took up his position at the post, with a colleague on each flank some distance off. One was a Trooper Niekirk of the Natal Hussars, the other, like

Kent, was attached to the Mounted Infantry. As Kent settled into his position, five Zulus suddenly sprung up without any warning, and fired a volley at him. Kent's horse was hit, reared up, threw off its rider, and galloped away towards the fort, streaming blood. Kent hardly had time to gather his wits about him before the Zulus were on him. There was a brief struggle, and he fell with seventeen or eighteen stab-wounds. The other two vedettes saw the attack – which must have been over in seconds – and turned their horses, riding away to raise the alarm. A group of the 'Uhlans' were immediately dispatched to the scene, supported by a company of the 99th, and Kent's body was recovered. The Zulus had taken his gun and ammunition. A charge of cowardice was later brought against the two vedettes on the grounds that they had failed to go to Kent's assistance, and a court of inquiry was convened. Trooper Niekirk, who was generally held to be a brave man, argued in his defence that the Mounted Infantryman had retreated first, and that he saw no point in staying alone; it was unfortunate for him that he had overtaken his comrade and reached the fort first. The result of the inquiry is unknown –although rumour suggested that the Mounted Infantryman was liable to a five-year sentence – but it was decided that in future a body of infantry should sweep the outlying area each morning before vedettes were posted. It is interesting to note that this decision was only taken ten days after the unsuccessful attack on Carson. Private Kent was laid to rest alongside a fellow member of the 99th, Private Venn, who died of enteric fever that same day.

The flickering communication from the Thukela brought good news for Courtney; he had been promoted captain. He had, in any case, taken over as acting commander of Engineers while Wynne was sick, and was busily continuing Wynne's work. On the 17th he ordered the old cattle laager, which had never been satisfactory, to be broken up, and he used the wagons to build two new circular laagers to the south of the fort. If the siting was preferable, however, the suffering of the oxen continued, for that night twenty were struck dead by a tremendous thunderstorm. Pelly Clarke's sense of humour still had not deserted him, and of the move he wrote, 'What a site for a future mealie field would that of the old kraal be, being in many places three feet deep in muck!'

Courtney also organised the replacement of some of the wagon traversing, replacing them with a sod wall. This meant that a number of men who had been sleeping under the wagons were evicted, but this proved to their advantage, as tents were allocated to those who lost their 'homes' in this way. Courtney himself was still happily free of illness, but he reported that on 19 March Willock had joined Wynne and about nineteen other men of the Royal Engineers on the sick list. The next day Captain Beddoes of the Natal Native Pioneers also reported sick. Wynne and Davison were now both extremely ill, neither of them able to keep up their diaries or letters.

The gloom that had pervaded the garrison for some time was lifted on the 19th when a great cheer heralded the arrival of a runner from the Thukela. This was the first man to run the gauntlet of the Zulu outposts and complete the journey since 11 February, thirty-six days before. He brought with him full details of the force being assembled at the Lower Drift, and the news that it was due to advance on the 29th. The joy that this news brought to the weary and dispirited garrison was immense; at last there was a definite prospect of an end to their isolation. The runner also brought other letters which contained news of the progress of the war and reactions from home, and these were duly posted on the fort's notice board for everyone's enlightenment. Pearson was invigorated by the news, and immediately ordered a foray to be made the next day, selecting a Zulu homestead across the Mlalazi river as a target. This was known to be used as a shelter by some of the Zulu outposts who had been harassing the cattle guards. The raid was a minor affair, but it was successful; a couple of shells were fired into the circle of nine huts, and a party advanced and burnt it.

On Sunday 23 March a number of messages were received from the signal station on the Thukela, one of which stated that a report had come in indicating that the Zulus were planning to try to entice the garrison out of the protection of the fort. Shortly after this communication was received, two Zulu messengers approached the fort under a white flag. Quite where they had obtained this white flag is not explained; certainly, as late as the Boer War twenty years later, the erratic use by the Boers of the white flag was excused on the grounds that they knew nothing of the Geneva Convention, and its terms were hardly likely to have been the subject of after-dinner conversation among the black population in 1879. Perhaps John Dunn had told Cetshwayo to send his envoys with a white flag, as it signalled peaceful intentions, or perhaps Chelmsford's own staff had suggested the idea in earlier diplomatic exchanges. One surviving Zulu 'white flag' proves to have been nothing more than a white handkerchief skewered through the corner with a stick. In any case, the garrison were clearly suspicious, and the messengers were blindfolded and taken before Colonel Pearson, to whom they explained that they were envoys sent by King Cetshwayo. They had an interesting offer to make; if the British retired to the Thukela without destroying any of the mealie fields along the way they would not be molested. They also assured Pearson that the local Zulu commanders, including Prince Dabulamanzi, supported this offer. Nevertheless, Pearson was unconvinced, and the offer seemed particularly doubtful in the light of the message the garrison had recently received. As a result, he treated it with disdain, and ordered the envoys to be arrested as spies.

In fact, the offer was almost certainly genuine, for as March drew on, King Cetshwayo had realised that a new bout of fighting was imminent. Chelmsford had refused all peace offerings, and reinforcements were flooding into Durban on a daily basis, and the king was anxious to make a last diplomatic effort to

35. Lieutenant Evelyn of 'The Buffs', who carried the Colours at Nyezane, but died of disease at Eshowe on 30 March.

36. Captain H.J.N. Williams of 'The Buffs', the senior officer to die of disease at Eshowe during the siege.

37. The poignant cemetery on the slope of the ravine to the west of the fort, where the British victims of the siege were buried; the photograph was taken in late 1879. *(S.B. Bourquin)*

38. The view along the north-western ramparts, *c*. June 1879. This photograph gives a good impression of the extent of Wynne's fortifications, and suggests why the Zulus declined to assault them. *(S.B. Bourquin)*

39. Inside the abandoned fort, *c*. June 1879; the mission bell, which had rung the alarm throughout the siege, lies overturned on the right; note the remains of the tree, cut down by the garrison, in the foreground. *(S.B. Bourquin)*

40. The main path through the centre of the old fort, built by Wynne's Engineers, with the ruins of the church on the left and the mission graves on the right. *(S.B. Bourquin)*

41. The force at the Lower Thukela were hardly better equipped for signalling than the Eshowe garrison; Chelmsford *(right)*, with Commodore Richards, inspects the St Andrew's signal station on 23 March; the unconventional apparatus is visible in the background. A sketch by Lieutenant-Colonel J.N. Crealock. *(Sherwood Forresters Museum, Nottingham)*

42. The Gatling, crew and officers of HMS *Boadicea*'s Naval Brigade, who fought at Gingindlovu. *(S.B. Bourquin)*

43. HMS *Tenedos*'s Naval Brigade, with Royal Marine detachment *(right)*.

44. The officers of the 91st Highlanders in Zululand towards the end of the war. *(National Army Museum)*

45. The 91st Highlanders on the march in Zululand, late 1879; a splendid photograph of a full imperial battalion in the field. These are the men who held the southern face of the laager at Gingindlovu. *(National Army Museum)*

46. An intriguing photograph of the NNC, which has persistently defied definitive analysis. Since the men are armed with firearms and in uniform, it clearly post-dates the unit's reorganisation, and the men probably belong to the 4th or 5th Battalions – both of which were present at Gingindlovu – and were photographed *c.* June 1879. *(National Army Museum)*

47. The relief begins: Lord Chelmsford's column starting from Fort Tenedos during the miserable weather of 29 March.

48. A panoramic and atmospheric sketch of Chelmsford's sprawling column crossing the amaTigulu river.

49. Lord Chelmsford, the British commander-in-chief in South Africa, who led the Eshowe relief column in person. *(Ron Sheeley Collection)*

50. Captain W.C.F. Molyneux, 22nd Regiment, one of Lord Chelmsford's ADCs, and his laager-master on the relief expedition; it was Molyneux who planned the laager at Gingindlovu. Photo *c.* 1872. *(MOD)*

51. A panoramic view of the Zulu army streaming up from the Nyezane valley to attack Lord Chelmsford's square at Gingindlovu, 2 April 1879; a sketch by Captain C.P. Cramer of the 60th. *(Killie Campbell Africana Library)*

52. Perhaps the most accurate representation of the scene inside the laager at the height of the battle: the 91st Highlanders defend the southern face (*right*), with the *Shah*'s Gatling visible beyond, in the centre of the picture. A rocket leaves a fiery trail (*background right*) as it arcs out towards the Zulus, concealed by the heavy smoke. Note the civilian wagon-drivers firing from their wagons (*left*); John Dunn was among them.

53. The *arme blanche* in action: Mounted Infantry pursuing Zulus after Gingindlovu. Despite their unfamiliarity with their weapons, the MI inflicted heavy casualties as the Zulu retreat collapsed into a rout.

54. The graves of the British dead just outside the rampart at Gingindlovu.

55. Lieutenant George Johnson, the 99th's Instructor of Musketry, killed at Gingindlovu.

56. Lieutenant Colonel Francis Northey, 3/60th, mortally wounded at Gingindlovu.

57. Captain Hugh Gough, formerly of the Coldstream Guards, who served with Nettleton's Battalion of the NNC during the relief expedition, and was present at Gingindlovu.

58. Second Lieutenant Arthur Clynton Baskerville 'Bunny' Mynors, 3/60th.

59. An impressive trophy of Zulu arms collected from the battlefield of Gingindlovu by the 91st Highlanders: a war-shield and spears *(centre)* flanked by percussion firearms, cow-tail body-ornaments and headdresses, and, below the shield, a magnificent ceremonial waist-covering. *(National Army Museum)*

60. Grim testimony to the losses suffered by the Zulus at Gingindlovu; skeletons lying on the field, late 1879. *(S.B. Bourquin)*

61. 'How are you?': the meeting between Lord Chelmsford and Pearson, 3 April, 1879. *(S.B. Bourquin)*

62. Relief at last: the 60th Rifles march into Eshowe along Pearson's new road late on the evening of 3 April. The artist has stressed the weakened state of the garrison cheering them in; note the graveyard *(left)*, and the mission spire on the skyline.

63. Retribution: Lord Chelmsford's expedition to destroy Prince Dabulamanzi's eZulwini homestead, 4 April, 1879. The party is harassed by Zulu snipers on the hilltop (*left*).

64. Three Zulus apparently captured at Gingindlovu – probably found wounded on the battlefield – photographed at the Lower Thukela after the withdrawal. Their guards are thought to be men of 'The Buffs'. *(Bryan Maggs Collection)*

65. The officers of the 2nd Battalion of 'The Buffs', photographed in September 1879, at the end of it all; an interesting contrast to the smart battalion photographs taken before the war. They are *(back row, left to right)* Captain Wyld, Lieutenants Campbell-Johnson, Somerset, Knight-Bruce, Hughes, Backhouse and Howarth, Captain Alexander; *(middle row, left to right)* Lieutenants Connellan and Martin, Lieutenant-Colonel Parnell, Captains Forster and Mcclear, Lieutenant Patterson, Major Halahan and Captain Harrison; and *(front row, left to right)* Lieutenants Middleton, Blackburn, Vyvian and Gordon, Lieutenant and Quartermaster Morgan. *(Bryan Maggs Collection)*

66. Herwen military hospital, Stanger, where many of the sick from the siege were nursed back to health. *(Bryan Maggs Collection)*

67. The cemetery at Fort Pearson, 1879.

head off the horrors of a new invasion. But Pearson was in no mood to take chances now, with the end of the siege in sight, and there was an air of expectancy about the garrison which was only dampened by the rising toll of disease; Private Coombes of the 99th died of enteric fever and was buried on 21 March.

There was now little work left to be completed on the fort. Courtney continued pulling wagons from the defences and replacing them with sod traverses, for the protection, now, of the future garrison. The transport officers began to organise any repairs they felt were necessary to their vehicles. An order was passed which forbade any more private messages being sent from Eshowe by sun-signal; this link with the outside world had proved such a novelty that for a fee of five shillings soldiers had been allowed to send messages to wives and friends in Natal. Some of these messages seem positively bizarre, under the circumstances: on 20 March a Sergeant Sherer of the NNC asked if Captain Hart would send £15 to his wife in Cape Town, while three days later the Thukela signal station enquired whether Colonel Walker wanted his flannel shirts sent up with the relief column. Several men – Lieutenant Lewis among them – sent messages to assure friends and relatives that they were well. Even Pearson had succumbed to temptation in this regard; he was concerned for the health of his wife who had been expecting a baby when he left to prepare for the invasion; he had heard no word since he had arrived at Eshowe. The signallers flashed his message, 'How is Mrs Pearson', and after a short delay the reply came back, 'Mrs Pearson is . . .'; and at that point a cloud intervened, the sun disappeared, and signalling had to be abandoned. Lieutenant Lloyd, who was sitting with Pearson at the time, speculated on the next word, '. . . dead, or alive, or what? I shall never forget my general's face when the sun having again shone out we read the letter "W", and he knew at once the word would be "Well". His look was that of intense relief.' Eventually the private message service became so popular that it interfered with official communication, and the ban was imposed. The money that had been raised was pooled into a 'relief fund' which had been started at Eshowe for the dependants of those who had died while serving with the column.

The easing of work around the fort did not apply to those engaged in caring for the sick in hospital. The steady, mournful processions of bodies being respectfully carried out to the cemetery continued. On 26 March Private Roden of the 99th died of enteric fever, to be followed next day by Private Tarrant of 'The Buffs' who had been suffering from bronchitis. Sadly, on that same day poor Lieutenant Arthur Davison, only twenty-two years of age, one-time adjutant of the 99th and keen amateur botanist, also died. Davison, who first reported sick on 12 March had lost his fifteen-day battle against enteric fever; he had stopped writing in his diary a few days before, and his last entry had been both poignant and ominous – 'Coker died last night.' Enteric's deadly harvest continued right to the end of the siege; on the 28th Private Lewis of the 99th died, and was buried shortly after a heavy thunderstorm. His grave became so flooded that his body floated on the surface of the water until enough earth could be shovelled in to weigh him down. Courtney was pleased to report that he felt Wynne and Willock seemed a little better, although the doctor remained anxious about Wynne, whose lungs had become infected.

The food supplies at Eshowe were now almost exhausted, but with the day of relief moving ever closer Colonel Pearson was not unduly concerned. He received a flashed message from Lord Chelmsford on Saturday the 29th requesting him to support the column's advance: 'Come down with 500 fighting men, when I am engaged. Four thousand men will leave Thukela today or tomorrow, and arrive at Eshowe on the 3 April. Expect to be hotly opposed.'

Having considered his position Pearson replied to Chelmsford that he did not feel able to risk an advance. He explained that the health of the garrison was so reduced and weakened by the shortage of food that he would have insufficient fit men to defend the fort while the supporting force moved down to the Nyezane. At his last check Pearson had 120 men receiving treatment from the hospital. As a compromise Chelmsford advised Pearson that at first light on the day he intended to reach Eshowe he would fire two artillery pieces to alert the garrison; if he were attacked on the march and appeared to be getting the worse of the engagement the garrison were asked to send what assistance they could.

On 30 March the excitement began to build in the fort. With a telescope it was possible to see the relief column advancing towards the amaTigulu river, closer to the coast than Pearson's column had travelled. At night, all were able to pick out the pinpoints of light that marked their campfires. Gunner Carroll joined the men watching the fires: 'Everyone is in eager anticipation of what they will bring, how many letters from home. Whether any tobacco will be brought us, or not'. But amidst the celebrations and with relief so close at hand, enteric fever claimed another victim. That evening Second Lieutenant George Evelyn of 'The Buffs', who had been on the sick list for a month, died. He was twenty-one years old and had only been with his regiment for sixteen months. The next day Chelmsford's cavalry scouts, operating far in advance of the main column, were observed scouring the path ahead, just over ten miles from Eshowe. Chelmsford's men were slowly and carefully edging closer to their goal, anticipation in the fort was growing hourly, and spirits soared.

In response to Chelmsford's request for assistance, should it be required, Pearson ordered preparations to be made for a party to be ready to march out at a moment's notice on 1 April. Accordingly the force turned out, consisting of about 350 infantry, the Naval Brigade, fifty Royal Engineers, the Natal Pioneers, one RA gun and the Mounted Infantry; each man was to carry eighty rounds of ammunition. However, the relief column's march was uninterrupted by enemy activity that day, and the heavy rains that came on in the afternoon confirmed that there would be no need for Pearson's men to sally out. From the heights at Eshowe Chelmsford's men were observed making their laager for the night on the plain below, about ten miles to the south-east of the fort, as the crow flies. Very few of the garrison turned in at lights out, the men were talking excitedly until late, and many found it hard to sleep at all. Lieutenant Lloyd was up early the next morning, eagerly anticipating the day's events, wondering if there would be a battle, and hoping to hear the firing of the two guns that would signify the commencement of the final march on Eshowe:

> At the dawn of day I crawled out as usual from under my wagon ... some few other restless creatures like myself had left their resting places, but as yet there was little stir. I was looking over the parapet at the horses in the ditch below, when I heard quite distinctly the 'boom' of a gun in the distance. I at once said to myself 'the column is about to commence its march'. I ran towards the middle of the fort to inform Colonel Pearson, but he was already astir; in fact, the whole camp was alive as if by magic. We listened for the second gun; the clear sounding 'boom' again fell on our ears, but was quickly followed by a third report! The battle had commenced!

CHAPTER 7

'War-songs Again'

If the implications of the disaster at Isandlwana had dawned slowly on Pearson's command, cooped up at Eshowe, they had been made brutally and immediately clear to Lieutenant-General Lord Chelmsford himself. Chelmsford had divided his command in the early hours of January 22, believing that the main Zulu army lay across his line of advance. He had moved out before dawn to confront it, leaving a caretaker force of 1700 white and black troops to guard the camp at Isandlwana. In fact, the Zulus had already slipped around Chelmsford's flank, and at noon on the 22nd they streamed down and took the camp. Chelmsford was too far away to participate in the fighting; by the time he returned that evening, the bodies of 1300 of his men lay ripped open and stiffening in the bloody grass at the foot of Mount Isandlwana. For a few desperate hours, bivouacking on the terrible field, Chelmsford and his command were torn between the desperate hope that some part of the garrison had managed to fall back to the border, and the dread that the victorious Zulu army had pushed forward to ravage Natal.

The truth was revealed when Chelmsford returned to Rorke's Drift the next morning. There were no organised troops left from the Isandlwana command; the survivors were few and had scattered along the length of the Mzinyathi river – the first of them was even then half-way to Pietermaritzburg with the news. Yet the Zulus had made no serious attempt to mop up, and their one foray across the river, little more than a pillaging raid by the disgruntled *amabutho* who had formed the reserve at Isandlwana and missed the fighting, had been checked by the stubborn defence of the post at Rorke's Drift.

Even so, Isandlwana was a disaster of stunning magnitude, and Chelmsford's invasion plan lay in tatters. His strongest thrust had been bloodily repulsed, and his remaining columns were unsupported. In the breezy self-confident days before the outbreak of hostilities, neither the military nor the civilian authorities in Natal had thought to implement a thorough defence policy within the colony. Local magistrates had been empowered to raise auxiliaries from among the black clans living along the border – a Border Levy, distinct from the NNC – but there had been little time, money or determination to implement a proper military infrastructure. The shortcomings of this approach were now woefully apparent; when Chelmsford left the remains of his Centre Column, now badly demoralised, at Rorke's Drift, with the order to hold the border at all costs, there was little else to protect 200 hundred miles of rugged border country, from Wood's Column in the north to the complex of forts at the Thukela mouth, apart from a handful of white Volunteers and the poorly armed Border Levy. If the Zulus chose to follow up their advantage by crossing into Natal at any one of dozens of inaccessible drifts, there was little to stop them. Small wonder that settlers across the colony shivered in their beds at night in hourly expectation of attack.

Chelmsford himself rode back to Pietermaritzburg as panic swept through the colony, and exposed settlers flocked into laager or made for the nearest town. If his immediate concern was to shore up the colony's defences, he was also faced with the grim task of informing his political masters at home that a war they had not sanctioned had gone disastrously wrong within the first fortnight of hostilities. Critics had suggested that Chelmsford had begun the campaign with insufficient troops for his strategy, and certainly now there was no prospect of renewing his offensive until his losses at Isandlwana were made good. His order to Pearson, dispatched on 27 January, with its bald implication that the coastal column was on its own, is certainly suggestive of the despair which Chelmsford felt in the first days after the disaster. Yet, in truth, there was little else that he could say.

In fact, though the British had little idea of the Zulu intentions, King Cetshwayo neither wanted to follow up his victory, nor was he able. He felt, quite rightly, that his kingdom had been the victim of unwarranted British aggression, and, despite the astonishing blow his army had dealt the invaders, he suspected that the British must inevitably get the better of any protracted struggle. Isandlwana had, indeed, cost the Zulus dearly; the regiments which had fought there had been the cream of the army, the youngest and fittest men in the kingdom, and over a thousand of them had been struck down. Perhaps as many more were suffering from the terrible heavy-calibre rifle wounds inflicted by the Martini-Henry, and would die a lingering death over the next few months. Few families within the kingdom had escaped unscathed, and there would be a limit to the number of times the king could risk his army in such a way. It was customary for the Zulu army to return to the king after a campaign, so that he could question his commanders on the army's performance, and to enable the warriors to undergo post-combat purification rituals. After Isandlwana, however, many of the exhausted warriors simply returned to their personal homesteads to recuperate. Cetshwayo was depressed at the heavy losses, and angry at the regiments who had crossed into Natal against his wishes to attack Rorke's Drift. Their commander, Dabulamanzi, retired to his eZulwini homestead, under a cloud of royal disapproval, and it was to be two months before the king and his councillors were able to call the *amabutho* together again. The king seized the opportunity afforded by this lull to open a diplomatic campaign, hoping that Isandlwana might have undermined the British determination to pursue the war. He sent messages to Bishop Schreuder's missionary outposts along the middle Thukela in an attempt to discover what terms the British might now offer for peace; his approach to Pearson had been part of the same campaign. He clearly hoped that the fact he had held his hand when the border lay open before him would buy him political bargaining power.

Yet, ironically, each day that passed had the opposite effect. Isandlwana may have been a blow to the self-confidence that had prevailed at Chelmsford's headquarters at the start of the campaign, but, far from causing them to reconsider, it provoked a determination to restore British honour at all costs. There could be no peace negotiations until the Zulus had been made to pay for Isandlwana, and the lull in hostilities merely gave Chelmsford time to draw in reinforcements. King Cetshwayo had misjudged the situation; his magnanimity, however pragmatic, merely allowed his enemies a breathing space to regroup.

The first reinforcements were rushed to the front as soon as the news of Isandlwana passed down the lines of communication. The 2nd Battalion of the 4th Regiment had been one of only two infantry battalions the home government had agreed to dispatch in response to Chelmsford's request before hostilities began (the other was the 99th): it arrived in South Africa just as the ultimatum expired. Three companies had been left at Cape Town, and as soon as the news reached them they were embarked for Natal, where the remainder of the battalion had already been moved up to protect the vulnerable hamlets on the Mzinyathi hinterland. Four companies of the 88th Regiment, still on garrison duty on the Eastern Cape Frontier, were also ordered up to Natal. And so it was across the Empire; when the news reached St Helena on 6 February, the local garrison, a company of the 88th and a battery of artillery, was immediately embarked for South Africa. HMS *Shah* had reached St Helena en route to England after a spell on the Pacific station, and she immediately took the troops on board. Her commander, Captain Bradshaw, felt justified in disobeying his original order, and on 6 March the *Shah* landed a Naval contingent of 400 men at Durban.

It took over two weeks for Chelmsford's telegraph breaking the news of Isandlwana to reach the War Office in London. It had to be taken by ship from the Cape to Madeira, the nearest point connected directly by cable to London; it was this delay which Frere had skilfully exploited when engineering the war, but the fact that the news of the defeat did not now reach London until 11 February merely heightened its impact, and it was greeted with uproar. With his dispatch, Chelmsford had modestly asked for sufficient troops to make good his losses, but the War Office, keen not only to restore Britain's reputation but also to bring the war to a swift conclusion before it interfered with more serious troubles in Afghanistan, hurriedly ordered no less than two full regiments of regular cavalry, two batteries of artillery, six battalions of infantry, and supporting companies of the Royal Engineers, Army Service Corps, and Army Hospital Corps to prepare to sail to South Africa. The excitement among those troops ordered out was intense; officers at Staff College or on leave were hastily recalled, and there was a frantic dash to ensure that the ranks were up to strength. The 91st Highlanders were in barracks at Aldershot when the 'sudden order' was received on 12 February. They were badly under strength, and in the week between the 12th and their departure from Southampton on the SS *Pretoria* on the 19th, no fewer than 374 volunteers were drawn from eleven different regiments to bring them up to an active strength of 919 officers and men.

The prospect of active service in exotic Africa also spurred many gentlemen adventurers – both within the army and outside – to volunteer. Officers in regiments not selected to go out rushed to secure special service or staff postings, and more than one civilian booked a ticket on the month-long steam passage to Durban in the hope of finding a commission in a local volunteer unit when he arrived. Hugh Richard Dawnay, the 8th Viscount Downe, a captain in the Life Guards, secured himself a post as an extra ADC, while his brother, Guy Cuthbert Dawnay – who had no military experience at all – merely packed his bags and set sail for Africa without any very clear idea of what he would do when he got there. Guy Dawnay was a rather distinguished thirty when the war broke out, a dedicated sportsman who, in 1870, had joined one of John Dunn's hunting parties in Zululand. He was motivated by nothing more than a search for adventure, though he had fond memories of the Zulus, and consequently had reservations about fighting them. Nevertheless, he trusted to his place in the worldwide network of the British officer class, into which he had been born, to find a niche in the war, and his diary gives a revealing insight into the breathless pace at which the reinforcements departed for the scene of action:

> On Wednesday, February 12th, on coming down to breakfast at Baldersby, I first heard of the Isandlwana disaster; and forseeing a chance of a rising in Natal, I got a few things ready for a hurried start, and ordered my rifle and cartridges to be packed, loaded &c. by Henry. On Saturday, the 15th, on coming back to Beningborough from a bad day at Brafferton, I found a telegram from H., saying he was going to Zululand on General Marshall's staff, went up to London that night, settled next day to start on myself by if possible the very first troopship leaving for the Cape, and to try to make myself of use as to getting horses for him &c., went back to Yorkshire again that night, packed up the few things I wanted on Monday morning, rode over to Beningborough that after-noon, found a telegram from E. saying he had got a berth for me on the *Pretoria*, to sail the next day but one, went to London that night, had a very busy day on Tuesday, getting different things, ordering a carbine – which H is to bring for me – and next morning, Wednesday 19th, said good-bye, and left Belgrave Square at 10.30 for Waterloo.

On reaching Southampton, I found our ship had already left the docks and gone a few miles down the river, and we had to follow in a little tug, a long job as we had to take a lot of baggage, but we left at last amidst the cheers of an enthusiastic populace and got on board the *Pretoria* by 4 o'clock, and were lucky enough to get the baggage on board, just before a very heavy rain came on ...

Among the officers, at least, Dawnay's enthusiasm was typical. The 3rd Battalion, 60th Rifles, had been quartered at Colchester, in Essex, when it received orders to depart on the same day as the 91st. They, too, were significantly under-strength, and, although the battalion included a number of senior NCOs, most of the men in the ranks were between the ages of nineteen and twenty-three, and the deficiencies had, in any case, to be made up with raw recruits. Nor were the officers particularly experienced: the battalion was commanded by Lieutenant-Colonel Pemberton, who had lost two fingers on his left hand in action in the Indian Mutiny, with the handsome, bewhiskered Lieutenant-Colonel Francis Northey as his second-in-command. Northey, who was in his early forties, had seen action in the Mutiny, but apart from a few captains who had served in China and the Fenian Raids in Canada, there was little enough experience of a full-scale war. When the battalion marched out of Colchester, it was cheered through streets decorated with flags and bunting, and given a farewell address by the Mayor. Six companies of the 60th embarked on the SS *Dublin Castle* at Gravesend on 19 February (two companies remained temporarily behind; they embarked on the *Danube* a week later).

Second Lieutenant Arthur Clynton Baskerville Mynors, a fresh-faced, fair-haired, twenty-three-year-old Old Etonian – one of several in the battalion, including Northey – known to his friends as 'Bunny', wrote regularly of his adventures to his mother, chronicling the battalion's experience in a style that now seems typical of the period; breathless, excited, sentimental, occasionally arrogant, and definitely quaint. He confided to 'dear Mamma' on board the transport was 'rather fun', but that 'we live in hopes of getting to Natal soon, where I hope we shall have some better fun'. Though the *Dublin Castle* was 'sailing about eleven knots an hour, I wish we were going faster'. Rough weather in the Bay of Biscay dampened the enthusiasm of many on both ships, and both Dawnay on the *Pretoria* and Mynors of the *Dublin Castle* were seasick: 'I was awfully ill,' admitted Mynors, but added cheerfully 'in fact, so was everybody.' He described the confusion of the first storm:

Our cabin, which is on deck, was turned upside down, portmanteaus and everything flying about, we had to hold tight to stay in bed at all. Keith Turnour, my Captain, is in my cabin. Saturday night the storm continued, the hatches were battened down to prevent the water going over the lower decks. You know the boats slung up by the side of the ship, actually touched the sea when we rolled; also the sea broke over into the engines.

In its wake the storm left several casualties; the *Pretoria* had six horses on board, 'and one was lost the first rough night, the poor brute falling out of its box when the ship gave a heavy lurch to port, and having to be killed.' On board the *Dublin Castle*, two horses died; their carcasses were thrown overboard after their manes, tails and hooves had been removed, presumably as souvenirs; another impenetrable Victorian custom. Even Mynors' spirits were dampened:

> It is awfully slow, nothing to do but read. The men also have nothing to do. I wish we were in Natal, I do so detest the sea. It keeps very rough the whole time and the ship rolls horribly. The men have an awfully bad time of it, packed so close they have scarcely room to breathe.

With little to occupy them, the officers took a keen interest in the daily progress of their beards. Queen's Regulations specified that, while moustaches were desirable, beards were to be forbidden in peace-time, but they were allowed on campaign, where they had certain practical advantages, and by the time they arrived in South Africa most of the reinforcements were sporting them to varying degrees of success. When the transports docked at Cape Town, the troops eagerly caught up on the latest news of the war's progress. Commandant Rupert Lonsdale, who had commanded an NNC battalion in the Isandlwana campaign, was at the Cape raising a troop of volunteer horse, and both Mynors and Dawnay recalled his story of how he had ridden into the camp at Isandlwana, unaware that it had fallen. 'He saw the Zulus putting on the red coats of those they had killed', wrote Mynors with wonder, 'and consequently mistook them for our own men. He galloped off, and was not killed, although shot at.' More significantly, Dawnay recalled that 'we heard ... that a relieving column was to start yesterday from D'Urban to try to reach Pearson and if only I could have once got the horse business settled I might have tried to catch them up'. Horses, indeed, were a major preoccupation among the officers, for whom they were not only a practical necessity, but often a point of pride. Some had brought magnificent chargers out from England, but found that they had suffered on board ship, and did not always take to the local grazing. Others, who thought themselves more canny, planned to buy hardy local animals when they arrived at Durban, only to discover that they were in short supply and that demand had pushed up the prices.

The transports were soon under way again, and as they neared their destination, the officers indulged in some much-needed target practice. Revolver practice was not a formal part of their training, and many officers could not be bothered with it, with inevitable consequences in the field. As the transports approached Durban, however, there was a sudden outburst of enthusiasm, and officers lined the decks to blast away at anything appropriate. Seagulls were a particular favourite, and would have been in greater danger had the shooting been better; according to Dawnay, whose hunter's instincts were clearly aroused, the officers of the 91st found a particularly unusual target: 'Yesterday afternoon there was a deal of revolver practice, an old shark coming right alongside during it, and getting a heavy fire, though I don't think he was much the worse for it.'

Nor were the officers the only ones who needed to hone their military skills; many among the new drafts who had brought the 91st up to strength were young recruits who had not even completed their musketry instruction courses.

The *Pretoria* arrived on 17 March, and the *Dublin Castle* three days later. Lieutenant E.O.H. Wilkinson, the adjutant of the 3/60th and another Old Etonian, was not impressed with his regiment's readiness as it arrived at the seat of war:

> ... no time was given to us even to disembark the ordinary necessities for a camp life as we actually marched out of Durban without Torren's Camp Kettles and with our bandsmen deficient in rifles; the former caught us up after four days delay, the latter with cases of flannel shirts (essentials in this country) and boots have never turned up yet ...

Inevitably, the fresh troops were prey to the rumours sweeping through the colony. Dawnay, who was now desperately trying to find a Volunteer corps which would have him, was told a common story that at Isandlwana the Zulus hung up the drummer boys of the 24th on meat hooks. Perhaps this rumour explained why the 91st marched out of Durban with their pipers, but left their drummer-boys behind. Lieutenant Edward Hutton of the 60th recalled that Chelmsford addressed the battalion on its arrival, and that:

> The impression left on our minds was that the Zulus were very formidable foes, and we soon found that this unfortunate sentiment prevailed on all sides, and that hesitation and vacillation were the natural result. Our men, especially the young soldiers, were not slow to share the general feeling of uneasiness which the disasters at Isandlwana and elsewhere had caused.

Indeed, as Frances Colenso, the daughter of the Bishop of Natal, who, with her family, was bitterly opposed to the war, noted, 'the spirits and courage of our army are flagging, and they seem to be beginning to *fear the Zulu.*' Mynors's account suggests just how far the image of the remorseless and indefatigable Zulu warrior was taking root in the minds of the new arrivals:

> No one knows where the Zulu armies are; one day they are seen at one place, another at another; one meal lasts them for three days; and the bush they can creep through like snakes. Being nothing but Zulus (natives) about the country

here, they come and watch us; in fact they know everything that goes on. They are awfully wily; they are never to be caught in an open country, and never will be unless at Undini; the only time they will attack their enemy is before daybreak, and at night when we encamp; and then they won't attack a very big force.

It is easy to see how the stories of Isandlwana – grim enough without the inevitable exaggeration that so often accompanied them – had a disturbing effect on the minds of young troops fresh out from England. Most of them had never been abroad before, and Africa itself was a wonderful and frightening place when compared with the rural villages or urban slums which had previously defined their world. The open spaces, the light, and the extreme weather conditions were unsettling enough, but on the leaden frontier nights, every strange cry of an unfamiliar animal, every rustle in the bush and swish in the grass, must have whispered of the closeness of the dreaded black men and their fearsome spears. It remained to be seen how the new arrivals would cope when the real thing put them to the test.

The 60th and the 91st were to form the backbone of Chelmsford's Eshowe Relief Column. They were joined by the 57th Regiment, who arrived on 11 March from Ceylon, and who had, therefore, rather more experience of service in the tropics. King Cetshwayo's failure to exploit his advantage after Isandlwana by raiding into Natal freed Lord Chelmsford to concentrate on Pearson's beleaguered garrison. The last of the three original invasion columns, No. 4 under Colonel Wood, was holding its own in northern Zululand, and could be left to its own devices for the time being. A solution to Pearson's predicament was an obvious precursor to the development of any new grand strategy.

Since the troops sent back by Pearson had arrived at the river at the end of January, life there had been a curious mixture of boredom and anticipation. The rumour of Isandlwana may have greeted Coates's command and the mounted men as they arrived back at the Lower Drift, but nevertheless, perhaps because their posts were so secure, the garrison there seems to have been immune to the panic which swept through the rest of the colony. 'The Buffs' remained at Fort Tenedos, while the three 99th companies crossed the river to occupy Fort Pearson. The odd two companies of the 99th still on the lines of communication were ordered up, and even when the Volunteers were dispatched for Thring's Post, and the NNC disbanded, the Lower Drift still seemed quite secure. When the trickle of messengers from Eshowe dried up, the garrison passed into limbo, with no very definite purpose beyond holding out until the war passed into its next phase. Lieutenant Backhouse felt, if anything, more frustrated now that he was back within reach of civilisation. He missed his wife, who was in Durban, and complained bitterly to his diary that her letters were not reaching him quickly enough: 'These wretched Natal people think it is unsafe to send the runners, when we know here that no Zulus have crossed the river at all.'

Indeed, unlike stretches of the Mzinyathi upriver, where small parties of Zulus occasionally crossed over to loot deserted homesteads on the Natal bank, there was little for the local colonial defence forces on the Lower Thukela to do. Before hostilities had begun, the civilian administration had appointed Captain Gould Lucas, a retired officer of the 73rd Regiment, to be commandant of the Lower Thukela border, designated Defence District No. VI. Lucas had taken up his duties with a mixture of military enthusiasm and bureaucratic inefficiency, and his attempt to establish a system of Border Levies drawn from local African groups, to watch the drifts, had seemed to both Lord Chelmsford and the Lieutenant-Governor, Bulwer, excessive. In the aftermath of Isandlwana, however, they seemed all too necessary, but in fact Lucas's sector remained one of the quietest along the frontier. There were no attempts by the Zulus to cross the river even in small numbers, and the only action that Lucas's men saw in February and March 1879 consisted of shouted exchanges and the odd pot-shot across the Thukela. At Fort Tenedos, the garrison watched eagerly for Zulu patrols, who could sometimes be seen on the hilltops opposite, observing the British movements; once or twice, Barrow – who had remained at the Drift – sallied out with the Mounted Infantry to drive them off, but there were no significant clashes. Occasional rumours that the Zulus were mustering in force to attack the forts proved unfounded.

Life at the forts was uncomfortable and dull. At Fort Tenedos, the men of 'The Buffs' were kept busy perfecting the defences, keeping the ramparts in good repair, setting wire entanglements, *troups de loup* and mines. At strategic points about the fort holes were dug 6 or 8 feet into the ground, and filled with 100 pounds of explosive, to be detonated by an electric charge from inside the fort. The days were alternately suffocatingly hot and humid, or very wet. For the first three weeks after Isandlwana, the garrison was allowed to pitch tents outside Fort Tenedos in daylight hours, but they had to be struck at night, and the men were compelled to sleep against the parapet protected from the regular deluges by nothing more than a waterproof sheet. Backhouse, for whom the inactivity only heightened his absence from his wife, became increasingly grumpy in his observations. He complained repeatedly to his diary of 'disagreeable and wet night[s], lying with the lower part of my body drenched all night'. He bathed regularly in the Thukela and his company occasionally did the same, but it was impossible to swim because of the current and the fear of crocodiles. It was difficult to keep the men healthy; diarrhoea was common, and a few men began to succumb to dysentery.

Despite the fact that the lines of communication back down towards Durban remained open, the garrison at the Thukela mouth was largely reliant on rumour to keep it informed of the state of the campaign. Backhouse was a prolific writer of letters, and at last managed to find excuses to ride down to Stanger, or even Durban, on duty, where his wife came out to meet him. He quite clearly knew of the arrival of reinforcements at Durban, but there is a significant absence of references to orders from above.

On 12 February, however, Chelmsford himself visited the border. It seems that he had little in mind but to see for himself the state of things, yet news that he was coming caused a flurry of excitement on the Lower Thukela, since it was assumed that he was about to form a Flying Column to march to Pearson's relief. On the 11th the troops held a practice parade in expectation of the general's visit, an exercise presided over by Coates of the 99th. Backhouse, who shared the low opinion of the 99th in general and disliked Coates in particular, commented that 'a more absurd farce I never saw'.

In the event Chelmsford arrived the following day with his staff, and inspected the forts, but without parading the men. He was not impressed by the site of Fort Tenedos – his Military Secretary, the waspish Lieutenant-Colonel John North Crealock, commented 'It was *very lucky* the Zulus did not attack this place. Fort Tenedos . . . is completely open to the fire of a long, strong, stony hill 300 yards off! And no one seemed to know that danger until we arrived!' Chelmsford's solution was to order the garrison to build a new supporting post on the hill in question. For a few days it seemed that a march on Eshowe was indeed imminent; Chelmsford and his staff rode out with an escort to observe the lie of the land, and on the 14th Lieutenant-Colonel F.T.A. Law, Royal Artillery, arrived at Fort Tenedos to take command of the troops along the Lower Thukela. On the 17th the men were ordered to parade at 6.30am ready for the general's inspection, which they did with some anticipation. When Chelmsford had not arrived by 7 o'clock, however, the men were allowed to stand down, only to be recalled half an hour later when he finally turned up. Chelmsford's speech was a disappointment; he talked mostly, according to Backhouse, 'about the 24th Regt. disaster, [he] said nothing about a Flying Column, but said we must wait for reinforcements.' He then rode out on the road to Durban. A few days later the plan to fortify the outlying hill was abandoned.

There had, indeed, been a plan to march out to Eshowe, but it had been thwarted by the collapse of communication with Pearson's men. Chelmsford had proposed that Pearson should sally out towards the Thukela, and that Law should lead a column half-way to meet him. However, were such a plan to succeed, given the weakened state of Pearson's command, and the relative weakness of Law's, it would have needed careful coordination. This was the plan Pearson heard about on 11 February, but at that point communication broke down, and Chelmsford remained as uncertain about Pearson's intentions as Pearson was about Chelmsford's. A comment by Crealock undoubtedly sums up the prevailing indecision among the staff at this time: '[Lord Chelmsford] very naturally does not wish to risk anything until the reinforcements come out, but with such a vast frontier, and the important centres of preparation being so far apart it is a fair puzzle to know what is best to do.'

Another month was to drag by before the arrival of the first reinforcements galvanised Chelmsford into action. In the meantime, John Dunn had at last been drawn into the conflict. Since crossing the Thukela with his followers at the beginning of January, Dunn had been living on a location appointed for him a few miles south of the river. Dunn had already compromised his relationship with King Cetshwayo by accepting sanctuary in the colony, and soon after his arrival, he had offered the service of his retainers as a border guard, hoping, no doubt, to reconcile Natal to his presence, and to protect himself from Zulu retaliation. Life on the location, however, had not proved pleasant. Lord Chelmsford had a habit of blandly promising cattle or land to settlers he wished to suborn, and John Dunn was not the only one to observe sourly 'Lord Chelmsford broke his promise as to feeding my people and I had to do so myself at a very heavy expense ... so much for the word of anyone representing the authority of a military government.' Dunn was obliged to slaughter his own cattle, and buy grain from the army commissariat at inflated prices. Worse, dysentery broke out in the cramped conditions on the location, and over a hundred of Dunn's followers died. If Dunn was unimpressed with Chelmsford, however, his circumstances forced him into an alliance. His position in Zululand was now questionable, and there was little to gain by remaining neutral. Chelmsford, indeed, increasingly pressed him to abandon his neutrality:

I think it will be very advantageous if you yourself were to accompany me as far as the Inyezani river. I would not ask you to go further. Your presence with me would ensure the efficient scouting of your men, and I feel sure that I should myself derive much assistance from your experience of Zulu warfare and from your knowledge of the country passed through.

Chelmsford had a point; almost all of the country from the Thukela up to Eshowe had been Dunn's fiefdom, and he knew it intimately. Furthermore, he had a nucleus of 150 trained hunters among his followers, who were far better shots and scouts that almost any other black auxiliaries to whom the British had access. Dunn considered his options, and reacted with a pragmatism that had characterised his career in Zululand:

I could see that I could be of service in pointing out the means of averting another disaster, and besides, I knew that in the fighting between the boers and the English at the Bay (D'Urban) my father had suffered by remaining neutral, so I made up my mind to go with Lord Chelmsford to the relief of the Eshowe garrison.

This decision was, in many ways, a turning point in Dunn's life. By agreeing to fight with the British, Dunn irrevocably betrayed his friendship for his old patron, King Cetshwayo. Whatever the outcome of the war, Dunn's future fortunes were unlikely to thrive in Zululand so long as it was dominated by the king or his superiors. From that day Dunn became an implacable enemy of the Zulu Royal House.

Throughout the end of February and beginning of March, the first reinforcements began to arrive at the Lower Drift. It was decided to recall the men of the Native Contingent, who were to be reorganised into new formations under their old officers. The old system of regiments, divided into battalions, was now abandoned in favour of a simplified one of battalions, and the old men of the 2nd Regiment now found themselves enrolled in the 4th and 5th Battalions, Natal Native Contingent. Major Graves, who had previously commanded the 2nd Regiment, had been transferred to other duties, and Captain Geoffrey Barton, 7th Regiment, formerly Durnford's senior staff officer, took over command of the revised 4th Battalion. Commandant W.J. Nettleton remained in command of his old battalion, now redesignated the 5th. Previously, only one man in ten had been issued with firearms, but now attempts were made to ensure that every man had access to a gun of some description. The 5th Battalion, notwithstanding that it was likely soon to be in the field, seem to have been short-changed; the 3rd and 4th Battalions were issued with Martini-Henrys and Sniders respectively, but the 5th Battalion had to make do with whatever was left over. Most of its guns were probably outdated Enfields and Tower muskets; it was, in short, little better armed than its Zulu enemy. Many of the men had now also been issued with surplus red jackets, which added to their martial appearance and their morale, but left Lieutenant Backhouse, for whom life on the frontier no longer held any delights, unimpressed; he merely observed that 'we shall soon have the brutes shouting their war-songs again'.

There were new mounted auxiliaries, too. Because the disaster at Isandlwana had devastated part of the original NNC, it had been necessary to look further afield for black reinforcements, and a contingent of both infantry and cavalry were raised at Ixopo in southern Natal. They were to be stationed at the Middle Drift, but the cavalry, under their chief Jantje, were temporarily attached to the column slowly assembling at the Lower Drift. The *Natal Mercury* was impressed by what it saw of these men:

They were well mounted, and armed with the Martini-Henry rifle.... Jantje himself heads his own men. He wears a sword and conducts himself like a brave captain of old. His men are drilled and disciplined and will no doubt give a good account of themselves in the forthcoming operations ...

Their uniform consists of an ordinary tan cord suit, blucher boots, leggings, and felt hat with turkey red badge. Horseflesh and saddlery they provide themselves.

On 21 February the first regular infantry company arrived at the drift. It was a company of the 88th, one of those who had been rushed up from the Cape. Its arrival was timely, since the coming night was the night of the new moon, and there was a feeling that perhaps the Zulus might use it to mask an attack. In fact, nothing happened, and as two more companies from the same regiment arrived over the next fortnight, it became clear that any chance the Zulus might have had of storming the forts was gone. By 12 March Backhouse noted in his diary that a Zulu prisoner had informed his captors that an *impi* was mustering to drive the British back across the river, but, Backhouse noted confidently, 'if they do, they come too late, for we have the 88th over here now'. The continued inactivity of the Zulus was almost disappointing; Barrow's mounted men, supported by Dunn's scouts, brought in a number of prisoners, both civilians and warriors, who were eagerly questioned about the Zulu intentions. They had little new to report; it seemed that the Zulus, too, were content to sit and wait.

In the meantime, the only excitements were the routine ones of military life. On 25 February Private Woodman of B Company of 'The Buffs' was given fifty lashes for leaving his post on sentry duty. This, too, Backhouse considered a farce, since 'Drummers Reilly and White flogged him ... they never hurt him at all.' On 13 March a private of the 99th ran out from the hospital tent on the Natal bank and committed suicide by throwing himself off the top of Fort Pearson. Major Coates of the 99th, who had also failed to impress the staff when Chelmsford had visited the garrison, sold his commission and returned to England. Backhouse noted with a certain smugness that Coates had 'made a good bolt out of it, and ought to be ashamed of himself.'

Communication with Pearson, meanwhile, proved no easier for those based at the Thukela than it had at Eshowe. There was no signalling equipment at either Fort Tenedos or Fort Pearson, and although a bedroom mirror had been purloined from Smith's hotel and pressed into service, it was only occasionally successful. On 14 March it was decided to push out an advanced party to the deserted St Andrew's mission, about three miles on the Zulu side of Fort Tenedos, which was thought to offer a better vantage point for signalling. Nearly 400 men from HMS *Shah* had arrived at the Drift only the day before, and when two companies of 'The Buffs' marched out that afternoon at 4pm, it was to the sound of the *Shah's* 'penny whistle' band. 'The Buffs' reached their objective before dark, but Backhouse, who was with them, complained 'I think it is a most absurd move, and I pity us, if the Zulus come down tonight, for none of us will ever leave this alive.'

The first night, officers and men dined together in the church for safety's sake, using the altar as a table. Daylight did not improve Backhouse's temper; when parties were sent out to clear the long grass away from the post, they found it to be full of snakes. One, which Backhouse proclaimed a black mamba, was 9 feet long. Nevertheless, he had reluctantly to admit that the post was successful enough for signalling, and for the first time regular communication was opened with the Eshowe garrison. When, two days later, a party of nine sailors from HMS *Shah* arrived with a Gatling gun, it, became moderately secure.

By this time, the long-awaited reinforcements were arriving at the Drift. The march up from Durban had been an arduous one, as extracts from Mynors's diary suggest:

Started at four am, to march in utter darkness; unpitched camp, packed up and off; marched six miles on awful bad road to Verulam; the hilliest and prettiest country I ever saw; forded two rivers; stopped eight hours at Verulam; bathed, washed my clothes; and started at three o'clock pm in the afternoon, our baggage drawn by oxen, sixteen to twenty oxen in each wagon ...

... The march on Sunday night to Victoria was fearful, dreadfully hot; the sun right on our heads; and carrying ammunition and arms, almost heartbreaking. We got there just in time to see to pitch our tents and tumble into bed for a few hours, and on Monday morning up again at 2.20 in the dark, see nothing and find nothing; started; crossed and bathed in the Tongaati, up to our waists crossing, so wet and wretched. Our halt for mid-day in Compensation Flat in the sun, no shade to be found, and no rest; waited til 2.30 and marched nine miles, the longest and weariest I ever marched; the men were almost dead with the heat. Had only coffee and tea twice a day, nothing else ...

Still, if the march was hard, it had one compensation; by the time the reinforcements arrived at the Lower Drift, they had shaken off any lingering stiffness from the long voyage out, and were becoming better used to the country and its climate.

The 57th were the first to arrive, on 22 March. The 91st marched in on the 25th, together with a new Naval contingent, 200 men from HMS *Boadicea*, which had docked at Durban on the 15th. The 60th reached the Drift on the 27th, and the NNC were moved up to the Thukela from their camps below the border at about the same time. The sprawling camps on either bank now housed a very considerable force, and an advance was at last imminent.

Chelmsford had finally been spurred into action by a message from Pearson, received on 16 March, that his supplies would run out by 4 April, and the general was convinced that he must start 'not later than the 28th inst.' On the 25th he sent a dispatch to the Secretary of State for War outlining his plans. The final paragraph suggests just how much the Isandlwana affair had sapped his confidence:

Thanks to the prompt dispatch of reinforcements from England, I shall be in three days' time able to advance with a strong column, strength as per the margin, to relieve the garrison at Ekowe, which has now been holding that post for upward of ten weeks.

As none of the Major-Generals ordered out have yet arrived, and Colonel Pearson, who at first commanded the column on this line, is shut up in Ekowe, and as there is no other senior officer available for the duty, I have decided to take command of the relieving column myself, assisted by Colonel Pemberton, 60th Rifles, and Lieutenant-Colonel Law, Royal Artillery.

The Column will not advance by the road which Colonel Pearson's column took but by one which runs nearly parallel to it, but nearer the coast. The advantage of this line is that the road runs through an easy open country for three quarters of the distance, whereas by the other line the road runs through bush country nearly the whole way.

The force will advance without tents, and with only a blanket and waterproof sheet for each man.

Notwithstanding, however, this reduction of weight, the convoy carrying one month's provisions for the garrison and 10 days' supplies (without groceries) for the relieving column, will consist of 44 carts and about 100 wagons ...

It is probable that the column will be attacked when moving along the last ten miles of the road between this place and Ekowe ...

I have suggested to Colonel Pearson, by sun signal, that he should be prepared to make a diversion in support of the relieving column with every available fighting man that can be spared from the defence of the post.

I should feel no doubt about being able successfully to convey the convoy and fresh garrison into Ekowe, and to bring out the present garrison with its train of empty wagons, were the transport of different quality.

A force moving, however, with a transport through a difficult country is heavily hampered, if attacked determinedly by large numbers, and while feeling every confidence in the ability, courage, and determination of those under my command, I trust that, should our efforts fall short of what is no doubt expected of us, circumstances may be duly taken into account.

Chelmsford was, indeed, weathering a growing storm of criticism about Isandlwana. It was argued that his own standing orders were lax, and that he had failed to insist that the camp at Isandlwana be properly laagered – which was true. His staff had attempted to shift the blame on to those actually commanding the camp's garrison, and both an updated version of the Field Force Regulations, published in February, and Chelmsford's own orders to the relief column's commanders, addressed issues raised by the fighting at Isandlwana. The Field Force Regulations specified that even temporary halts on the march should be protected by a wagon-laager and, where possible, entrenchment. Yet forming a laager with a large number of wagons, even when the drivers were experienced, was a difficult enough business, and the march to Eshowe would be characterised by chaos each night as the drivers attempted to

Chelmsford's relief column on the march, with the Naval Brigade carrying their 24-pounder rockets in carts.

form their wagons into a defensive perimeter. It then had to be disentangled the
next morning before the column could move off. Chelmsford's intelligence of
the Zulu movements was no more complete than it had been during the
Isandlwana campaign, but the steady trickle of reports and rumours from the
Lower Thukela all confirmed that the Zulus intended to make some sort of a
stand before Eshowe. In battle, there would be no more open formations, as
there had been at Isandlwana, nor would anything be allowed to interfere with
the free supply of ammunition. Chelmsford specified:

> Companies must be kept together in close order. Files may loosen out, but not be
> extended.
>
> Each wagon and cart with the convoys must have some ammunition boxes
> placed on it in such a position as to be easily got at. The regimental reserve boxes
> must have the screw of the lid taken out, and each wagon or cart will have a
> screwdriver attached to one of the boxes so that it may be ready for opening
> those in which the screw has not been taken out.
>
> The supply wagons containing stores for the garrison of Ekowe must be
> loaded with a proper proportion of each article of consumption. The force will
> form a square laager of the wagons every night with a shelter trench round it,
> 9 ft. from the wagons, and will bivouac, as far as possible, in the order of march.
>
> The European portion of the force will bivouac between the wagons and the
> shelter trench; the natives, cattle and horses will be inside the laager.
>
> The troops will be under arms at 4am every morning; and the column will
> prepare for its further advance so soon as it is daylight, and so soon as the scouts
> (which should be pushed forward when the force gets under arms) have reported
> that the enemy is not in the immediate neighbourhood. No bugle sound to be
> permitted, except the 'alarm' which will be the signal for every man to stand to
> his arms. Combined parties of 6 Europeans and 6 natives will be placed half a
> mile in advance of each face of the laager at night as outlying sentries. Native
> scouts will however be pushed forward at least a mile. These parties will remain
> quietly on the alert. No smoking, no talking above a whisper, and then only
> regarding matters of duty. Their duty is to listen. Should the enemy be dis-
> covered by the native scouts they will fire volleys and fall back on the picquets
> who will retire quietly and give the alarm *without firing*. Care must be taken not
> to fire upon the scouts when running in.

This last point was to prove particularly relevant. Once the column crossed into
Zululand, the Zulu presence began to prey on the men's minds.

When Chelmsford himself rode up to the Thukela on 23 March, the camps
came alive with excitement. Even Backhouse, who returned from St Andrew's
on the 28th when the column was almost ready to move, was forced to admit
that 'a most exciting scene is going on at the Drift, preparing for the move.'
Natal blacks shouted across to Zulus on the other side of the river that 'the cow

was about to calve.' The 57th, 60th and 91st were all appointed to the relief column; to their disgust, the 88th were ordered to stay behind and garrison Fort Pearson. One of Lord Chelmsford's ADCs, Captain William Molyneux of the 22nd Regiment, gave a vivid impression of the confusion as the troops were ferried across to their starting positions on the Fort Tenedos side of the river:

> From March 25th to the 29th we were hard at work all day and half the night ferrying the force over the Tugela by pont. The Naval Brigade worked the machine, and were quite in their element. It would take only one wagon and its team at a time, so that more than a hundred trips over and back were required for the transport alone; and as the river when high is about half a mile wide, it will be understood that the Blue-jackets had no light task.... By the night of the 28th the whole force was across, and bivouacked on the left bank in a terrible storm of rain, which put out all the fires and turned the ground into a swamp.

The imminent advance brought a crowd of stragglers hurrying to the front. On the advice of one of Lord Chelmsford's staff, Guy Dawnay had abandoned his plan of joining one of the Volunteer units, but while in Durban, dining at the Natal Club – 'the new and best one here' – and bemoaning the fact that he could not find a servant prepared to cross into Zululand with him, and that the price of horses had gone up by 20 per cent in the ten days he had been in the country, he had bumped into an old friend, Captain the Hon. Hugh Gough. Gough had served with the Coldstream Guards, but had sailed for South Africa in December 1878, and had taken a commission in Nettleton's Battalion of the then 2nd Regiment, NNC. He had marched up with Pearson and been present at Nyezane, and had returned to the Thukela with his regiment at the end of January; his obituary later noted that 'with characteristic generosity [he] gave up his horse on the way to non-commissioned officers, marching more than half the distance.' Gough had taken advantage of the reorganisation of the NNC to take leave at Durban, but when Dawnay met him he was most unwell; he had apparently contracted dysentery. Using the favourite word of the day, Dawnay pronounced him 'seedy'. Nevertheless, Gough swore he was improving, and had rejoined his battalion, despite a comment from Lord Chelmsford himself that 'young Gough was going about too early.' Nevertheless, it was Gough who invited Dawnay to attach himself to the 5th Battalion NNC; in such casual ways did gentlemen go to war in the 1870s.

Dawnay and Gough rushed to the front, arriving on the 29th in time to see the rearguard of Dunn's scouts disappearing across the river. Pausing only to make a final selection of his campaign kit – Dawnay took with him 'a waterproof, a blanket, waterproof sheet, brush and comb, sponge and tooth-brush, a small tin or two of cocoa and milk, Liebig's and Revalenta Arabica, biscuit or two, a small kettle, cup, a knife, fork and spoon ... My revolver,

Snider carbine, glasses.' – they crossed the Thukela and reported to the NNC mess. Here Gough introduced him to Nettleton, and Dawnay secured permission to attach himself to the 5th Battalion 'for the time being'. He held no official rank, but nonetheless assumed the duties and privileges of an officer.

Charles Norris-Newman, the correspondent of the *Standard*, who had scooped his rivals by being the only journalist present during the Isandlwana campaign, had been anticipating fresh activity with some enthusiasm. Throughout February and March, he had ridden repeatedly up to the frontier, but when the advance came it nonetheless took him by surprise. He arrived at the Thukela from Durban on the 28th, to find that a veritable army of 'specials', who had come out with the reinforcements, had beaten him to it:

> I found I had been preceded by Mr Francis of the *Times*, Melton Prior, *Illustrated London News*, Fripp, *The Graphic*, Dormer, *Cape Argus*, and Mr W. Peace, who represented the *Daily Telegraph* until the arrival of Mr P. Robinson from Afghanistan. Other English, Colonial, and Provincial papers were represented. Some of them, however, did not accompany us past the Tugela ...

Curiously, Melton Prior was among them. Arguably the most famous 'special' of his day, Prior usually thrived when the presence of danger promised a good story, but on this occasion he had a premonition of his death, and he decided not to go with the column; Crealock offered to supply him with sketches instead, and Prior accepted.

The Natal Volunteers were still encamped at Thring's Post, and most of them had volunteered to join the relief column. To their disgust this offer was refused, and they were not allowed to return to Zululand under their own officers, but fifty-nine of them, led by Captain Friend Addison of the Stanger Mounted Rifles, and two other officers, were formed into a temporary scratch unit, the Natal Volunteer Guides, and attached to the column. Trooper John Robinson Royston – inevitably known as Jack – had managed to join the Isipingo Mounted Rifles against the wishes of his father, despite the fact he was only sixteen years old. When Royston applied to join the Volunteer Guides, however, he was refused; he promptly went absent without leave, and caught up with the unit on the road. He was not the only one to do so; four men from the Durban Mounted Rifles tried the same trick, but were arrested and sent back to the border.

Reveille sounded on the Zulu bank at 5am on the 29th, and by 6 o'clock the column was underway. Chelmsford and his staff, who had lingered at Fort Pearson, crossed the river at 8am, with John Dunn's men just behind, and caught up the advance. Chelmsford had divided the column into two Brigades; the first, under Law's command, consisted of the 91st, five companies of the 99th, two of 'The Buffs', the Naval Brigades of the *Shah* and *Tenedos*, which included two 9-pounder guns, two 24-pounder rocket tubes and a Gatling, the Mounted Infantry and Volunteers under Barrow, Jantje's mounted troop, and the 5th Battalion NNC. Dunn's men also accompanied this brigade. The second brigade, under Pemberton, consisted of the 57th, 60th, the Naval Brigades from the *Boadicea* with one Gatling and two 24-pounder rocket tubes, the 4th Battalion NNC, and two troops of mounted men, one black and one white. The total force consisted of over 5500 fighting men, of whom over 3000 were white.

The column followed Pearson's old road as far as the St Andrew's mission, and then veered off to the right, keeping closer to the coast. The ground was wet and soft, and the wagons soon churned the track to a sea of mud. By the end of the first day's march, the front of the column had reached the Nyoni river, about ten miles from Fort Tenedos, but the rear had only travelled five miles by noon. According to Molyneux, who had been appointed commandant of laagers, '... that night the wagon drivers, who had had no practice in laagering, got so out of hand that the laager was made anyhow, and it would only hold one third of our oxen. So much for our first laager on our first trek'.

That night it rained in torrents again. Without tents, the men had to find what comfort they could, most simply sleeping out in the mud with a blanket over them. Guy Dawnay made himself comfortable under a wagon, but awoke to find himself covered with 'tar'. Bunny Mynors's lot was a more miserable one, as he stated with commendable honesty, 'I and Keith (Turnour) on outpost duty all night; (blue funk) and both dark and wet. Luckily no enemy came.'

The next morning was misty, which delayed the start of the advance, and the wagons had to be dragged across the steep banks of the Nyoni in single file. Still, by late afternoon that day – the 30th – the column had reached the south bank of the next natural obstacle, the amaTigulu river. Once again the camp was laagered, and Molyneux thought 'this was better than the previous day's work: we had covered seven miles in seven hours, and the laager this time was large enough and fairly well made.' But, he added, 'the performance was not good enough for the critical eye of John Dunn.' Dunn was now serving with a British army in enemy territory for the first time, and found himself singularly unimpressed with their fieldcraft and shooting. 'We shall have to do better than this,' he commented sharply, 'if we are to beat Cetewayo's *impi*'.

That night it rained again. The laager had been built in a rough square, with a trench dug round it, and the earth piled up inside to form a rampart. The trench had been dug a few yards outside the wagons, and, since the transport oxen were contained inside the laager, the troops were required to sleep in the gap inside the rampart. It was a miserable experience; 'Slept on mud,' commented Dawnay succinctly, 'as usual'. The deluge had not made the amaTigulu any more passable, and in the morning it was found to be forty yards wide and four feet deep. It was obvious that crossing it would take up most of the day, so

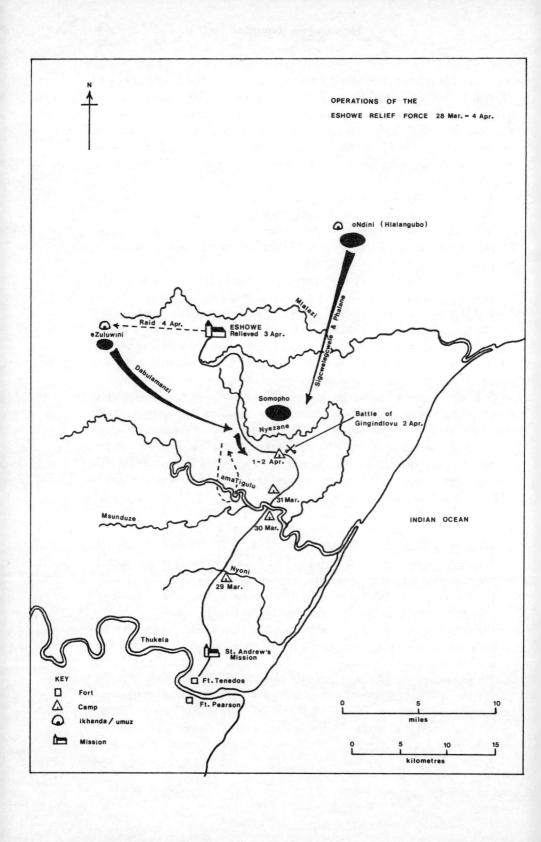

N

OPERATIONS OF THE
ESHOWE RELIEF FORCE 28 Mar. – 4 Apr.

oNdini (Hlalangubo)

Mlalazi

Raid 4 Apr.

eZuluwini

ESHOWE
Relieved 3 Apr.

Sigcwelegcwele & Phalane

Dabulamanzi

Somopho

Battle of
Gingindlovu 2 Apr.

Nyezane

1–2 Apr.

amaTigulu

31 Mar.

Msunduze

30 Mar.

INDIAN OCEAN

Nyoni
29 Mar.

Thukela

St. Andrew's
Mission

Ft. Tenedos

Ft. Pearson

KEY

☐ Fort

△ Camp

⌓ ikhanda / umuz

⌂ Mission

0   5   10
miles

0   5   10   15
kilometres

Chelmsford selected a spot for the next night's camp less than two miles beyond the river. Most of 31 March was taken up with moving the column across; Dawnay, who had learned a little Zulu on his hunting trip nearly a decade before, found that it was particularly useful that day. Since none of the commissariat officers spoke any, he found himself directing the traffic across the river. He worked from 7am until 1pm, and it took the rest of the day to move the wagons to the new campsite. Molyneux described the advance:

> Barrow's mounted men and Dunn's scouts began the passage; then followed the first Brigade, and then the convoy of wagons and carts. The Brigade took two hours to cross, the wagons six, losing an ox or two, but on the whole making the passage in fine style. The second Brigade brought up the rear, wading up to their arm-pits, rifles and pouches on their heads. The whole column was in camp before five, after nearly eleven hours work, everybody as wet as a sponge.

Dawnay considered the amaTigulu laager badly sited, and there was a general feeling throughout the column that a battle was imminent. Small bodies of Zulus had been seen during the day, and Barrow's men had ridden out about fifteen miles towards the Mlalazi, and had burned a large deserted homestead which, it turned out, belonged to Prince Magwendu kaMpande, the king's half-brother. Mynors recorded that there were rumours that two Zulu armies were reported in the vicinity, and that the rear of the column might be attacked. More significantly, Captain Hay of the Native Contingent reported that his men had spotted signal fires on the hills near Eshowe.

The march continued the next morning, 1 April, at 7am. To ring the changes, the second Brigade advanced to the front, and the 57th led the way. The path now veered to the left, approaching the Eshowe heights, and Norris-Newman noted a change in the scenery:

> Hitherto, the Column had traversed rolling grassy plains, with gentle slopes, wooded knolls, and small streams at intervals, diversified with an occasional deserted kraal and patch of cultivated ground. We now entered a more wooded country, with large patches of high and strong Tambookie grass bordering the road, and many treacherous boggy places, which had to be crossed or circumvented as best as could be done. On this day's (Tuesday's) march it was found necessary to make occasional halts, to allow the Column and convoy to close up, and on two occasions the regiments in front were sent out in extended order to sweep through the long grass and clumps of bushes, so as to avoid any ambush or attack, and Barrow's mounted men were patrolling some distance ahead, on the high hills overlooking the Inyezane valley.

Because of the poor laagering performance, and because of the increase in enemy activity, Chelmsford decided to simplify the laagering procedure. In future, the laager would be an exact square of 130 yards – which allowed for thirty wagons or carts to fit in on each side – and the shelter trench was to be dug 15 yards in front of it on all sides. Accordingly, as the column moved into the Nyezane valley, a few miles downriver from the spot where Pearson had stopped the Zulu attack on 22 January, Molyneux rode out with John Dunn and four orderlies to select a camping site. They found one less than a mile south of the river, on a low rise, near the ruins of the kwaGingindlovu *ikhanda*, which Pearson's men had burnt three months before. Molyneux was happy with the choice:

> ... it was only slightly commanded on the south side, with regular glacis-like slopes on the three others. I at once placed my four mounted points; the column soon appeared; and the laager was finished and the shelter trench marked out in no time. The distances worked out beautifully; we had guns, rockets, or gatlings, at the angles of the trench; an opening in the middle of each face to let the horses and cattle in and out, with four wagons ready to run in and close it at any moment.

The 60th formed the front of the camp, lining the north-eastern rampart, with the 99th and 'The Buffs' on the left face, and the 57th on the right. The 91st were situated at the rear. The Naval Brigades, with their artillery, were positioned in the corners; the Native Contingent were placed behind the 91st.

It seemed obvious to everyone that there were indeed Zulu concentrations in the vicinity. Barrow's scouts had seen small parties of warriors beyond Misi hill, which lay a mile and a half off to the left of the camp, and Dunn was convinced that the Zulus who were camped in the hills around Eshowe would move down to block their path in the Nyezane valley. That evening a mist rose in the valley, and Dunn was convinced it masked the smoke from Zulu camp fires. He suggested to Molyneux that the two of them ride out to investigate. Molyneux was given permission, 'was told to take care of myself' and the two rode out unescorted. Dunn's plan was that they should ride to the river, then dismount, and, leaving Molyneux to hold the horses, he would swim across and investigate. Once they were alone, Dunn had a pertinant question to ask Molyneux, a question that bitter experience would prove all too relevant before the Zulu War was over:

> Now you know we are in for a dangerous job, and as I have never been out with English officers before, I should like to be certain before I start across, that our ideas are the same. In Africa a white man must stand by a fellow while there is life in him; if his friend is dead, then he may save himself. Do you agree?

Molyneux satisfied Dunn on that point, and the two approached the river in silent single file. It was to prove an extraordinary adventure:

The rain began to fall again in perfect torrents, which was all the better for us, as any scouts about would be likely to crawl back to their fires. After a couple of miles Dunn turned off into the bush, pushed through to the Nyezane, and stopped to listen. Not a sound was to be heard but the patter of rain drops and the roar of the river. Beckoning me up to hold his horse, he stripped, tied his clothes up in a bundle which he gave to me, took his rifle, swung himself into the torrent, and, holding on to the branches of a tree that had fallen across it, landed on the other bank and disappeared. The good old horses stood like lambs; but a Kafir crane found me out in his peregrinations in search of a dinner, and made off with rather more noise than I thought necessary. It was rather uncomfortable work as the dusk began to fall, and I was not sorry to see my naked friend wriggling down through the grass on the far bank. I don't know how he managed to get back, for the river had risen ten feet in an hour, and the trunk of the tree was submerged, but he swung himself across somehow, landing blue with cold. We were soon on the march again, he drying his rifle and changing the cartridge as we made our way through the bush, and as soon as we reached the open, away we went at a gallop for the laager. As we rode he told me that he had seen an *impi* and a lot of bivouac fires, that he had been nearly discovered by one of their scouts, who, when the clattering crane rose, had advanced to within a few yards from where he lay, that he had been obliged to lie low till the fellow was satisfied and went back, and that he wanted a gallop now to warm himself.

When we reached the laager the trench was completed but full of water in places, and the state of the ground inside it defies description. When 5000 human beings, 2000 oxen and 300 horses have been churning up five acres of very sodden ground for 2 or 3 hours it makes a compost neither pretty to look at, easy to move about in, nor nice to smell. There were unpleasant reptiles about also, for two puff adders had been killed close to our wagon.

Dunn's report confirmed what the scouts had suggested during the day. The Zulus were apparently drawing close, and a battle seemed likely on the morrow. Chelmsford decided not to start early the next morning, but to send out the NNC to feel for the enemy first. The men were left to get what sleep they could. The night, again, was dreadful. A heavy thunderstorm broke over the camp, and Dawnay – who noted that he had camped with Dunn on almost the same spot nine years before – commented that 'sheltering under the wagons was useless, as there were soon two inches of water on the ground, and we were all wet through, and having no change had to remain so.' Mynors noted that 'our feet had been wet for the last two days; in fact, we are never dry. No clothes to change, or anything.' The weather had brought a relapse to Captain Gough of the NNC, and he became so ill that he was ordered to the ambulance wagon. A tot of rum was issued to keep the men's spirits up, but just as they were drinking it, there was a smatter of shots from the picquets outside the laager. Immediately, the whole camp rushed to their posts, expecting to be attacked at any moment; but after about an hour it became clear that it was a false alarm, and they stood down.

The next morning, Wednesday, 2 April, broke surprisingly clear, although a dense mist hung in the valley of the Nyezane. Just as the NNC were being prepared to march out, several shots were heard from the night picquets still on duty. A large Zulu force was advancing under cover of the mist; the battle of Gingindlovu had begun.

CHAPTER 8

'Talk About Pluck!'

It had become clear to the Zulus throughout March that the war was about to enter a new active phase. The king's peace overtures had been steadily rebuffed, and the efficient Zulu intelligence network was fully aware that fresh British troops were marching up to the frontier daily. For more than a month the warriors who made up the main army had been resting at their homesteads, recovering from the traumatic experience of Isandlwana. By the middle of March, however, the king felt able to order his district *izinduna* to recall the *amabutho*, and the army began to reassemble at oNdini.

Two problems faced the king and his council as they met to discuss how best to proceed with the campaign. In the north, Evelyn Wood's column had remained on the offensive, raiding local homesteads, driving out the king's supporters and looting cattle. The local Zulus, particularly a royal section known as the abaQulusi, and the followers of a renegade Swazi prince, Mbilini waMswati, had struck back wherever they could, but they were driven increasingly on to the defensive, and both groups sent repeated messages to the king begging for assistance. But if Wood's column remained the strongest and most immediate threat, the king was extremely angry that Pearson seemed to have taken root in Zululand, and the arrival of troops at the Lower Thukela Drift in the last week of March clearly indicated that the British were preparing to advance on that front. Either they would have to cross the river into Zululand, or Pearson would have to move out to meet them; either eventuality suited the Zulu commanders. Despite the casualties they had suffered at Isandlwana, the Zulu army remained convinced that they could defeat the British if only they could catch them in the open field. Once again, the king and his council decided on a divided strategy; the main army assembling at oNdini would be sent north to counter Wood, but part of it would be sent as reinforcements to stiffen the forces camped around Eshowe. These would be supported by auxiliaries drawn from the northern coastal peoples, the Tsonga, whose chiefs were clients of the Zulu kings. In this way Cetshwayo hoped to neutralise the existing British threats before Lord Chelmsford had time to mount a fresh invasion; he was increasingly aware that his only chance of an outright victory lay in the hope that he could prolong the campaign beyond the will of the British to pursue it.

The fires which both Chelmsford's scouts and Pearson's men had seen on the hills south of Eshowe and down into the Nyezane valley had been evidence of

'Friends at a distance': two sketches showing the attempts to improvise signalling equipment at Eshowe during the siege.

Captain Friend Addison, who commanded the composite force drawn from the Natal Volunteers, known as the Natal Volunteer Guides, during the Gingindlovu campaign. *(Sketch by Edward Hutton. Africana Museum, Johannesburg)*

Two members of the Ixopo Mounted Contingent, some of whom fought at Gingindlovu.

the gathering of this *impi*. These warriors were under the command of Somopho kaZikhale, the chief of the Thembu, who was a typical representative of the king's inner circle of trusted commanders; he was a close friend of Cetshwayo, and held the post of *induna* of the emaNgweni *ikhanda*, which lay north-east of Eshowe. He was also the royal armourer, in charge of the king's attempts to manufacture gunpowder and lead. Somopho's command consisted of about 3000 Tsonga, augmented by about 1500 men from the *amabutho* who were attached to the kwaGingindlovu *ikhanda*. Prince Dabulamanzi, the king's half brother, had remained in command of the warriors in the immediate vicinity of Eshowe, who were based at eNtumeni, while Sigcwelegcwele kaMhlekehleke, the commander of the iNgobamakhosi and a veteran of Isandlwana, commanded about 3000 warriors from the iNgobamakhosi, uKhandempemvu, uNokhenke, and uMbonambi *amabutho* who were quartered at Hlalangubo, the old oNdini *ikhanda*. A further 1500 men of the iNdluyengwe *ibutho* were quartered at another *ikhanda*, isinPuseleni, nearby. Sigcwelegcwele's co-commander was Phalane kaMdinwa, chief of the royal Hlangezwa section, which inhabited the lower stretches of the Mhlatuze river. All of these men had strong local ties, and knew the area well.

The Zulus apparently began to draw together to oppose Chelmsford on the 29th. The rumour that Mynors had heard that day, that an *impi* was threatening the column's rear, was not entirely without foundation, as a body of warriors had apparently crossed the amaTigulu upstream from the British column, and watched its progress. The Zulus were not in a position to attack, however, as the various elements of their force were not yet assembled. It was not until the evening of the 1st that Sigcwelegcwele and Phalane's detachment joined the main Zulu camp on the hills below Eshowe. Some of the Zulu commanders wanted to attack the British immediately, but Dabulamanzi, showing uncharacteristic restraint, persuaded them to wait until morning. In any case, the new arrivals were tired and hungry, and the Zulus, whose scouts had been kept back by Barrow's enthusiastic patrolling, were not entirely sure of the British dispositions. Instead, they moved down before dawn, and when the early morning sun began to burn off the mist, the British spotted a dense column, shaped like a coffin, advancing on the far side of the Nyezane, and another west of the laager, on the Misi hill. An anonymous officer of the NNC described the first encounter, which took place at about 6.30am:

On the evening of the 1st I was out on outlying picket with fifty natives and a company of the 60th Rifles. It rained nearly all night, and the next morning, at about daylight, one of my boys came to me and asked if I saw Zulus down in the valley. I saw nothing. But a few minutes afterwards I saw swarms of them all rushing for the laager about half a mile off. I at once fell my men in and ran for the camp.

(Left) Sigcwelegcwele kaMhlekehleke, the commander of the iNgobamakhosi *ibutho*, and a Zulu divisional commander at Gingindlovu. *(Sketch by Edward Hutton. Africana Museum, Johannesburg)*

(Right) Chief Somopho kaZikhale, the senior Zulu commander at Gingindlovu. *(Sketch by Edward Hutton. Africana Museum, Johannesburg)*

(Left) An incident during the pursuit at Gingindlovu; this may be Sergeant Anderson's famous duel. *(Sketch by John North Crealock. Sherwood Foresters' Museum, Nottingham)*

(Right) Prince Dabulamanzi kaMpande, sketched by Edward Hutton at the end of the war. Dabulamanzi led the right horn at Gingindlovu. *(Africana Museum, Johannesburg)*

According to Norris-Newman, one of the 91st's picquets had wandered off to fetch water, and was surprised by the advancing *impi* and speared to death. If so, it must have been Private R. Marshall, the only man from the 91st to have been reported killed that day.

The picquets fired a few shots which were clearly heard in the laager, and Norris-Newman proudly claimed to have drawn the attention of the staff to the Zulu approach. By that time, however, the Zulu columns were clear to everyone on the north and west faces of the camp, and the bugles rang out the alarm. The men fell in, lining the space between the rampart and the wagons four deep on all sides. Molyneux recorded that there were few enough orders issued: 'Stand to your arms – saddle up – no independent firing – volleys by companies when they are within 300 yards'. This last order was vital if the men were to make the most effective use of their fire; the disciplined crash of volley fire was believed to have a devastating effect on an enemy attacking in close formation, as the British expected the Zulus to do. Independent firing, while it gave good shots the chance to excel, was difficult to control, especially where inexperienced troops were concerned. In the excitement of the moment, it was all too easy to fire off round after round without taking proper aim, and a great deal of ammunition was liable to be wasted. Yet at Gingindlovu, the order to hold fire condemned the troops at the front of the square to the nerve-racking spectacle of the Zulus deploying to attack without a shot being fired to stop them. It was a sight that was to strain the nerves of the untried men of the 60th.

The main Zulu body split into columns, then crossed the Nyezane at two drifts about a mile apart, and, as it advanced up the slopes towards the laager, it fanned out into the traditional 'chest and horns' attack formation. Their approach required them to shift their line of advance, and the most easterly column, the left horn, curled sharply to the right to attack the north-eastern corner of the laager, while the remaining body, the chest, streamed in a more gentle curve towards the northern face. A separate body, coming up from beyond Misi hill to the west, formed the right horn. Sadly, few Zulu accounts of the battle have survived, and it is impossible to determine the disposition of the individual *amabutho*, but it seems that most of the regiments had representatives present, and that the total force numbered in excess of 11,000 men. Chelmsford had issued his officers with a pamphlet which described the distinctive uniforms worn on ceremonial occasions by the various regiments, and those officers who had yet to see them in action had expected to see the Zulus thus attired. Some undoubtedly were; one correspondent referred to 'their white shields, their headdresses of leopard-skin and feathers, and the wild ox-tails hanging from their necks', while the 91st were later able to recover sufficient headdresses and cow-tail ornaments to form a fair-sized trophy. The majority, however, were wearing nothing more than a loin covering about their waists and necklaces containing charms to ward off evil around their necks. Typically, it seems that

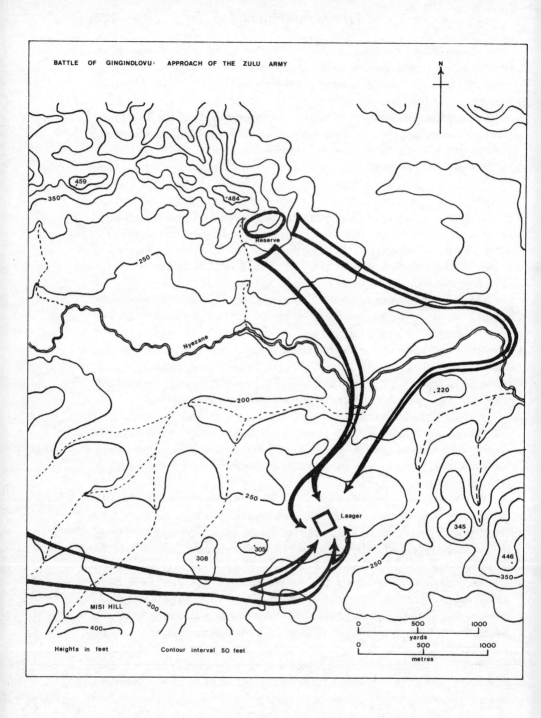

BATTLE OF GINGINDLOVU: APPROACH OF THE ZULU ARMY

N

459

·484

350

250

Reserve

Nyezane

·220

200

250

Laager

345

305

250

308

446

350

MISI HILL

300

250

446

400

0   500   1000
yards

0   500   1000
metres

Heights in feet   Contour interval 50 feet

only those warriors who were quartered closest to the scene of the fighting had turned out in some part of their regalia; those who had longer to march wore little or none. Captain Edward Hutton of the 60th noted 'contrary to precedent, they did not wear their full war costume, but carried rifles, assegais, and small shields'. To young Jack Royston, the dappled war-shields rippling through the grass looked like nothing so much as a swarm of multicoloured beetles. Hutton, indeed, marvelled at the skill with which the Zulus skirmished:

> The dark masses of men, in open order and under admirable discipline, followed each other in quick succession, running at a steady pace through the long grass. Having moved steadily round so as exactly to face our front, the larger portion of the Zulus broke into three lines, in knots and groups of from five to ten men, and advanced toward us. . . .
>
> The Zulus continued to advance, still at a run, until they were about 800 yards from us, when they began to open fire. In spite of the excitement of the moment, we could not but admire the perfect manner in which these Zulus skirmished. A small knot of five or six would rise and dart through the long grass, dodging from side to side with heads down, rifles and shields kept low and out of sight. They would then suddenly sink into the long grass, and nothing but puffs of curling smoke would show their whereabouts.

For perhaps a hundred yards around the laager, the turmoil of men and animals the afternoon before had trampled the grass flat, though here and there a clump had survived around a tree or cluster of bushes. Beyond that, there had been no time to clear the ground, and the grass grew in some places 4–5 feet tall. It was excellent cover, and the Zulus used it to good effect.

The corners of the square were held by detachments of the Naval Brigades, with their respective artillery. On the front left corner there were ninety Royal Marines and men of HMS *Boadicea*, under the command of Lieutenant Carr, with two rockets. The front right was held by a company of Marines under Captain Phillips, and a company of seamen also from HMS *Boadicea* – 143 in all – with their Gatling gun, while the right rear corner was held by the Headquarters detachment of the Naval Brigade, 175 men from the *Shah* and a Gatling. Lieutenant Kingscote of the *Tenedos*, with two 9-pounder guns and 158 men from the *Shah*, completed the formation in the left rear corner. The advancing Zulus were clearly visible to the *Boadicea*'s Gatling crew, and the petty officer in charge begged to be allowed to fire. According to Molyneux,

> 'Beg your pardon, sir,' he said, 'last night I stepped the distance to that bush where those blacks are, and it's just 800 yards. This 'no firing' seems like throwing a chance away. I've got her laid true for them; may I give her half a

Men from HMS *Shah*'s Naval Brigade at the ramparts of the south-west corner of the laager at Gingindlovu during the battle.

turn of the handle?' The Chief [Chelmsford] who was close by, did not object to the range being tested, providing he stopped at once. A final sight, and, I am sure, quite two turns of the handle was the response, and there was a clear lane cut quite through the body of men. The effect of the fire of a machine gun is awful if it is served by a cool hand; the gun has no nerves, and, provided the man is steady and the cartridges do not jam, nothing can live in front of it. The captain of this gun was a veteran, and afterwards during the fight his exhortation to his crew would have made, when carefully expurgated, an admirable essay on behaviour under fire.

Awesome as it was, however, the Gatling did not slow the Zulu advance in the slightest, and as the warriors closed to 400 yards, the order was given for the 60th to open volley fire. Lieutenant Hutton remembered that he could hardly make himself heard above the clatter of the Gatling, and that not ten minutes had elapsed since the Zulus had first appeared on the far side of the Nyezane. The first volley crashed out with a roar that was deafening; Guy Dawnay, experiencing his first taste of action, 'never imagined even such a crash of sound as the whole thing'. To the correspondent of *The Daily Telegraph*, it seemed that 'the whole front of our camp broke into a sheet of flame which ran from corner to corner without intermission, in rattling volleys of a frightful close-range musketry. Nothing, it might be thought, could live before this terrible and perpetual roll of the breech-loader'. Yet this impression was misleading, as Hutton admitted; the first volley 'could hardly be expected to have done much execution, since there were but a number of darting figures at irregular intervals and distances to aim at'. He tried to keep his men firing 'very steadily'. Wilkinson, the adjutant, recalled that the 60th were 'firing volleys by sections in order to prevent the smoke obscuring the enemy, and we had repeatedly to cease fire to allow the smoke to clear off, as some young aspirants out of hand paid little attention to the section firing.'

Most of the non-combatants with the force had moved inside the laager, where the wagons protected them from the worst of the Zulu fire. John Dunn was among them, but he had no intention of shirking the fight. He climbed up onto a buck wagon from where he cast a professional eye over the 60th shooting. He was not impressed:

> . . . I noticed that the bullets of the volleys fired by the soldiers were striking the ground a long way beyond their mark, and on looking at their rifles I found that they still had the long-range sights up, and that they were firing wildly in any direction. I then called to Lord Chelmsford, asking for him to give orders for lowering the sights. This was done, and the soldiers began to drop the enemy and consequently check the advance; but again, when I had my sight down to 100 yards, as the Zulus came nearer I noticed that the soldiers had up the 300 yard sights.

... I was much disappointed in the shooting of the soldiers. Their sole object seemed to be to get rid of ammunition or firing so many rounds per minute at anything, it didn't matter what.

Nevertheless, there were some marksmen among the 60th, and they were making good practice – according to Wilkinson, one man of the 60th dropped four running Zulus at 400 yards with consecutive shots. These losses, coupled with the psychological effect of the booming volleys, caused the Zulu attack to lose momentum. They went to ground in the long grass, wriggling forward, rising up on their elbows now and then to fire at the defenders. As they reached the open space in front of the line, some of them, 'brave to madness' according to one observer, charged forward with their shields up and their stabbing spears drawn back. At that range, however, nothing could survive before the 60th fire; clumps of bodies were found here afterwards, only 30 yards from the shelter trench, and Mynors claimed to have paced out one or two at only 20 yards. As the attack ground to a halt, the men composing the Zulu 'chest' began to filter to their right, past the corner of the square, and attempted to attack the companies of the 99th on the left face. The left horn, meanwhile, probably supported by elements of the chest, had pushed forward to where a concealed donga in a hollow allowed them the cover of some dead ground only a few yards in front of the front right corner. According to Hutton:

> The donga to the right of my company appeared to be full of Zulus, who by groups of ten or fifteen began to make rushes for a clump of palm bushes ten yards from us. Numbers succeeded in reaching it, but the cover proved delusive, for when it was all over we found a pile of dead bodies in this place. After a short time the enemy, unable to make headway against our fire, gradually withdrew, slinking off through the long grass like whipped hounds.

The Zulu attack, directed particularly at the Gatling, seems to have been very determined. Jack Royston recalled years later that one big Zulu had seemed to run right up to the gun, touching it with his arm, before he was cut down. Someone saw an *induna* 'haranguing them "as to what the Zulu maidens would say when they heard the Zulus had fled before British dogs," the force came on again, and was literally mown down'. Standing near the Gatling was George Hamilton-Browne, a hard-bitten Irish adventurer who had led an NNC battalion through the Isandlwana campaign, and who had slipped away from his current duties – training a unit of irregular horse in Natal – on the pretext of carrying a message to Chelmsford. Hamilton-Browne was looking to avenge the friends he had lost at Isandlwana, but that did not stop him marvelling at the extraordinary endurance of the Zulus; he saw one young Zulu lad, a mat-carrier, dash right up to the rampart, 'where one of the blue-jackets spotting him, leaned over, grabbed him by the nape of the neck and collected him, kicking and squirming, inside the work, where after he had been cuffed into a state of quietude his captor kept him prisoner by sitting on him till the end of the engagement.' The youth was apparently adopted by the *Boadicea*'s crew as a mascot, and later passed into the Navy. Generally, however, it was impossible for the warriors to linger in the face of such an intense fire, and they fell back to the dubious shelter of the donga.

The attack nevertheless apparently provoked a crisis among the 60th. The Zulu fire was extremely heavy, but, as usual, inaccurate and mostly high. This was itself disconcerting, however, since the rampart behind the shelter trench was only about 3 feet high, just big enough to provide cover for a man kneeling. For the rest, as Lieutenant Backhouse – who was with two companies of 'The Buffs' on the left of the square – noted 'the ground sloped upwards towards the wagons in our rear so that only the two front ranks were sheltered, the rest exposed.' He added 'It was amusing to see the men bobbing their heads when the Zulus first opened fire on them.' Lieutenant Wilkinson of the 60th recalled 'We had some narrow escapes; one officer of ours received a shot in his ammunition pouch, and another officer, Lieut. R.H. Gunning, had part of his rifle carried away as he was aiming.'

Among those to go down was Lieutenant-Colonel Francis Northey of the 60th. Northey was standing with his adjutant, Wilkinson, on the right of the line, near the Gatling; according to the Regimental History, he walked over to the Gatling to discuss the range when he was hit by a Zulu bullet which struck him high on the left arm. Molyneux, who was near by, thought the wound must have been slight, for Northey coolly gave the order for the next senior officer to take command of the battalion, and allowed Wilkinson to help him off to the ambulance wagon inside the laager. Both Hamilton-Browne and Royston noticed that, with the Zulus pressing on in front and Northey down, the 60th became unsteady. Hamilton-Browne, who thought the 60th 'half-baked nervous boys', commented that for a moment they were 'worse than wobbly', and Jack Royston was afraid the square might cave in. Even the officers of the 60th admitted that their men were difficult to control: Hutton noted that a 'few men showed signs of firing wildly, but a smart rap with my stick soon helped a man to recover his self-possession'. Baskerville Mynors, himself under fire for the first time, was as refreshingly candid as ever:

Our men were awfully frightened and nervous at first, could not even speak and shivered from funk, so we – the officers – had enough to do to keep the men cool...

...I myself did not quite like the first few shots as they whizzed over our heads; but found I had such a lot to do to keep the men in order and telling them when to shoot, that I did not mind it a bit.

Somehow the officers managed to steady their men, and they stood their ground, and as the Zulu rush faltered, the crisis passed.

Northey's wound was more serious than anyone thought. The bullet had passed through his shoulder and lodged close to his spine. He was given medical attention and his wound bandaged, but when a fresh burst of firing heralded a new attack, he struggled to sit upright and cheer his men on. The effort ruptured an artery, and he collapsed in a sudden haemorrhage, blood spurting out through the dressing.

Meanwhile, a second serious attack had developed as the Zulu centre had moved to its right to try to assault the left face of the British square. Once again volley fire rippled down the ranks, obscuring the battlefield with thick greasy smoke. Lieutenant George Johnson was the 99th's Instructor of Musketry; he was twenty-seven years old, and a veteran of Nyezane, who had returned to the border with Coates's convoy. Nonetheless, his looks were so youthful that Lord Chelmsford had once pointed him out to a staff officer, and asked who he was, and whether he had seen active service before. Johnson tried energetically to control his men's fire, and at one point jumped clear over the shelter trench so that they could see him better. Back inside the entrenchment, one eye-witness noted that he had taken a Martini-Henry rifle from one of the men, and 'was fighting manfully, as if he was at Rorke's Drift, fighting for his life.' He was standing near a group of officers – Major Walker, the senior officer of the 99th, and Backhouse of 'The Buffs', who knew him well, among them – when he suddenly clutched his chest, and, exclaiming 'I am shot!', fell to the ground unconscious. Norris-Newman saw him fall. He was rushed to the hospital wagon but died shortly after; a Zulu bullet had gone through his heart.

Johnson's death seems to have spurred Norris-Newman into joining the fray. Victorian war-correspondents made no pretence of the impartiality so nurtured by their modern counterparts; they were, after all, a product of the same ideological school as the armies they accompanied. Some were sensitive enough to see some justice in the cause of those opposing Imperial expansion, but few were prepared to cross the great divides of race and culture which separated them from the black warriors on the other side of the shelter trench. They were, in any case, automatically marked down by their white skins as enemies by their opponents, and almost all of the great Victorian 'specials' were happy to defend themselves when caught up in a fight; Norris-Newman had seen the devastated field of Isandlwana, and does not seem to have suffered moral qualms for a moment:

> During this time I and a friend of mine named Palmer, who had accompanied the expedition as conductor, with a lot of wagons, had each got a rifle and were steadily taking pot-shots, at any native who made himself visible, from the top of the wagon, which position gave us great advantage. Palmer (who is a crack

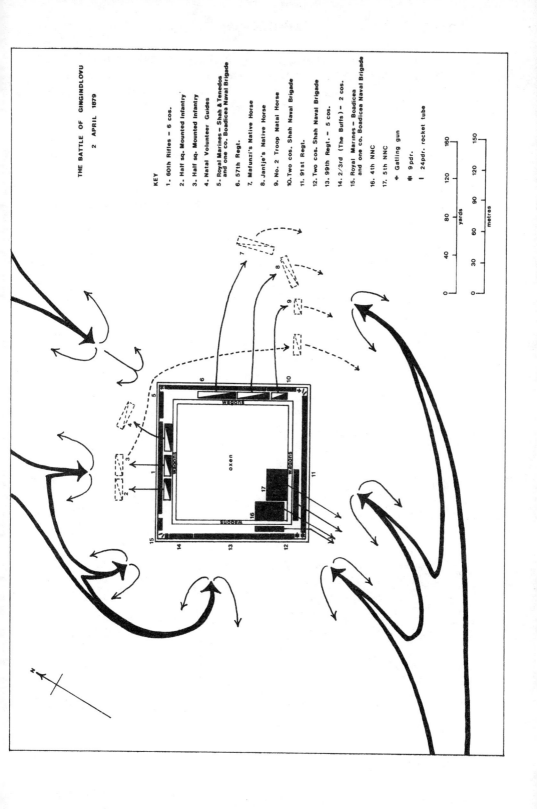

THE BATTLE OF GINGINDLOVU
2 APRIL 1879

KEY

1. 60th Rifles – 6 cos.
2. Half sq. Mounted Infantry
3. Half sq. Mounted Infantry
4. Natal Volunteer Guides
5. Royal Marines – Shah & Tenedos
   and one co. Boadicea Naval Brigade
6. 57th Regt.
7. Mafunzi's Native Horse
8. Jantje's Native Horse
9. No. 2 Troop Natal Horse
10. Two cos. Shah Naval Brigade
11. 91st Regt.
12. Two cos. Shah Naval Brigade
13. 99th Regt. – 5 cos.
14. 2/3rd (The Buffs) – 2 cos.
15. Royal Marines – Boadicea
    and one co. Boadicea Naval Brigade
16. 4th NNC
17. 5th NNC

✛ Gatling gun
❋ 9pdr.
❘ 24pdr. rocket tube

oxen

0   30   40   60   80   90   120   120   150   160
        yards
        metres

shot, having hunted large game in the interior for years) brought several to the ground. One shot in particular was a great success; about a hundred yards off, – straight in front of us, three Zulus had managed to gain the shelter of a thick bush, whose roots formed an impenetrable barrier to even our hot fire, and it was from this bush that the shot was fired which killed poor Johnson. His death was, however, quickly avenged, as we both arranged to wait quietly until the Zulu fired again, and then taking good aim we both fired together as two of them had raised themselves on their knees to get a fair aim. The one aimed at by Palmer sprung high in the air, with outstretched arms, and fell backwards dead, shot clean through the forehead, as we found out afterwards. The one I aimed at was only wounded, but in a little while both he and the third Zulu were killed by some men of the 99th.

The Zulus were able to make no more headway against the left face of the square than they had at the front, and the attack stalled. At about this time, however – and the battle had so far been raging for probably no more than fifteen minutes, if that – the regiments in the right horn approached rapidly from Misi hill, and deployed to attack the rear face of the laager. They were led by an *induna* on horseback, believed to have been Prince Dabulamanzi himself. Even above the din of battle the British could hear the Zulu shouts of command, and the cries of 'uSuthu!' and 'They are encircled.' Apparently, the Zulus saw the glitter of the sun on the bayonets of the 91st, who held the rear face, and mistakenly assumed that they were the spears of the Native Contingent. Certainly they may have seen some of the NNC themselves, who were nervously squatting together between the 91st and the wagons. As the Zulus rushed closer, Dawnay heard the first of their shots 'whishing up the line of our trench'. The men of the 91st seemed to have reacted well to the first fire of the Zulus; they were no more experienced than their colleagues in the 60th, but they had been spared that agonising ten-minute wait, watching the menacing sight of the Zulus deploying, but unable to respond. As soon as the Zulu attack developed, the 91st presented arms; Dawnay joined their adjutant, Lieutenant St Clair, behind the Highland ranks, and thought 'the general fire of the men did little except make a smoke and spoil our shots; but as a whole the 91st behaved excellently. Our sights came down from 500, 400, 300, 200 to 100 yards; but no Zulu got nearer to the shelter trench than 31 yards.' As soon as the shooting began, Captain Gough, sick though he was, rushed out from the ambulance wagon, and took up a rifle. For a few minutes the return fire was very hot. Dawnay

... heard more bullets whizzing past us in the first five minutes than in any other quarter of an hour of our fight, but then now came several narrow escapes. St Clair was just raising his head after showing me a Zulu to fire at, when a bullet caught his helmet fair in the middle, and knocking it off onto my shoulder without touching him; at the same moment a native just straight behind Gough and myself was killed, and the next moment the assegai of another standing within a foot of us was cut in half by a bullet.

Chelmsford was so concerned about this fresh assault that he ordered two companies of the 60th out of the front face, where the pressure had slackened, and sent them across to act as a reserve for the 91st. In the left rear corner of the square, Lieutenant Kingscote's two 9-pounders showered the Zulus with shrapnel, while at the other end of the 91st's line, the Gatling and rocket tubes also opened up. Dawnay saw them come into action, but had his misgivings about their effectiveness: '... the rockets and shells were tried at them; I can't say, though, I was impressed by the accuracy of either. One rocket struck the ground not a quarter of a mile away and came straight back over the camp!'

Molyneux was similarly sceptical: 'Rockets look awful instruments of destruction; but they do none at all except when used to frighten horses or to set tents on fire. The Zulus evidently thought them living devils, for I saw many men fire at them as they passed over their heads ...'

Nevertheless, the British were able to put down a terrible barrier of fire around the square. The same anonymous officer of the NNC who had been out on picquet duty earlier described his own part in this stage of the fight:

... the natives were all round [us] in swarms, shooting as fast as they could. Fancy, there were some of them twenty yards from the trench. Talk about pluck! the Zulu has all that. They were shot down one after the other, and they still came on in hundreds.

... I can only swear to one man that I shot. He was creeping in the long grass about one hundred yards from me. I took a good steady aim, and saw him jump in the air, and when the fight was over I went and looked at him. I hit him, just where I aimed, in the ribs. The ball passed through him, so I have done some good for Natal in ridding it of one Zulu. I may have shot more, only I can't tell, so many firing at once.

For the rank and file of the NNC, however, the experience of battle at Gingindlovu was particularly unpleasant. They squatted in a block behind the 91st, and, as Molyneux describes, received some rough treatment from their officers and NCOs:

They had been ordered to keep their muzzles pointing to the sky and not fire at any price, their white officers being in front of them and facing them; but they are an excitable race, and gun after gun was let off in the air, sometimes at no very great elevation. Then came bad words and hard boots....

Molyneux, indeed, had been having an adventure of his own. Apparently, when the Zulu attack faltered against the front face of the laager, Chelmsford had ordered Barrow's mounted men to try to clear them away from the long grass and bush. According to Molyneux,

> ... [a rocket] went skimming just above the grass, and the Zulus in that direction fell back a bit from its flaming tail, [so] the General told Barrow to take out the Mounted Infantry on the right face and keep them on the run. But the Zulus, quickly recovering from their panic, and showing no fear of the horsemen, and the attack, which had come on our left and rear, extending round to our right face, the Chief [Chelmsford], fearing Barrow might be cut off, ordered me out to recall him. It was done only just in time, for we had to fight our way back. One fellow missed me at close quarters, and paid the penalty by a revolver bullet in the forehead, but another shot straighter; the bullet entered poor old Lampas just below the seat of the saddle; he carried me over the trench and then succumbed, sending me headlong into the miry mess. Barrow and two of his men were wounded, three horses and men were wounded.
>
> It is a curious sensation when a horse going at a gallop under you gets a mortal wound. He falters in front, picks himself up and drops behind, gets his hind legs under him once more, makes one supreme effort, and then turns a complete somersault; it is much the same sensation as trying to sit the mechanical horse when bucking, an exhibition that I had visited in London in my youth. My poor brute lay still but alive; so I gave him his quietus, cleared him of saddle and bridle, and saw under the saddle on the opposite side to the wound a lump like a warble; one touch of a knife and the bullet dropped out, a very badly cast spherical thing, half hollow, with the waste lead still left on it.

Barrow merely states that at '6.40am I advanced out of the laager by the front face with the volunteers and mounted infantry, and opened fire on the enemy who had retired into the long grass out of fire from the laager.' It was another twenty minutes before he made any further move, however, and it was presumably during this time that he was recalled. It is possible that Barrow's men remained outside the laager, hugging close to the right-front corner, since there are no reports apart from Molyneux's which suggest they returned inside the entrenchment. As an ADC, of course, it was Molyneux's duty to return to his commanding officer's side. Barrow himself was wounded at some point, though it is not clear when; it may have been at this time, although Royston claims to have seen him earlier, knocked off a wagon, where he had been watching the attack on the front face, by a flung spear which caught him in the thigh. Barrow later reported a gunshot wound in the leg, although this does not necessarily contradict Royston, since, curiously enough, all wounds sustained at Gingindlovu were reported as gunshot injuries.

The Zulu attack, meanwhile, had recoiled from the rear face of the square, and rolled round to attack the right face. So far the 57th had not been heavily engaged, since the left horn seems to have been halted at the start of the battle, but for a few minutes there was a determined attack on their position. The ground ran level for perhaps 200 yards in front of the 57th's line, then sloped sharply away. The Zulus were able to assemble in the dead ground beyond, but cresting the rise at such a short range exposed them to such a terrible fire that they could not press their charges home. Captain Hinxman of the 57th was wounded in the leg and another man killed by the Zulu fire, but the 57th, who – apart from the two 'Buffs' companies – were the most seasoned men in the square, replied with volleys that rang out 'as clear as if they were at Aldershot. If every regiment had possessed such seasoned men as those', commented Molyneux, 'we could have walked to Ekowe and back without having to burrow in the ground like ant-bears.' Once again, the Zulus went to ground.

On the whole, the battle of Gingindlovu was a soldiers' battle. Chelmsford had prepared his ground well, but once the fighting had begun, there was little for him to do; it was not a battle of movement on the British side, and he was called upon to make no great tactical decisions. It fell to his officers to control and direct their men's fire. The general paced about on foot, urging them on; Norris-Newman saw him 'on foot, with his red nightcap on, encouraging the men, directing their fire, and instructing them to fire low and steady.' Chelmsford's staff followed him on horseback, a dangerous position given the wild nature of the shooting. Two of them suffered lucky escapes; Crealock was hit in the arm by a spent bullet which he found among his clothes, while one of his ADCs, Lieutenant Milne of the *Active*, had a bullet pass through his sleeve, grazing his arm.

Inside the laager there was a scene of indescribable confusion. Bellowing oxen were jumbled up with civilian wagon-drivers and others, all at the mercy of stray bullets which sometimes struck among them at random. They reacted in different ways to the stress of combat; Norris-Newman found his groom, 'a cockney lad who had probably never seen a shot fired in earnest before in his short life of seventeen years', calmly preparing a stew for breakfast, and making 'droll remarks' on the battle raging about him. Many of the drivers were standing on the wagons, which allowed them to fire over the heads of the soldiers, and pick their own targets. Molyneux spotted John Dunn among them:

Noot [his batman] was sitting on the top of a wagon alongside John Dunn, loading for him and beaming with joy. 'Here's about the first man killed on our side', he said, as he got down. 'It's our forelooper; he went and lay under the wagon in a fright; I told him to come out as it was all luck, and that minute a bullet hit him in the head. And there's the first drunk man', he added, pointing to one of the Native Contingent who lay under a commissariat-wagon breathing stentorously. A Martini bullet had pierced a cask of rum, and the nose of the native had detected the well-loved smell even amidst the 'villainous saltpetre'; he had caught the stream in his mouth and was, when discovered, quite insensible. 'I tell you that gentleman is a fine shot', my man went on, 'he never misses them; he has his own and my rifle; he shoots, I load.' 'Well, get on with the other horse, and clear as much of the filth off the saddle as you can,' I said, and mounted up alongside Dunn. 'I've picked out an *induna* or two', was his only remark . . .

Dunn himself admitted that he had fired over thirty shots, 'and missed very few'.

By about 7am, the Zulu attacks were stalled on all sides, but the warriors showed no signs of retiring, and clung tenaciously to the cover of the long grass. Chelmsford decided the time had come to give them a push; 'I now directed Captain Barrow to advance across the right or east face and attack the enemy's right flank.' It was a grand moment for the mounted men. The Mounted Infantry had been armed with swords shortly before the expedition set off, and Barrow, the Hussar, had been delighted. Now was the opportunity to test the effectiveness of the 'arme blanche'. Norris-Newman, with his journalist's eye for the dramatic, noted that '. . . the gallant Major led the charge in person, having formed his men in two lines, with instructions to the rear rank to protect any of their comrades in the front rank, who might fall, from being surrounded and assegaid by the Zulus'.

Barrow, accompanied by his staff officer, Lieutenant Courtenay, rode out with Lieutenant Rawlins' half-squadron of the Mounted Infantry to try to drive back the Zulu right horn. For a moment or two the Zulus stuck in the long grass, and there was a flurry of fighting; gradually, however, they began to retire, and the rest of Barrow's command fell in along side him, with Lieutenant Cook's Troop of the Natal Horse on his immediate left, and Mafunzi's and Jantje's men beyond them. Behind them, Lieutenant Sugden's half squadron of the Mounted Infantry, and the Natal Volunteer Guides harried the warriors still lingering across the front of the 57th and 60th. Barrow was delighted at the effectiveness of the swords carried by Rawlins' men:

> The half squadron drew swords and charged the Zulus, who were in large numbers, but utterly demoralised. The actual number of men killed with the sword was probably few, but the moral effect on the retreating Zulus as the swordsmen closed in on them was very great . . .
>
> . . . The Natal Light Horse followed up in support, but were unfortunately unable to charge owing to having no arme blanche or revolver. They fired however with effect.
>
> I have no hesitation in saying, that had a regiment of English cavalry been on the field on this occasion scarcely a Zulu would have escaped to the Umisi Hill.

For the most part, the Zulus fell back rapidly in front of Barrow's advance, but

The shock of impact: Major Barrow's Mounted Infantrymen drive into the retreating Zulus at the start of the pursuit at Gingindlovu.

here and there a few turned and made a determined stand. Barrow himself, Courtenay, and a sergeant in the Mounted Infantry, Anderson of the 6th Carabineers, all distinguished themselves in the fight, riding the Zulus down, and slaughtering them with dextrous use of the sabre. Anderson was apparently the man Molyneux was referring to when he described how:

> There was one warrior who would not fly, but set his back to a thorn bush and defied his foes. 'Leave him to me', said a Sergeant of the Greys who was instructor in the Mounted Infantry. A ring was formed and at it they went, sword mounted against assegai and shield dismounted. The soldier was the more skilful, but the Zulu was in better condition. Cutting was tried at first, but it was turned by the shield invariably; at last the point went through shield and man, and the hero found the death he courted.

According to one account, Anderson's last cut took the back of the Zulu's head clean off. Mynors, too, saw something of these duels: 'I saw one cavalry sergeant kill two. The second one he killed lay down, and he could not reach him with his sword. The nigger assegaid his horse. The sergeant jumped off and killed him with his sword.'

Barrow later estimated that perhaps fifty or sixty Zulus were killed by the sword during the pursuit. Not everyone thought this performance impressive; George Hamilton-Browne, who was not convinced that the infantrymen had taken well to their steeds, thought that most of them 'looked as uncomfortable as a lot of moulting devils squatting on icebergs', and felt that most of them were wanting in the basic principles of sword drill, too:

> Now it came to pass as I, riding my own line and being very busy using only the point, chanced to notice a big fine Zulu louping along through the grass, and had half a mind to go for him, but at the same moment he was charged by a MI man, who galloping recklessly past him made a most comprehensive cut at him, which, however, although it failed to annihilate or even wound the Zulu, still drew blood, as it lopped off the ear of his own horse, a proceeding that the animal resented by promptly kicking off its clumsy rider. The Tommy was however true grit, for in a moment he regained his feet, and hanging on to the reins which, good man, he had never let go, he turned on the astonished Zulu and discharged onto the latter's hide shield such a shower of blows that the noise sounded like a patent carpet-beater at work and effectually prevented him from using his assegai. Again, I was on the point of going to our man's assistance and had swung my horse ready to do so, when up from the rear galloped another Tommy who, holding on to the pommel of his saddle with his left hand, flourished his sword and shouted, 'Let me get at the bleeding blighter, Dick,' and then delivered a terrific cut which in this case missing the crow etched the pigeon as it nearly amputated poor Dick's sword hand, who might well have

ejaculated 'Lord save me from my friends.' This, nor any other pious cry he did not use, as his remarks, on receiving the wound, were of a decidedly declamatory nature and were sufficiently comprehensive so as to embrace not only his enemy and his rescuer but also all things animate and inanimate within the district. The blighter had however come off badly for he had been knocked end over end by the rescuer's horse, and before he could regain his feet the rider, whether voluntary or involuntary, was precipitated on top of him and without further delay, discarding his sword, grabbed the Zulu's knobkerrie with which he proceeded to bash its owner over the head, so seeing that they were all right I devoted my attention to my own work.

Perhaps this was the incident of which Lieutenant Knight of 'The Buffs' heard tell the next day:

> One gallant trooper, anxious to distinguish himself, rode valiantly after one of the flying Zulus who tried to cut him down. After hacking ineffectually at him for some time the Zulu thought it was his turn, and going for his persuer with his assegai slashed his fingers off, and picking up his sword, which he naturally dropped, made off in triumph.

If the story were true, the soldier was too shamefaced to admit it, for the official returns for the Mounted Infantry indicate that only gun-shot injuries were reported.

As the Zulus retired before the horsemen, Chelmsford ordered the Native Contingent to follow up and clear the ground behind them. This was the work for which the NNC were best suited, and they rushed enthusiastically over the shelter trench, and fell on the wounded Zulus lying in Barrow's wake. John Dunn's Scouts, led by Dunn's headman Moore, followed them out. The regulars cheered them on; 'The natives assegaid all the wounded they could find', wrote a piper of the 91st. 'It was brutal work; still, it was nothing more than they would have done for us, if it were possible.' It was the moment Guy Dawnay had been waiting for; few of the NNC officers had their horses ready, and most of them, including Gough, had to fetch theirs and saddle up, but Dawnay decided to go out on foot. This was a dangerous decision, given the number of wounded Zulus about, and he certainly found the adventure he craved:

> On reaching the ridge not thirty yards in front of us, we found a lot of Zulus in the hollow; but they only stayed to fire one volley, and then 'balekile'd'; the volley dropping three men. We ran as hard as we could, had to cross a bit of swampy grass, which gave me the worst stitch I ever had, fired at them as they collected on the next hill and pulled up to shoot at us, and then followed on, the Zulus now running for their lives. I tried in vain to stop the assegaing the

wounded, but it was perfectly impossible in the heat of the pursuit, as the Zulus, however badly wounded, always turned round with their assegais when we neared them. We followed a mile or mile and a quarter down to a kloof of bush, palm and long grass, and then I had my last shot at a Zulu I just saw going to fire at us, from a mealie field. The men stood on the near side, and blazed away at nothing into the bush or up into the air; but they would not come down into the bush with assegais as I begged them, and they nearly as possible shot me half a dozen times by accident as I got in front. One of them had previously run up to me with an order, as he said, for the men to retire; but I wasn't going to give the order, and I could see no white officer any where about near us. The natives were wasting their ammunition too ridiculously firing at nothing, and I had to take away three of their rifles, and lick a fourth man who wouldn't cease firing. At last I saw Burnside and later Drummond, and we got them to cease firing and return to the camp.

The NNC officers were not the only ones to have some narrow escapes outside the laager. Generally, the soldiers were strictly prohibited from leaving the ranks to pursue the Zulus, since Chelmsford was worried that the Zulu retreat might be a feint. Commodore Richards had impressed on the bluejackets from HMS *Boadicea* the dreadful things he would be obliged to do to them if they disobeyed the order, but the sight of the Zulus in full flight proved too much for Richards himself. 'Come along', he called to his flag-lieutenant, and the two of them rushed out on foot, 'hacking and slashing', according to Molyneux, 'while the tars, who obeyed orders and never stirred, yelled with delight. "Go it Admiral!" they would shout, "Now you've got 'em! Look out, sir, there's one to the right in the grass!" till everyone was roaring with laughter.'

Barrow recalled that Sugden and the Volunteers had some difficulty in pursuing the Zulus along the front of the square, owing to the boggy ground and the wild fire of the NNC following them up, but that his own detachment chased the Zulus for one and a quarter miles, until they were checked by a spruit. There can be no doubt the pursuit was ruthless; the black troops habitually killed enemy wounded in the heat of the moment, while the white soldiers exulted at the revenge they exacted for Isandlwana. Private Edward Powis of the Mounted Infantry, whose parent unit was the 2/24th, which had been through the Isandlwana campaign, cheerfully admitted in a letter to a lady friend that his comrades had caught three wounded men, 'trying to make for the bush. We cut off their heads, the three of them, and let them lay.'

If the Zulus had begun their retreat 'sullenly', the pressure from the mounted men and NNC turned it into full flight. Two large bodies of reserves had lingered beyond the Nyezane river, and they too fell back as the broken regiments struggled across. Some of the right horn attempted to rally on Misi hill, but a few shells from the *Shah*'s 9-pounder dispersed them.

The ceasefire was sounded at about 7.15am, or perhaps a little later – no more than an hour and a half after the Zulus were first spotted. Barrow's men and the NNC trudged back to the laager, the latter singing victory songs. The soldiers lining the ramparts were keen to go to examine the evidence of the fight, but most were ordered to remain in their places. Lieutenant Hutton of the 60th secured special permission from his colonel to explore the ground occupied by the Zulus, and found that the long grass concealed a slaughterhouse:

> With Colonel Pemberton's permission I got the loan of a horse and rode round the laager and the position lately occupied by the enemy. The Martini-Henry bullets had indeed committed frightful havoc – every man struck, almost without exception, was stone dead – not so much, I conclude, by the deadliness of the wound as by the combined shock to the system of impact, and the short range. In the afternoon I was repaid for my curiosity by being told off to superintend the burial of the dead in our front, a most unpleasant task. We buried sixty-one Zulus who had been killed within 500 yards of our line, more we had not time to bury. The bluejackets on either flank were very jealous about their bag, and some little tact had to be shown when Jack claimed his 'birds'. The marines made no extravagant claims.
>
> The total number of Zulus buried by the troops close to the laager amounted to 520. The total Zulu loss in killed was estimated at 1000, and numberless wounded. Many dead bodies were found by the mounted men, so Barrow told me, on the following day close to the Inyezane, and all along the banks of the stream, half concealed by the long grass, the bodies lay thick. The bodies were presumably those of men who had crawled or been supported by their friends from the field of battle, and then been abandoned when it was found impossible to carry them across the swollen river. All those who were desperately wounded and unable to get away with their retiring friends were doubtless assegaid by our native troops, and the proportion of killed to wounded was very large.

Hutton's estimate of the Zulu dead is a little higher than most other witnesses, and probably reflects the fact that he covered more ground than most. Lieutenant-Colonel Law reported that 248 dead and two wounded Zulus – a proportion which confirms Hutton's comments about the ruthlessness of the pursuit – were found in front of the left and rear faces of the square. Norris-Newman noted that 473 bodies were buried within a 500 yard radius of the British position, but observed that 'the whole valley [was] strewn with dead bodies.' Chelmsford's official dispatch records that 471 bodies were buried, and that '200 have since been found near the scene'. By general consensus, the true total was at least a thousand, perhaps as high as 1200. At least two chiefs and several sons of chiefs were among the slain. Many more were wounded, although it is impossible to compute how many; Dabulamanzi was among them, having been hit in the thigh during the attack of the right horn. If the *izinduna* tried to rally their demoralised warriors, they had no effect; the garrison at Eshowe saw long lines of them in full retreat. They gathered for a while at an *ikhanda* in the Mhlatuze valley, then moved on. Others, presumably those who lived locally and had taken an active part in the siege, retired to neighbouring forests or to the difficult hill-country in the Thukela valley, while most who had been sent from oNdini and who lived elsewhere in the country simply went home.

Bunny Mynors, who had survived his baptism of fire unscathed, found that once the excitement of the battle had passed, the Zulu dead were a sobering spectacle. 'It was a fearful sight,' he wrote, 'so many of these brave chaps lying about covered with blood, and gore'. Backhouse of 'The Buffs' was also moved to sympathy: 'I went over the field where the dead Zulus were lying in the afternoon, it was a ghastly sight, such fine men too, they were as thick as peas in some places.' The British collected up the Zulu firearms, and were keen to find evidence that their attackers had fought at Isandlwana. They found surprisingly little of it; the Nyezane was found choked with firearms where the Zulus had crossed, casting their weapons aside in their hurry to get away. In all, more than a wagon and a half were collected, a total of 435 guns. Of these, however, only five were Martini-Henrys; one was unmarked, three bore the mark of the 24th Regiment, and one of the 32nd. Curiously, there had been one man of the 32nd present at Isandlwana, Lieutenant W. Cochrane, attached to the Native Horse. He had survived; perhaps a Zulu had looted his rifle from the camp. Of the remainder, there was one revolver, presumably another piece of Isandlwana loot, and four 'double fowling pieces'; the rest, to the staggering total of 425, were antiquated flintlock and percussion pieces, 'mostly "Tower" and Prussian.' Molyneux recorded that

... in some of the dead Zulus' pouches and bags was found stationery captured at Isandlwana which they had been using as wadding for their smooth-bores, ration returns, letters, English newspapers, and all sorts of odds and ends. From off one Zulu an English officer's sword was taken and brought to the Chief. Crealock's clerk, who had been an assistant in the orderly-room of the battalion annihilated at Isandhlwana, at once recognised it as having belonged to Lieutenant Porteus of the 24th; it was accordingly preserved and sent to friends.

Norris-Newman and his friend Palmer went out to the place where they had seen the Zulu snipers fall, and found three bodies lying together in a clump. They stripped them of their weapons and regalia, 'most prized and hardy won spoils.' Nevertheless, their colleague F.R. Mackenzie, whom someone claimed to have seen chase a Zulu and beat out his brains with his own knobkerry during the pursuit, was generally thought to have overstretched the bounds of 'fair play'.

A party of the NNC led by Guy Dawnay came across a wounded Zulu, shot through the stomach and side. Dawnay was astonished at his composure: 'He walked along quite jauntily, and replied freely to all our questions.' So much devastation had been wrought by the expenditure of little enough ammunition. Hutton noted that the average number of rounds expended by the 60th was probably 'rather under seven' per man, 'that of the marines next to me was sixteen.' Norris-Newman was of the same opinion – 'Though in some cases the number of shots fired per man in a company ran up to fifteen, yet the general average would not much exceed seven or eight; the 57th Regiment, however, were as low as five rounds per man.' No doubt the 57th's lower rate was due both to the steadiness of their fire, and the fact that the attack on their face of the square was less well sustained than elsewhere. Figures which survive for the 5th Battalion, NNC, record that they expended a total of 10,911 rounds during the battle and in the pursuit. Their losses were officially listed as four killed and twelve wounded, although privately Dawnay felt that the NNC losses must have been significantly higher.

As Chelmsford himself realised: 'Our casualties are small considering the easy mark the laager afforded the assailants, and had it not been for the cover afforded the troops by the broad shelter trench, I should have to report a much heavier loss.' Chelmsford's loss amounted to only nine dead and fifty wounded, several of them, including Northey, dangerously. Nonetheless, it was sufficient for Dawnay to pronounce 'the wounded, and the stretchers of dead and dying, a sickening sight.'

The rest of that day, 2 April, was spent burying the dead, and reducing the size of the laager to a more compact form. Chelmsford intended to leave part of his force at the laager, and march on with a flying column. Accordingly, noted Molyneux, 'the trenches had to be levelled first, then the oxen inspanned, and the left and rear faces of the wagons moved in 30 yards'. The work was apparently interrupted briefly by sudden shouts and screams from the long grass, but it proved not to be a fresh attack, but merely the NNC butchering some wounded Zulus who had escaped their previous attentions.

The British were clearly elated at their victory – 'The garrison at Eshowe now flashed their congratulations,' noted Molyneux, 'to which the Chief replied, and we all felt very pleased with ourselves.' Yet the easy victory seems to have done little to destroy the soldiers' dread of the Zulus. If anything, they were more impressed than ever: 'This was my first experience of these savages,' wrote Molyneux, 'and I was certainly astonished at their pluck'. Norris-Newman thought:

No praise can be too great for the wonderful pluck displayed by these really splendid savages, in making an attack in daylight on a laager entrenched and defended by European troops with modern weapons and war appliances. This fully confirmed the opinion I had never failed to express, that they would fight us again and again, no matter how often they were beaten, as soon as any trusted Chief could assemble some thousands of them.

Such sentiments, which showed little understanding of the true extent of the Zulu defeat, seem to have made for no more relaxed a night in the laager after the battle; Dawnay commented tersely, 'Another false alarm at night, and a 91st man bayonetted.' There seemed to have been little enthusiasm for the morrow's work, when Chelmsford planned, at last, to end the sufferings of Pearson's men, and to relieve Eshowe. Lieutenant Backhouse of 'The Buffs', whose usually copious writings include only the briefest account of the battle, summed up what may have been the feelings of many in the laager that night:

The force hope to reach Ekowe tomorrow evening, possibly they will have another fight either going up or coming down: I would rather go up with them than remain here, for I should not feel too safe if we were attacked by large number of Zulus, the laager being too big for the numbers we shall have to defend it.

CHAPTER 9

'Nothing to be Gained....'

The relief of Eshowe, when it came at last, was greeted by a mixture of elation and anti-climax.

From their position on the heights near the fort, Pearson's men had witnessed Chelmsford's victory at Gingindlovu 'very plainly'. They had seen the Zulus advance and be driven back, and their delighted reaction was in marked contrast to that of the Zulu prisoner taken at Nyezane; when he heard the distant thud of the guns, he had broken down and wept. A curious exchange of messages then took place. Pearson's men, using their improvised signalling equipment, flashed their congratulations to Chelmsford. They then spotted a distant twinkling from the direction of the Thukela, which turned out to be a message relayed from Colonel Wood's column in the north.

At the same time that Chelmsford had been nerving himself for the dash to Eshowe, Wood's column had been involved in some of the heaviest fighting of the war so far. Keen to distract attention from the Eshowe front, Chelmsford had ordered his other commanders to make what demonstrations they could to confuse the Zulus about the British intentions. Most of these demonstrations had been minor border raids, but Wood had taken the opportunity to mount a major assault against a local Zulu stronghold, Hlobane mountain. His attack began at dawn on 28 March, but was badly conceived and poorly executed, and at its height, by pure chance, the main Zulu army sent by the king from oNdini entered the fray. Wood's men were caught against the mountain slopes, and after suffering heavy casualties, fled the field. The disaster at least gave Wood advanced warning of the Zulu presence, however, and when, the next day – just five days before Gingindlovu – the Zulus attacked Wood's base at Khambula, he was waiting for them. For several hours the Zulus repeatedly assaulted the entrenched British position, and when they at last faltered, Wood's irregular cavalrymen chased them from the field.

Since Chelmsford's column had no line of sight to the Thukela from the low, undulating country at Gingindlovu, the general received his first news of this crucial victory from Pearson, who now flashed the message back to him.

Within a few days, therefore, the British position in Zululand had dramatically improved. For the first time since the war began, the Zulus had been uncompromisingly beaten; Khambula and Gingindlovu had scattered both the king's main striking arm, and his local holding forces on the coast. The two

215

defeats, at either end of the country, had cost the Zulus 3000 dead, and marked
a turning point in the campaign.

Not that this was immediately apparent to either Chelmsford or Pearson.
The relief of Eshowe was characterised by the same nervousness which had
marked the operations so far. Chelmsford's force marching out from
Gingindlovu on the morning of 3 April still considered the possibility of a Zulu
attack to be a very real one, while the garrison at Eshowe remained concerned
that the retreating Zulus might yet rally.

Chelmsford had replied to Pearson's messages with his instructions to the
garrison: 'Ekowe will be evacuated after relief and an entrenched post put
somewhere else near here (Inyezane). 3 regt. will leave here for you tomorrow,
you will bring all you can and destroy the rest.' In a dispatch dated 10 April to
the Secretary of State for War, Chelmsford explained his decision to abandon
the post: 'My reasons for ordering Colonel Pearson to evacuate Etshowe was
that I found the last 15 miles of the road of a most difficult nature, far more so
than I had been led to believe by the reports furnished me before Colonel
Pearson crossed the frontier in January.'

Yet, as his message to Pearson indicates, Chelmsford had clearly decided
against the continuing occupation of the site before he marched those last miles
from Gingindlovu to Eshowe. The fact was that with his original invasion plan
in tatters, the fort at Eshowe was redundant. With Chelmsford concentrating
reinforcements in Natal for a new invasion, it made far more sense to withdraw
to the border, and start the campaign again afresh. It served no great strategic
purpose to retain Eshowe, and the effort required to keep it provisioned would
tie down a disproportionate number of troops on convoy duty, and expose them
to constant risk. As Chelmsford went on to say: 'Every advantage from a
military point of view in our present intention of destroying the Mangwane and
Undine kraals can be equally gained by occupying a strong post on the coast
road.'

This was a sound and pragmatic decision, but it was a difficult one for
Pearson's men to accept. 'As you may suppose', wrote one of them:

> We were very sorry to hear that our impregnable fort was to be given up. The
> fort that had taken us so much trouble to construct, and which we had held for
> ten weeks, was to play no further part in future operations, but was to be
> abandoned to the Zulus after all! We could not help feeling greatly disappointed
> about it. . . .

Lieutenant Lloyd of the Artillery found the news 'disagreeable', and thought it
'too annoying . . . that all our work had been done in vain'. Nevertheless, orders
were orders, and, as they waited for Chelmsford's force to arrive, Pearson's men
set about preparing the post for evacuation. At first, it was decided that any

munitions which could not be taken away should be thrown down the well in the centre of the fort, in the hope that 'when covered in, the Zulus would never look for them there'. A number of Tower muskets and 'odds and ends' were duly tossed down, until Pearson's transport officer calculated that if the relieving force brought up 400 oxen, he could take away all of the wagons at the fort, and with them everything of military value. A message was flashed to Chelmsford, who replied that the oxen would be sent.

Chelmsford's force, meanwhile, began its advance at about 7.30 on the morning of the 3rd. They took no wagons with them, just fifty-eight carts, laden with supplies for the Eshowe garrison. Dawnay was surprised to discover at the last minute that the NNC were detailed to remain behind at Gingindlovu, but he prevailed upon Commandant Nettleton to let him go with Chelmsford. With them, too, went Norris-Newman, and the army of special correspondents, eager to be among the first into the fort. Barrow's men fanned out ahead of the column, and Bunny Mynors noted the prevailing opinion that 'the ground was very favourable to an attack by the enemy.' According to Norris-Newman, however, the lighter carts, which required only six oxen to draw them, but which on this occasion had eight, 'were able at times to go ten carts abreast', a line that was 'neither long nor straggling'. The march got off to a high note; a mile and a half from the laager, the column found a large homestead, and the correspondent of the *Cape Argus*, 'with that youthful impetuosity and bravery which is natural to him', gallantly put it to the torch.

The line of march was littered with evidence of past campaigning. Zulu shields, spears, firearms and other accoutrements were strewn along the banks of the Nyezane, where the long grass concealed many dead from the previous day's battle. Beyond the river, no less than eight broad tracks were found in the grass, marking the paths by which the Zulu force had assembled to attack the laager. The column had just crossed the river when it received Pearson's request for the oxen, and a halt was made for two hours – 'much too long', according to Dawnay – while they were sent for. Further on, as the road began to climb up the first of the series of steep ascents which lay between Chelmsford's men and their objective, there lay the Nyezane battlefield. Norris-Newman was delighted to find that 'I recognised [it] at once, having had the whole thing explained to me some time ago by the aid of a plan and sketch through the kindness of an officer who was present.' The specials explored the site of the old fight, and Norris-Newman marvelled that 'with so few men as were actually engaged such a large body of the enemy could have been driven out with so little loss of life,' a comment in marked contrast to the easy confidence of the time, and which reflects the very different attitude that the British had towards the Zulu fighting capability after Isandlwana. The column was pleased to discover that the rough wooden cross which marked the spot where Pearson had buried his dead was overgrown, but untouched. The column wound up

The relief column crosses the Nyezane river on the final stage of the march to Eshowe, 3 April 1879.

through the hills, and John Dunn pointed out 'to the right down below in a gorge' the remains of a campsite, where part of the Zulu force investing Eshowe had evidently stayed for some time. A little further on they came across the wagons deserted for Colonel Ely's convoy on 28 January. Norris-Newman was meticulous in his description of what was a rather eerie spectacle:

> I came up to the first wagon ... It bore the mark W.D., with the broad arrow, and had written upon it 'Commissariat reserve'. It was very much smashed up, and its contents lay scattered around in a state of putrefaction, horrible to smell. Further on there was another, No. 74, and then quickly following one another I came upon five others, Nos. 4, 48, 15, 18 and 49. Many of these were not injured at all, while some merely had a wheel or disselboom off. Furthest of all and nearest to Eshowe, one wagon had been turned right over and rolled down a precipice; we could see its remains all over the place.

None of the supplies were serviceable, and no attempt was made to gather them up. The march went on throughout the day, and by late afternoon the forced pace was beginning to take its toll on the men. According to Dawnay:

> The men had had no food all day, the constant stops and the fording steams took it out of them, and they were falling out right and left. I took pity on one Naval Brigade man who was dead beat, and lent him my horse – thundering good animal too – and he rode it into a sore hack in no time, as in the dark I couldn't find him when I wanted to tell him to tighten the girths as he went on.

Baskerville Mynors commented simply that it was 'the longest and hardest march I ever remember.' Molyneux – who denied that any men had actually fallen out during the march – nonetheless acknowledged that they had been on their feet for sixteen hours, and had climbed 1400 feet in fifteen miles.

As the column drew near the fort, it came to the point where the road built by Pearson's Engineers intersected the old road. By now, the specials were excited at the prospect of at last meeting someone from the garrison, and several of them suddenly spurred on ahead. Norris-Newman, however, stole a march on them:

> ... I went on ahead with my boy following, and kept my eyes open for [the new road]. Two other 'specials' had already left us, and I saw them racing each other along the road a mile in front. They, however, did not think of the short cut, and only saw their mistake when they saw Col. Pearson at the head of 500 men coming down it from Etshowe. In the hopes of meeting him first, each of these two tried to cut across the country, and the last seen of them by me was that one had got stuck in a bog and the other could not get his horse, already pumped, over a nasty spruit. I profited by their example, turned up the short-cut, and had

the pleasure of being the first man to shake the hand of Colonel Pearson at the Relief of Eshowe.

Pearson had, indeed, set out from Eshowe with about 500 white troops, fifty black auxiliaries, the Mounted Infantry and one gun, intending – as Chelmsford had suggested on 31 March – to support the relief column if it were attacked. Even at this late stage, those left behind at Eshowe were nervous that the Zulus might take advantage of the absence of half the fighting force, and attack the fort; as one of the garrison wryly put it, however, they 'were not equal to the occasion, and contented themselves with only looking at us.' Chelmsford himself commented that the move 'would have been of great assistance had the enemy opposed our advance, but none were to be seen that day'. Chelmsford himself, with his staff, was ahead of the relief column when Pearson rode up. It was, perhaps, a very Victorian meeting, a little breathless, but without any undue expression of excitement; according to the *Natal Mercury*:

> All at once, Lord Chelmsford called out, 'Here's Pearson,' as that gallant officer on a grey horse, and looking very jolly, as well he might, dashed round the corner of a hill four and a half miles from camp, and hastened up to the General. 'How are you?' said his Lordship, as he grasped the hand of the Colonel....

With no enemy in sight, Chelmsford asked Pearson to send to his men, who had not yet come up, and order them to the fort. They were to be denied the pleasure of meeting the relief column for a few hours yet. Pearson and his Staff rode with Chelmsford, talking over the events of the previous three months.

Meanwhile, Norris-Newman had won his race with his rivals, and had reached the fort. Although, as Lieutenant Lloyd observed, the garrison were delighted to meet 'the first strange face we had seen for 72 days', Norris-Newman was not, apparently, quite who they had expected, and the meeting had a touch of the absurd about it. Said one who was there:

> A solitary horseman is seen towards 5pm galloping up the new road to the fort: he had an officer's coat on, and we could see a sword dangling from his side. Who is he? A special messenger from Lord Chelmsford, with important despatches? Our doubts were soon dissolved by the arrival of the horseman, who, dismounting, proved to be Mr N.N. of the *Standard*. 'First in Ekowe!' he exclaimed, with a self-satisfied air; 'proud to shake hands with an Ekowian', he continued, shaking hands with those round. We were all very much gratified at his condescension, and asked the 'news'. A second horseman appeared approaching the fort, his horse apparently much blown. 'Who is he?' we asked. 'That is the gentleman of the *Argus* newspaper.' They had had a race to see who should be first in Ekowe, the *Standard* winning by five minutes.

According to Lieutenant Main, one private greeted Norris-Newman's effusiveness with the dour quip, 'You're three months late.'

It was an hour later before the first troops arrived in the fort. They were the mounted men led by Barrow, and this meeting was a good deal more poignant:

> [They] were, as you may suppose, warmly welcomed by us. It was nearly ten weeks since they had left the fort; none of us thought then we should have been so long separated. After much hand-shakings, and congratulations on our being relieved, Major Barrow passed on to the camping ground appointed for Lord Chelmsford's column.

There followed a dreary wait for the rest of the column to come up. A few of the garrison gave up and went to bed, but most were too excited to sleep. It was not until nearly midnight that the skirl of the pipes cut through the still African night, and 'The Campbells Are Coming' – 'to most of us the sweetest music we ever heard,' according to Norbury – announced the arrival of the infantry, led by the 91st Highlanders. The garrison lined the ramparts of the fort, and 'greeted them with ringing cheers which were well responded to by the "relievers"'. 'The scene "beggars description"', wrote Lieutenant Main, 'some of our men were so weak and delirious with joy that they actually cried. One of the relieving force, mistaking me, I suppose, for a pal in the dusk, said, "However did you find this bally place?"'.

Generally, the relieving force was surprised at how well the garrison had withstood their ordeal. 'Many in our relief expected to see a lot of skeletons in the fort', commented Gunner Carroll, 'but thank God we were not so bad off as all that.' Molyneux observed more precisely that 'the universal cry was want of tobacco, tea-leaves and coffee-grounds being carefully preserved, dried and smoked; otherwise they were not in actual want, but coast fever and typhoid had claimed many victims, while rough fare, watchfulness, and anxiety had set their marks on all.' Indeed, some of the garrison prided themselves on their endurance, and at least one was indignant that one of the 'specials' 'described us as having passed weeks ago into a condition somewhat resembling that of the prisoner of Chillon!' Nevertheless, their true state was perhaps suggested by two final deaths at Eshowe; Able Seaman Alf Smith of HMS *Active* died of typhoid on 2 April, the day of Gingindlovu, and Private J. Monk of 'The Buffs' died of enteric on the 4th – the very day Pearson's men began their evacuation. Main later admitted that he lost more than two stone in weight during the siege. Perhaps the last word should go to Corporal F.W. License, one of Wynne's hard working sappers, who commented succinctly that 'we had fearful hard times of it at Eshowe.'

Initially, however, it was the relieving column who were in some need of comfort, as Lieutenant Lloyd explained:

The relief column had marched up on the shortest possible rations. They therefore informed us that they had suffered much from the pangs of hunger, and felt they undoubtedly had come to the worst place for assuaging their appetites. However, as luck would have it, much to their surprise, we managed to assist them, for we had carefully put aside three days full provisions, in case we should be forced at any time to cut our way back to British territory. These rations were produced, and our gallant 'relievers' enjoyed a hearty meal after their exertions of the past five days.

But it was remarked that most of the newspaper correspondents reported that the garrison of Ekowe had suffered but little from the scarcity of food, that they found the place well stocked with provisions, one of them went so far as to say that he never enjoyed a better meal in his life than that supplied by the starved-out heroes of Ekowe. The real truth being that they were gloating over these three days provisions which we had treasured for so many days, and had longed to 'be at' on so many occasions.

The object of this last barb was probably Norris-Newman, who noted with some satisfaction that the Naval Brigade 'gave me a better dinner than I had tasted since I left Fort Tenedos ... first came some excellent beef broth with pumpkins in, then a piece of roast beef (not very juicy or fat) with pumpkin fritters and fried cakes of new mealies crushed up by hand. We also each had a small share of good wheaten bread, and the meal was brought to a close with a cup of tea, and what do you think? a pumpkin tart, pastry and all! This, I thought was a feed worthy of a king, after going days with only tinned beef and biscuits.' Captain Pelly Clarke noted wryly that the 'specials' seemed greatly preoccupied with the subject of dinner, and that 'the next morning the gentleman of the *Argus* was in great trouble about his breakfast.'

It is, perhaps, Gunner Carroll, who has left the most evocative account of the relaxed atmosphere that prevailed that first night when Eshowe was relieved:

Everything and everybody was unable to rest during this happy night. Little notice was taken of the Bugles to put lights out or anything else. Puffs of tobacco smoke rose like the smoke from a furnace till everyone had satisfied their craving to the full. Tobacco which a few days (before) was eagerly bought at a guinea an ounce, had now fallen down to zero as we could now get plenty from those who came up today. The part of the Naval Brigade who had come up, brought our letters with them. A wagon load nearly and we were terribly busy for a few hours sorting them out by the light of a lantern. Some of the men walking off with at least two dozen and spent the greater part of the night reading them by the flickering light of a lantern.

At last, however, the soft night passed, and the men of the relieving column succumbed to exhaustion. Norris-Newman gratefully accepted the offer of a share of Father Walsh's wagon, 'and I was soon in the arms of Morpheus'. Guy Dawnay, who had arrived ahead of his prospective hosts, the 91st, had gone to the stream to fetch water, and stumbled in up to his waist. With no change of clothes, it promised to be a chilly night, and he could not locate his hosts in the dark. Instead, he transferred his loyalties once more and befriended Major Barrow – 'It ended by my staying with him' – and, using his saddle for a pillow, curled up with his ground sheet serving as both bed and blanket. The next morning he was up at 4.30, and enjoyed 'a jolly bathe' in the garrison's pool.

Military routine returned at 5am with the sounding of reveille. Chelmsford had confirmed his orders for Pearson to abandon the post, and wanted him to leave that day. The general, however, was determined to make one last gesture before he left. It was widely rumoured that Prince Dabulamanzi had retired to his eZulwini homestead on eNtumeni hill after Gingindlovu. Since Dabulamanzi had remained largely unscathed, despite Pearson's raid on eSiqwakeni on 1 March, the general 'determined' as Molyneux put it, 'to show the King's brother that he too had a long arm to strike with.' Accordingly, about 11am on the morning of the 4th, Barrow's mounted men were sent out at a canter to attack the homestead. Dawnay noted that the expedition 'assum[ed] larger proportions, as the General and staff, mounted volunteers, native pioneers, and Dunn's men under Moore came also.' According to Molyneux, however, a breach of etiquette almost robbed the sortie of one of its most experienced elements:

> . . . as I was on the point of starting I came across Dunn sitting on the ground in the middle of an *umkumbi* (circle) of his men. Apologising for the interruption, I told him that the General had just started. 'He did not ask me and my men to come', was the answer, and it was evident that the chief and his men were highly indignant. I told him that a notice had been sent round the camp, and that orders had been given to show it to him; that he knew of it was obvious, from the fact of his being offended. 'Of course the General wants you to come with him,' I said. 'I'll gallop on and get the invitation from him direct if you won't believe me.' He relented, was on his horse (with his 'after-rider' close behind him) in a moment, and away we went while the men stood up, raised their right hands to the sky, groaned Inkos [Chief], and raced after us. It is necessary to be most particular in your behaviour to a Zulu Chief; and Dunn, while amongst his men, could not afford to waive any portion of his dignity. He had by this time, moreover, assimilated many of his people's habits and modes of feeling; and I fancy they would all have thought it more correct if the General had sat upon his hams every morning with an *umkumbi* of all the heads of departments round him, hearing their reports, and deciding on the day's operations.

Despite the speed of the advance – 'very hard on us one-horse men', according to Dawnay – the expedition failed to catch the Zulus by surprise. Most had already climbed up to the top of a cliff overlooking eZulwini, about 1300 yards away. A few stragglers were still climbing up, and shouted a war-cry in defiance. Barrow's men chased after them, shooting two and capturing a third. Pelly Clarke saw him later, led into the fort by a Volunteer with a rope round his neck, and thought he 'presented a comical appearance'. They then set fire to the homestead. As the flames caught hold, Molyneux noted the splutter of gunfire from within the huts, and concluded 'there must have been many loaded guns left in them.' The explosions became so frequent that the staff were obliged to move further off, and as they bunched together, they presented a tempting target to the Zulus on the cliff-top. The shooting was remarkably professional, as Dawnay noted:

> Then came a puff of smoke, and a bullet whished over our heads, then came others, and lower and lower till we heard them hit the ground among us, and then we were ordered to separate and not give such a big bull's eye to them. As I led my horse away by his bridle, a bullet came right between my hand and my horse's head and went into the ground about fifteen feet further on. . . .

Dunn, with his hunter's eyesight, recognised that the marksman was Prince Dabulamanzi himself. Dunn had taught the prince to shoot in the happy days before the war, and he now took up his rifle to duel with his old friend. Watching through a naval telescope, the staff pronounced Dunn the winner; several times they saw the Zulus duck as Dunn's bullets whistled overhead. But the range was too long: 'As there was nothing to be gained by this sport', commented Molyneux, 'we destroyed their mealie fields and made our way back to Eshowe.' Their hunting spirits aroused, the British party were delighted when a duiker suddenly broke cover only 80 yards in front of them on the way back; Dunn took a shot at it, but narrowly missed, whilst Dawnay grumbled that Chelmsford strayed in front of his line of fire and prevented him shooting. That night, back at Eshowe, Dawnay and Dunn shared a nip of brandy and talked over their past adventures; that day they had seen the last sport of the Eshowe campaign.

Pearson's men had already left the fort. After Chelmsford's foray had departed, the original garrison spent a busy morning, dragging serviceable wagons out of the traverses, loading them with whatever materials were worth salvaging, and breaking up anything which the Zulus might remotely have found useful. It was mid-afternoon before they were ready to move off, and Norris-Newman was not alone in finding the moment a poignant one:

> Some of the pipers of the 91st came down to play us off, and after going a little way returned to camp amid the cheers of the men of Pearson's column. The band

of the Buffs then struck up and off we went. The sick had all been comfortably placed in the ambulances and wagons specially fitted for them, and they, with other wagons belonging to Col. Pearson, brought the number up to 116 – nearly as many as our relief column had. The order of march was as follows – Royal Engineers under Captain Courtney; RA, with guns under Lloyd; 3rd Buffs under Col. Parnell, and their wagons, followed by the 99th, under Col. Welman, and the Naval Brigade with their guns brought up the rear.

The length of the wagon-train was, indeed, a cause of some concern to Lord Chelmsford. Pearson's column wound down through the hills, following the old road, to a new campsite at the foot of the heights. The head of the column arrived at the appointed spot at about 5pm, when the tail was still leaving the fort; the last stragglers did not arrive until 9 o'clock that night. Norris-Newman, at least, was aware that the column was hardly in a fit condition to defend itself – 'We were not a strong column for such a convoy, even if the men had been all well, and the oxen fit and strong' –and it was stretched impossibly thin along the line of march. The fear of a Zulu attack was still very real, and at least one of Chelmsford's staff commented that Pearson seemed to have learned nothing from his previous experiences in Zululand. Chelmsford apparently administered a mild rebuke, although the general feeling in Pearson's column was that the proximity of Chelmsford's force ensured the column safe passage.

The next morning, 5 April, march was resumed at 7am. For many among the garrison, the implications of their freedom was only just sinking in. 'The sense of being free once again was delightful;' wrote Courtney, 'and our men, notwithstanding their long confinement, marched splendidly.' 'My mind seems so full of different things,' commented Corporal License, 'and I feel so strange after being shut up in that fort for so long.' The column passed its old battlefield at Nyezane, and the men were delighted to see that the Zulus had not interfered with the rough wooden cross which marked the resting place of the British dead. Captain Gelston of 'The Buffs' took down the old cross and replaced it with the one he had made at Eshowe. Near the amaTigulu they came across the site of the Zulu bivouac from the night before Gingindlovu, and marvelled at the evidence of the Zulu concentration. Surgeon Norbury described it:

Beneath every bush there had been a fire, and round them a circle of Zulus had slept, while the long grass was everywhere trampled down, proving that a considerable force had been present. One tree, which had drooping branches, had been covered over with long grass, so as to form a kind of hut, and this had probably been occupied by the principal *indunas*. This *impi* had left a large number of things behind, or they might have been thrown away by the fugitives after the battle – assegai sheaths, mats, armlets, and pieces of rug, and there was also the corpse of a Zulu, with a severe bullet wound in the abdomen. This man had probably been wounded at Gingdindlovu, and had reached thus far before he fell.

Pelly Clarke thought that 'the hills above it were literally seamed with the tracks they had made in coming to the place of assembly,' and wondered idly if the dead man would have 'gone so far with ... Snider-Enfield wounds?' Lieutenant Main recorded that at some point on the march they also came across proof of the danger their messengers had run: 'We found the dead body of one of our runners, who still had a packet of letters on his back (the Zulus would not touch a corpse) which Captain Williams had tied on to him just before Williams was taken into hospital.'

Chelmsford's column had marched off from Eshowe after Pearson that morning without fuss, and at last the post was deserted. When the column was a safe distance away, the first of the watching Zulus came down and rummaged through the ruins. They set fire to the buildings, causing some among the garrison – who saw the smoke rising in the distance from down on the plain – to wish they had booby-trapped the debris.

As the head of Chelmsford's column reached the foot of the hills, it ran into the rear of Pearson's, which had not yet pulled away. Progress was delayed because one of Pearson's wagons had overturned, and, despite the efforts of one of Pearson's transport officers, Lieutenant Thirkill, was blocking the road. This caused some irritation among Chelmsford's command, and the general decided to take his men off across a new track, farther to the left. To avoid further congestion at Gingindlovu, Chelmsford ordered Pearson's men not to march to the laager, as had originally been intended, but to head straight for the Thukela. This order was greeted with some dissatisfaction amongst the old garrison, who had first been disappointed to find that their colleagues in 'The Buffs' and 99th companies had not been part of the flying column, and who realised now that they would not be reunited with them at Gingindlovu either. Furthermore, some of the men were keen to take part in fresh operations, and were convinced that a move to the Thukela would result in them languishing until the sick had recovered. A few officers, Pelly Clarke among them, rode over to the laager at Gingindlovu, but were appalled at the stench of death which still hung over the laager, from Zulu dead who still lay hidden in the long grass. They were relieved to get back to their own campsite.

Under Dunn's guidance, Chelmsford's column struck eastwards across the veld. The country must have been full of wounded Zulus, for along the way Dawnay discovered one who had been shot through the foot and heel at Gingindlovu, 'and had crawled miles on his hands and knees, till the latter were swollen in the most horrible way and all the flesh worn off.' Dawnay saw to it that he was taken on board a wagon for treatment. Although the track itself was quite serviceable, it was desperately hot and humid, and the exertions of the previous few days were catching up with the relief column. According to Molyneux:

> This was a most trying day from the heat, the long grass, and scarcity of water. The men, too, now the excitement was over, were falling out every moment. There was no shamming; they did their best; but as one soldier said to me, 'Now those chaps are relieved you seem to begin to feel yourself, and I'm just as if I had no heart left at all and no legs.'

As the afternoon wore on, it became apparent that the column would not reach Gingindlovu that night, and Crealock and Dunn rode ahead to select a campsite. They found a suitable one near the deserted mission-station of eMvutsheni, overlooking the Nyezane river. The column was all in by 6.30 that night, and threw up a rectangular entrenchment around the camp. Despite this, however, the men's nerves seemed frayed by the day's exertions, and that night was to see a tragic postscript to the Eshowe saga.

Infantry picquets, four strong, had been placed 300–400 yards out in front of each face of the camp, with Dunn's scouts in clumps beyond them. At about 3.30 on the morning of the 6th, a picquet of the 91st apparently saw something moving in the gloom beyond him which he took to be Zulus. He issued a challenge, and when no reply was forthcoming, fired a shot, at which point all hell broke loose. A picquet of the 60th promptly fled to the rear, abandoning their officers, and even their helmets, in their hurry. Dunn's scouts, hearing the troops falling back behind them, naturally also retired to the laager. Dunn's scouts were hardly distinguishable from the Zulus in the daylight, and some of them had by this stage even lost the distinctive red rag they wore around their heads. The result was a nightmarish confusion, as Molyneux described:

> The men in the trench opposite them fixed their bayonets and, unable to distinguish friends from foes in the dark, met them with the point, the result being that five soldiers were wounded, and of Dunn's men two were killed and eight wounded. At the sound of the shot we were up; at the sound of the rush we were outside the tent and on our way to the trench. It was heartrending to hear the wild appeals of those outside to those within to keep cool. The poor scouts were the worst off, their only distinguishing mark from the enemy being the red cloth around their heads. They had been drilled by Dunn to answer 'Friend'; the best they could manage was 'Flend', and shrieks of 'Flend' were heard above all the din, yet they were stabbed unmercifully. Dunn was mad. 'They are killing my people! Are the men fools? Can't they hear them calling out? Oh my children!' he cried as he ran towards the trench; and then the soldiers recovered their wits, and we did what we could for the wretched victims of funk.

Chelmsford was furious. 'It was bright moonlight,' he wrote in his report, 'and I can offer no excuse or explanation of what occurred, beyond the youth of the men of the 60th, for it was perfectly well known to officers and men that these scouts were in front.' The next afternoon, when the column had reached the laager at Gingindlovu, a general courtmartial was convened, and a sergeant of the 60th who had been with the picquets was sentenced to be reduced to the ranks, and to five years' penal servitude. Curiously, the proceedings were subsequently quashed. Molyneux mused:

> It was supposed afterwards, when a more serious runaway was suffered to go unpunished, that this man could not in justice be brought to book. Others said that it had been forgotten to send a warrant to South Africa empowering the Officer commanding the Forces to assemble general and district courts martial. Few know the truth to this day.

The latter reason is clearly improbable, given the number of courts martial which did take place throughout the Zulu War. Perhaps the second was correct; the 'more serious runaway' was Lieutenant Jahleel Carey, 98th Regiment, who left the exiled Prince Imperial of France to his fate when their patrol was attacked by Zulus on 1 June. Carey's case became a *cause célèbre* after the Queen failed to approve a guilty verdict. In the light of these events, the military establishment was probably happy to draw a veil over the whole sorry story of the many panics that had characterised the war.

Chelmsford's column reached Gingindlovu about 11.30 on the morning of the 6th, and camped on fresh ground about a mile beyond. The reunion had its unpleasant aspects; the garrison had turned up Zulu dead who had been missed by the burial parties every day. By now, even the most stubbornly concealed corpse could be detected by the awful smell. Bodies had been found in the stream from which the garrison had drawn its drinking water; Dawnay rode over to the old camp taking fresh lemons, which he had foraged when crossing the Nyezane, to his friend Hugh Gough, and in the process stumbled across three unburied bodies in such an unpleasant state that he was almost sick. Gough he found worse than he had left him; the effort of joining the battle had exhausted him, and dysentery had taken hold again. Indeed, Dawnay thought most of the garrison looked 'seedy' – 'I am not surprised, as the stench is awful; a few hours of it gives one a headache'. A number of live Zulus, some bearing terrible wounds, had also been found and brought in, and Norris-Newman noted that there were as many as seventeen prisoners in the camp. Not all of the wounded had been treated so sympathetically, however; Jack Royston had witnessed an incident which would affect him for the rest of his life. On the day after the battle, he had been searching the field when he found two Zulus lying wounded in a donga, both shot in the chest. They were able to walk, however, and Royston led them towards the camp. Before he reached it he encountered a colonial officer who cursed him roundly for his compassion, promptly produced a revolver, and shot both Zulus dead. 'I was at an age when such things leave impressions,' recalled Royston, 'it took me a long time to get over it. The man was much older than I, and I was powerless to prevent his action though I knew it was wrong.'

There was bad news for the 60th, too. On the day that they arrived at the laager, Francis Northey died. Four days of constant medical attention were not enough to repair the damage caused by the haemorrhage of the 2nd. He was buried alongside the other British dead, outside the laager rampart. He had been a popular officer, and the 60th felt his death keenly.

Clearly, it was impossible to maintain any sort of permanent presence on the battlefield, and Chelmsford gave orders to move to a new campsite a few miles away. On the morning of the 7th the old laager at Gingindlovu was finally broken up and abandoned. Chelmsford himself marched for the Thukela with 'The Buffs' and 99th, leaving the 57th, 60th, 91st and NNC to guard the new post. According to Mynors:

> In the afternoon we moved up a small hill into a first-rate position, but water bad, and that a mile off, and even that not likely to last long. We have also on the next hill another laager for the natives and bullocks. It is, of course, a necessity to keep them out of the camp because they make the place smell so.

Most in Chelmsford's force were happy to be going, and Lieutenant Backhouse was probably typical when he longed for the end of the campaign, to meet his friends in his regiment once more, to 'be rid' of the despised 99th, and to see his wife again.

There was another blow to come for Dunn. As he rode back with Chelmsford and his Staff, they passed the site of Dunn's old homesteads, at eMoyeni and Mangethe. The Zulus had vented their frustration at his desertion on the buildings, and had looted and destroyed them. Molyneux described Dunn's reaction:

> Dunn's house (or rather houses) was a sorry sight. Everything had been looted or pitched outside: some things had been burned; but what vexed him most was the destruction of all his journals. He took it very stoically, merely observing, 'I have not done with the Zulus yet.'

Pearson's men reached the border at about 11am on 7 April, 'receiving', according to Pelly Clarke, 'hearty congratulations on our deliverance from "exile vile", from the garrison there'. Chelmsford's column rode ahead of his men and arrived that same day, and the officers of 'The Buffs' and 99th were later delighted to have the chance to seek out their old comrades and catch up on the news. 'So ended', in Norris-Newman's words, 'the march to Etshowe and the relief of Colonel Pearson's Column'. Chelmsford was well pleased with the results, and was fulsome in his praise of Pearson 'for so tenaciously holding on to Ekowe after the bad news of the Isandlwana affair had reached him. The occupation of that post, and of that one held by Colonel Evelyn Wood during a time of considerable anxiety had no doubt a very powerful moral effect throughout South Africa, and diminished the effect of what would otherwise have been considered as a complete collapse of our invasion of Zululand.' Yet, as Chelmsford now rode down to Pietermaritzburg to marshal the reinforcements arriving daily at Durban, and to make his plans for a fresh invasion, he must have known that the end of the Relief Expedition marked the real end of his first invasion; three months after the war had started, the British held no more than two fortified posts inside Zululand, close to the border. The Zulus had repulsed them entirely; it was their tragedy that in doing so they had suffered such body-blows as would cause their kingdom to wither.

The veterans of Nyezane and Gingindlovu settled into the mundane duties of garrison life, awaiting the new offensive. Some of the players went on their way to fresh adventures; Lieutenant Main was sent down to Durban to meet Engineer reinforcements arriving from home, while Guy Dawnay rode down to Pietermaritzburg in search of a fresh appointment. Charles Shervinton sought out his brother Tom, who had been ailing at Fort Pearson; he found him seriously ill. Tom Shervington was to die in February 1880, his health broken by the rigours of campaigning. Twenty-eight British dead had been left at Eshowe, two of them victims of wounds sustained at Nyezane, one killed on vedette duty, and twenty-five struck down by disease. Twelve lay beneath a spreading mimosa tree on the battlefield of Nyezane, and at least fourteen more at Gingindlovu. Yet the grim toll was not yet over; Pearson had brought as many as 200 sick down with him, who were carefully ferried across the Thukela to be treated in the hospital at Fort Pearson. They were not all to recover. Captain Warren Wynne, the Engineer officer whose ingenuity had been largely responsible for the impregnability of the defences at Eshowe, died on 19 April, the day of his thirty-sixth birthday. He was buried on the hillside near Fort Pearson. Pearson, who was suffering from typhoid himself, wrote in sympathy to his wife, and Courtney, 'the only officer present, the others being up country,' read the burial service. Corporal Garner of Wynne's company noted that Courtney 'was so deeply cut up he could hardly read the burial service.' Some of the more serious cases were sent back to Stanger, where a military hospital had been established at Herwen. Hugh Gough and Lieutenant John Thirkill were among them, but it was too late for both of them; Gough died on 19 April, the same day as Wynne, from an abscess of the liver. Guy Dawnay had been expecting him to recover, and to join him at Durban: 'I never was more shocked than on hearing it,' he wrote. Commandant Nettleton expressed the view that the NNC had lost 'a right good fellow and a pleasant companion ... a splendid soldier.' Thirkill died three days later, despite the devoted attentions of his batman.

Meanwhile, by a cruel twist of fate, disease also struck down more than one of those who had survived Gingindlovu. Life at the new camp there was dull, and hardly more healthy than at the old laager. There was little for the garrison to do beyond the occasional foray to burn a deserted homestead, and they were not allowed to go more than a few hundred yards from the camp except in large numbers. The arrival of convoys from the Thukela provided the only break in the monotony. Baskerville Mynors dreamed of hunting – 'Two rhinoceroses have been seen near here feeding, I wish I could get a shot at them, but can't get leave to go out,' – while the men succumbed to ennui, and the new camp became as insanitary as the old. The men had been without tents since the relief expedition had first crossed the Thukela on 29 March. Norris-Newman rode up to visit the camp, and was appalled at what he saw:

> ... I found on my arrival there ninety-three serious cases on the sick list, nearly all being cases of dysentery, colic, and diarrhoea. As for the officers, a more woe-begone lot it has never been my fortune to see. Thanks to the paternal care of Major Bruce, of the 91st, and some of the officers left behind on the Tugela, the officers of this admirable regiment presented a better appearance than did those of either the 57th or the Naval Brigade. Private supplies of food had been forwarded to them, and they had not been obliged for weeks to live on that utter abomination in the way of food, 'Chicago tinned beef'. They therefore looked better, though of course far from well. When, however, I came to the 60th Rifles, and saw them, so cadaverous were their looks, so utterly changed and wasted down from what I had left them but ten short days before, I felt quite dazed when they surrounded me. The colonel was sick and unable to move; the senior captain was doubled up, and a whole row of fine young fellows were lying for shelter from the burning sun under wagons, eking out their shade with an old tarpaulin – shaking with low fever, and exhausted by continuous dysentery – nine hundred men in the ranks, and only three officers fit to take charge of them, though others were manfully struggling against their sickness and holding the field.

Among the 'young fellows' lying in the shade was Second Lieutenant Arthur Clynton Baskerville Mynors. He had been 'taken awfully seedy in the night [of 11 April] with diarrhoea, and to-day, Easter Sunday [13th], I was obliged to go on the sick list, as my complaint turned more to dysentery.' On Monday he wrote home chirpily that 'my dysentery still sticks to me with bad pain in my inside, but I feel otherwise well in myself,' but the next day he complained of

feeling much weaker. At the end of the week, he was sent in a wagon down to
Fort Pearson, where a family friend, Colonel Hopton of the 88th, was in
command. Wrote Hopton:

> This morning early, I went to see him, having first asked the doctor in charge
> about him. He at once told me he feared the worst. When I saw him I did not
> think he could recover. His servant was with him, who was very attentive to him.
> We gave him what medical comforts could be got, such as beef tea and
> champagne. I stayed with him all the morning, until 2pm, and at his request, I
> read and prayed by his stretcher side, he was then quite sensible, and followed all
> I said, and repeated some of the prayers after me. All this time he was very weak,
> and hardly able to raise himself up, although his servant told me that yesterday
> he was able to stand and walk. The disease for some days seems to have taken
> hold of him. He passed nothing but pure blood, and when I first saw him, was
> reduced almost to a skeleton. About 2pm, having changed his shirt and made
> him as comfortable as I could I left him, telling him I would come back soon.
> Sometimes afterwards, I got a message from him, asking me to go back, which I
> did, about 5.30pm. I found Captain Cardew, one of the staff officers, with him.
> He had just read the 14th chapter of St John to him, which he listened to, and
> asked Cardew to read slowly, so that he might follow. A doctor was also with
> him. They told me that the end was approaching. We all stayed with him till
> about 7pm, when he gave a little sigh, and passed away ...

Lieutenant Edward Hutton, who considered Mynors 'the most promising
boy Eton has sent to our ranks for many a day', wrote in sympathy to Mynors'
father, adding a fresh touch to the typically poignant Victorian death-bed
scene. As Mynors' servant tried to rearrange his pillows, Mynors said 'Hush!
Don't touch me, I am going to heaven.' Bunny Mynors was buried the next day
close to Fort Pearson. The men of the 60th made a wooden headboard in the
shape of a Maltese Cross – the regimental badge – and Adjutant Wilkinson
wrote a tribute to him in the Eton College *Chronicle*.

And what had the campaign meant to the Zulus? Well over 2000 had died
in the battles of Nyezane and Gingindlovu, and in the skirmishes around
Eshowe. Countless more had suffered the horrific injuries inflicted by the heavy-
calibre Martini-Henry bullets; how many of them died over the weeks and
months following the battles will never be known. Their suffering was no less
intense than that of Northey, Wynne, Gough, Thirkill, or Mynors, and the
effect on their families no less devastating, for all that it has gone unrecorded.

The Anglo-Zulu War rolled on. By the end of May, Chelmsford had sufficient reinforcements to contemplate renewing his invasion. He abandoned his
old plan of invading in three separate columns, and opted instead to move with
two much larger forces. One, the 2nd Division, crossed into Zululand north of

Rorke's Drift, and, supported by Wood's old column, thrust straight at oNdini. The other, the 1st Division, was to advance up the coast, destroying surviving *amakhanda*, and opening a landing point on the beach. The arrival of no less than four major-generals, who had come out from the UK with the reinforcements, meant that some of Chelmsford's officers were no longer sufficiently senior to hold independent commands. Pearson was among them; the command of the 1st Division went to a newcomer, Major-General H.H. Crealock – John Crealock's elder brother – while Pearson was made a brigade commander under him. The Bulldog of Eshowe's constitution had not yet recovered from its ordeal, however, and in June Pearson was invalided home. The advance of the 1st Division was not, in any case, an exciting one; hampered by an enormous, yet still inadequate, baggage train, it crawled painfully up the coast, burning a few Zulu homesteads, and establishing a beach-head at Port Durnford. The Zulus, mustering inland to make one last stand before oNdini, made no attempt to oppose it. Indeed, with the tide of war flowing inexorably against them, a number of important Zulu chiefs who lived along the line of march surrendered to the 1st Division. Among them were the commanders of Nyezane and Gingindlovu; Mbilwane kaMahlanganiso, the *induna* of the kwaGingindlovu *ikhanda*, who had been present at both battles, was amongst the first to 'come in' on 4 July. The next day several important chiefs surrendered, including Somopho kaZikhala and Phalane kaMdinwa. Prince Dabulamanzi himself, who had achieved considerable notoriety among his enemies, held out a little longer; he surrendered on 12 July. By that time the outcome of the war had been decided.

The 2nd Division reached oNdini at the beginning of July, and the last great battle of the war was fought on the 4th, on the grassy Mahlabathini plain, overlooked by the king's royal residence. Chelmsford had learned something from Gingindlovu, though he was determined to face his final battle in the open, with no shelter trenches or protective laager. He formed his men into a huge square, and the Zulus attacked him on all sides. They were no more successful at penetrating the deadly zone of concentrated artillery, Gatling and rifle fire than they had been three months earlier, and after half an hour they wavered. Now Chelmsford had to hand not merely Barrow's scratch mounted force, but the 17th Lancers, the pride of the British light cavalry. The 17th chased the Zulus from the field. Several inside the square had been through the Eshowe campaign – Courtney and Main were left by chance in Chelmsford's camp on the White Mfolozi, but watched the battle in the distance – and they now witnessed the British army's final revenge for the humiliations it had suffered at the hands of these naked African warriors armed only with shields, spears and obsolete firearms.

Chelmsford withdrew from Zululand and resigned his command to General Sir Garnet Wolseley, who had been sent out from Britain to replace him. There was little for Wolseley to do beyond catching King Cetshwayo – who had abandoned his royal homestead on the day of the battle the British called Ulundi – and impose a peace-settlement on the defeated nation. A flying column, commanded by Lieutenant-Colonel C. Clarke, and consisting of the 57th Regiment and six companies of the 60th, was marched first to oNdini, and then north towards the Black Mfolozi river, the furthest point in Zululand penetrated by British troops throughout the war. It was from here that the king was run to earth by a party of Dragoons at the end of August. He was brought into camp, and from there escorted to Port Durnford by the 60th. The veterans of Gingindlovu, who had so nearly collapsed under the onslaught of his warriors, nevertheless appreciated the deep poignancy of the moment as the king was taken aboard a surf-boat, destined for captivity in Cape Town. Hutton – now promoted captain – made several sketches of his march, which were engraved and published in *The Graphic*. 'The Buffs', 91st and 99th had no such high point on which to end their time in Zululand; the capture of the king marked the end of the war, and the 1st Division was gradually broken up. By the end of September the troops had been marched back across the Thukela, and Zululand was left to its own devices.

The Eshowe campaign offered little in the way of glittering prizes. After his return to the UK, Pearson was presented with an ornate sword by the citizens of his home town, Yeovil, in gratitude for his services, and in December Queen Victoria herself decorated him with the Order of the Bath. There was a feeling that at least one man among the garrison had deserved a gallantry award; as early as July 1879 Charles Shervinton had prepared a statement regarding the incident on 11 March when he had saved the life of Private William Brooks. After the war, Shervinton's mother wrote to both Pearson and Chelmsford in an attempt to secure for her son the Victoria Cross. Brooks himself had stated that 'I feel confident that my life that day was saved by Captain Shervinton's gallant conduct, and for which I shall be forever indebted to him.' The campaign foundered, however, on a point of protocol, which, it seems, the senior officers lacked the interest to resolve. Pearson argued that he had mentioned Shervinton's name in dispatches, and that 'I also spoke of him personally to Lord Chelmsford. He did us *right good* service and I hope that he will be rewarded in some way or other.' Beyond that, however, he feared 'that I cannot do anything further towards recommending him.' Chelmsford himself merely responded that whilst he 'well remember[ed] the gallant conduct' of Shervinton, he was dependent on a recommendation for the VC being submitted 'by the officer under whose immediate command the individual was serving.' The buck was effectively passed back to Pearson, who clearly felt he had done enough, and at that stalemate the matter dropped. It was hardly a generous decision; the VC had been awarded to other colonial officers during the Zulu War for similar deeds, and Shervinton's persistent daring surely qualified him for some tangible recognition. Yet the siege of Eshowe had not captured the imagination of the British public in the same way that Rorke's Drift had, and in any case, there was a feeling within the military establishment that enough awards had already been presented – eleven were given for the defence of Rorke's Drift alone. Charles Shervinton did not receive the VC: nor, indeed, were any gallantry awards given for either Nyezane, the siege, or Gingindlovu.

Common threads linked the later lives of many of the British professional soldiers. Lord Chelmsford returned home the hero of oNdini (Ulundi) rather than the vanquished of Isandlwana; he was given a variety of impressive sinecure posts, but never commanded an army in the field again. He died in the middle of a billiards match in his club in 1905, at the age of eighty-one. Pearson, too, saw little further active service in a career which encompassed governorship of the military hospital at Netley, and command of the garrison in the West Indies. A number of 'Buffs' officers who had served in Eshowe accompanied him there, including his former ADC, Lieutenant Knight. Pearson retired with the rank of lieutenant-general in 1895, and died in October 1909. Molyneux served in Egypt in 1882, where the nationalist revolt of Ahmad 'Urabi collapsed before Sir Garnet Wolseley's fierce assault on the trenches of Tel-El-Kebir, and returned to South Africa in 1885 to take part in the Bechuanaland Field Force; he retired a major-general in 1887 and died a year later. Guy Dawnay, too, was at Tel-El-Kebir, and went on to serve in the campaigns against the Mahdists in the eastern Sudan. Dawnay became the Tory MP for the North Riding of Yorkshire between 1882 and 1885, but following an electoral setback he returned to Africa. His end was tragically appropriate to his life; he was gored to death by a wounded buffalo he had been hunting in Ngiri, East Africa, in February 1889. Percy Barrow's dashing career was brought to a premature end by a Mahdist spear-thrust at the battle of El Teb; he continued to serve for a while but succumbed to its effects in Cairo in January 1886. Lieutenant Main pursued a successful career in the Engineers but apparently saw no more active service before his retirement as a full colonel in 1907. Charles Shervinton's adventures were the most bizarre of all: after a spell fighting the BaSotho in 1880, he went to Madagascar, where he rose to the rank of colonel commanding Malagasy troops in their struggle against French colonial forces. His adventurous career ended on a sour note of defeat, however, and he returned to England in poor health, and died in 1898.

South Africa had proved a testing time for the 3rd Battalion, 60th Rifles, and was to demand more of them yet. In late 1880 the Boer republic of the Transvaal overthrew British annexation – thereby marking the final collapse of the Confederation policy which had provoked the Zulu War – and the battalion was among the troops marched up from Natal to suppress the revolt. Five companies were badly mauled in the action at the Ingogo river on 8 February 1881, when the Boers attacked a British column attempting to clear a threatened line of communication. The veterans of Gingindlovu spent a day pinned down behind boulders whilst the Boers sniped at them. They extricated themselves under cover of darkness, having sustained over a hundred casualties; among them was Lieutenant Wilkinson, who, crossing the flooded Ingogo river with medical supplies for the wounded, was swept from his horse and drowned. The British commander, Colley, described Wilkinson's as 'the saddest death of all – drowned returning from an errand of mercy.' Edward Hutton, however, survived the 1881 Boer War, Tel-El-Kebir – where his horse was killed under him – the Gordon Relief Expedition, and the second Boer War: he commanded a division in 1914, and died Lieutenant-General Sir Edward Hutton, in 1923.

For Zululand itself, the post-war period was characterised by misery and bloodshed. The British, reluctant to accept responsibility for the country directly, appointed thirteen chiefs who were to rule in accordance with British guidelines, under the watchful eye of a British resident. The settlement soon dissolved into a bitter wrangle between royalist and anti-royalist factions, however, and in an attempt to head off a crisis Britain restored Cetshwayo to part of his old territory in 1883. This merely accelerated the conflict, and open civil war broke out. Cetshwayo was defeated by a faction led by his erstwhile general, Zibhebhu kaMapitha, and he fled to Eshowe to appeal to the Resident. While the British government pondered their next move, the deposed king lived briefly in a small homestead nearby, but on 8 February 1884 he died. His death was variously attributed to a broken heart or poison. With wry symbolism, fate has decreed that the spot where he died is today marked by a concrete slab; it is on a traffic island in the middle of a road in the modern town of Eshowe. The king's followers took his body out to the remote Nkhandla forest, and buried it there. Unrest simmered in Zululand throughout the 1880s, and the British built another fort at Eshowe, Fort Cross; it did not see any action, however, despite the outbreak of a short-lived rebellion in 1888. Prince Dabulamanzi, who had achieved more fame among his enemies in 1879 than any other Zulu commander – largely, it must be admitted, because of his role as commander of the unsuccessful attack on Rorke's Drift, rather than because of the part he played in bottling up Pearson's men – remained an ardent supporter of the royalist cause, and played a prominent part in these disturbances; on 22 September 1886 he was involved in a fracas with two Boers in the northern part of Zululand, and shot dead. His followers carried his body in a wagon back to eNtumeni, where it was buried on the site of his eZulwini homestead.

True to his promise, John Dunn had, indeed, not done with the Zulus. When he returned to Zululand after the war, Sir Garnet Wolseley toyed with the idea of making him a white king of all Zululand, but opted instead to appoint him one of the thirteen kings. He was given control of all his old territories and more, from the Mhlatuze river in the north to the Thukela in the south. Many of the Zulu chiefs he had fought against at Gingindlovu – including Prince Dabulamanzi, Somopho and Sigcwelegcwele – were now under his control. Dunn accepted his commission from Wolseley on the understanding that King Cetshwayo would never be allowed to return to Zululand, and his rift with the Royal House became complete. To assert his authority he did not scruple to confiscate royal cattle found in his district, to Dabulamanzi's bitter and lasting resentment. When it was proposed that Cetshwayo be restored to Zululand, Dunn's old friend Guy Dawnay tried unsuccessfully to block the move in the British parliament. Dunn lost part of his territory to the king on his restoration, and his influence with his British patrons declined, but he continued to enjoy his unconventional lifestyle to the full. He entertained visiting sportsmen, imported his furniture and silver tableware from England, and behaved as a Zulu chief. When he died in August 1895, at the age of sixty-five, he mentioned twenty-three wives and seventy-nine children in his will. The struggle of his mixed-race offspring to secure their birthright has been one of the more poignant sideshows of the tragic saga of apartheid.

The missionaries who had shared Pearson's confinement had mixed fortunes. The Reverend Robert Robertson returned to Zululand after the war, delighted that the heathen kingdom of Cetshwayo had been overturned. To his disappointment, however, the Zulus still clung stubbornly to their traditional beliefs, and Christianity did not thrive. Robertson died in November 1897 at the age of sixty-seven. Father Walsh continued to follow in the footsteps of the military; he was Catholic chaplain to the garrison at Lydenburg in the Transvaal when it was invested by the Boers in 1881. Once again he found himself under siege, leading Sunday services with an energetic rendering of 'Hold The Fort'. Lydenburg's senior officer was a young and inexperienced lieutenant, and many credited Father Walsh as the mainstay of the resistance, which lasted for three months until the end of hostilities. In 1884, Walsh accompanied Sir Charles Warren's Bechuanaland expedition, where he bumped into Hamilton-Browne, who was still knocking around Africa, looking for adventure. Walsh died shortly after in Kimberley; Hamilton-Browne went north into Zimbabwe in the wake of Cecil Rhodes.

The fighting of 1879 left little mark on the landscape. In early June 1879, a correspondent for the *Illustrated London News* visited the battlefield at Gingindlovu, and found the trenches still visible, and the site strewn with debris, particularly Zulu shields. Three months later, Northey's body was exhumed, and returned to the UK, where he was laid to rest in the family plot near Epsom. In 1882, the traveller, Bertram Mitford, pronounced Gingindlovu 'one of the most God-forsaken places I have ever seen.' The trenches were still visible close by the British memorials, but Mitford found only one other gruesome relic of the fight – a solitary Zulu skull, gleaming in the long grass. Because of its hot damp climate, the coastal sector was ideal for the cultivation of sugar-cane, an important crop in Natal since the 1860s, and one which was introduced commercially to Zululand after the country was opened up to white farmers at the end of the 1880s. Much of the area is now swallowed up in a waving green sea of tall cane leaves. Until quite recently, the local farmer at Gingindlovu turned up cartridge cases, bullets, shell fragments and occasional human remains when he ploughed. At Nyezane, a new road runs just below the track Pearson followed up the spurs of Wombane mountain, and a stone memorial near by has replaced Gelston's cross on the site of his dead. Yet there are still Zulu homesteads on the slopes of the knoll where the Gatling once stood, and the site repays exploration on foot. The view from the top of Wombane, the Zulu position, is a commanding one. Wynne and Mynors still lie in the cemeteries near Fort Pearson, a peaceful spot, despite a new highway which bridges the Thukela at exactly the point where Pearson's ferry crossed in 1879. The trenches and ramparts of Fort Pearson are well preserved, but across the river, little remains of Fort Tenedos beyond the geometric outline still traceable in the cane.

At Eshowe, the KwaMondi mission was never reoccupied, and what the Zulus failed to destroy in April 1879 soon fell to ruin. The site now lies to the east of the modern town, on the outskirts of a black township. Bertram Mitford's description of the site in 1882 has a melancholic and enduring quality:

> Looking at the fort now, one would think it had been constructed twelve years ago rather than three. Long grass trailing from the earthwork almost conceals the ditch, whose brink is, in places, so overgrown with brambles and rank herbage as to constitute a source of danger to the unwary explorer; the buildings within, that did duty for storehouses and hospitals, are in a tumbledown state; in fact, the whole enclosed space presents a woeful and ruinous appearance.

Only an occasional trace of the foundations survive now to indicate the site of the buildings, but the trenches are largely intact. The luxuriant undergrowth defeats the efforts of local conservationists, but the ramparts and trenches are still formidable today. Wynne's work undoubtedly contributed to his death, but it has survived as a fitting tribute to his efforts. Near by, Midshipman Coker, Adjutant Davison, Lieutenants Evelyn and Williams, and all the rest who died with them during the 'fearful hard times' at Eshowe, lie on the grassy slope below a dirt track which was once Pearson's new road. Eshowe, which grew slowly once the British established a magistracy there in the 1880s, is now a fair-sized town, catering largely for the agricultural community; it celebrated its centenary in 1991. It has an interesting museum, housed in an architectural curiosity, Fort Nongqai, built in 1883 to house the Zululand Native Police. The troublesome anchor of HMS *Tenedos*, to which the pont hawsers had once been attached at the Lower Thukela Drift, stands outside, but, fittingly enough, the museum dwells not only on the siege and past conflicts, but on the continuing thread of Zulu cultural life.

Appendix One

Diary of a Siege

23 JANUARY–4 APRIL 1879

DAY 1.	Thu. 23 Jan.	Column arrives at Eshowe. Death of Pte Dunne, 'The Buffs', wounded at Nyezane.
	Fri. 24 Jan.	Reinforcements for Lt Col Ely's convoy sent from Eshowe. Trace of new entrenchment laid out.
	Sat. 25 Jan.	Work parties begin digging ditches. Lt Col Coates sent with convoy to Lower Thukela.
	Sun. 26 Jan.	Pearson receives Frere's note to the effect that Durnford has been defeated but that Chelmsford has won a victory. Death of Sgt Hydenburg, NNC, wounded at Nyezane.
DAY 5.	Mon. 27 Jan.	Garrison told news of Durnford's defeat. Barrow takes mounted men on reconnaissance towards Mlalazi; Coates reaches Thukela.
	Tue. 28 Jan.	Barrow on recce towards eNtumeni. Pearson receives Chelmsford's telegram instructing him to 'act in whatever manner you think desirable', and to be prepared for a major Zulu attack. Pearson decides to remain at Eshowe but to send back mounted men and NNC. Ely's convoy arrives. Tents abandoned, all men move into entrenchment. Barrow reaches Thukela.
	Wed. 29 Jan.	Pearson orders inventory of food and ammunition.
	Thu. 30 Jan.	Ninety oxen escape overnight. 1000 oxen are sent back to Lower Thukela; 500 are captured, the rest return to Eshowe.
	Fri. 31 Jan.	Ditch now completely surrounds entrenchment.
	Sat. 1 Feb.	Work begins on new cattle laager in ravine. Men placed on three quarter rations. Death of Pte Kingston, 'The Buffs'.
	Sun. 2 Feb.	Pearson receives full news of Isandlwana disaster, asks for more troops to be sent to Eshowe.
DAY 12.	Mon. 3 Feb.	Garrison given full details of Isandlwana. Large numbers of Zulus seen in area. Forty-four oxen die in laager overnight.
	Tue. 4 Feb.	Pearson told no extra troops will be sent to Eshowe.
	Wed. 5 Feb.	Work on fort continues; daily band concerts begin.
	Thu. 6 Feb.	List of officers' casualties at Isandlwana received, together

with story of Rorke's Drift. Chelmsford asks Pearson to reduce garrison and move to Lower Thukela. Pearson asks for twenty wagons of supplies.

Fri. 7 Feb. Powder magazine built, outlying defences commenced.

Sat. 8 Feb. Late start to general work due to overnight rain.

Sun. 9 Feb. Basic work on entrenchment completed; Zulus fire on Captain Shervinton's patrol.

DAY 19. Mon. 10 Feb. Vedettes under fire.

Tue. 11 Feb. Pearson receives second letter urging him to retire with part of garrison to Thukela. Council of War decides to stay at Eshowe; Pearson informs Chelmsford they will nonetheless march out if orders are confirmed. Work on roadway within fort; death of Artificer Moore, HMS *Active*.

Wed. 12 Feb. General work on fort.

Thu. 13 Feb. Range markers laid out around fort. Death of Pte McLeod, 'The Buffs'.

Fri. 14 Feb. Work started on caponnier in west face of fort.

Sat. 15 Feb. Death of Pte Oakley, 'The Buffs'.

Sun. 16 Feb. March to Lower Thukela cancelled as no confirmation of order received from Chelmsford.

DAY 26. Mon. 17 Feb. Very wet day, no work.

Tue. 18 Feb. Pearson writes to Chelmsford again; lecture by Rev Robertson.

Wed. 19 Feb. Pearson rides out on recce to Mlalazi.

Thu. 20 Feb. Second lecture by Rev Robertson.

Fri. 21 Feb. Oxen driven over a mile from fort for grazing. Firing heard from the direction of Thukela. Deaths of Lce Cpl Taylor, 'The Buffs', Ptes Shields and Knee, 99th.

Sat. 22 Feb. Cattle guards under fire; troops sent from fort to drive off attackers. Two *imizi* burnt, heavy rain at night.

Sun. 23 Feb. Fort flooded. Auction of foodstuffs left behind by Volunteers.

DAY 33. Mon. 24 Feb. Pearson accompanies one raid; one *umuzi* burnt.

Tue. 25 Feb. Early rain prevents work in morning.

Wed. 26 Feb. Work begins building wattle hut inside fort.

Thu. 27 Feb. General work continues.

Fri. 28 Feb. Late start to work due to bad weather; orders issued for major raid next day.

Sat. 1 Mar. Attack on eSiqwakeni *ikhanda*.

Sun. 2 Mar. Sun-flash signals observed at Lower Thukela.

DAY 40. Mon. 3 Mar. Part of received message understood.

Tue. 4 Mar. Hot-air message balloon completed, but bad weather prevents launch. Death of Pte Paul, 99th.

	Wed. 5 Mar.	Pearson orders a recce to find a route for proposed new road towards Thukela.
	Thu. 6 Mar.	Sun-flash message fully understood. Relief column to start on 13/3. Signalling screen completed. Heavy rain returns. Death of Drummer Mortimer, 'The Buffs'.
	Fri. 7 Mar.	Attack on Cpl Carson whilst on vedette duty.
	Sat. 8 Mar.	Strong winds destroy signalling screen. Rain collapses caponnier on south face. Last of slaughter oxen eaten. Deaths of Ld Seaman Radford, HMS *Active*, Pte Barber, Army Hospital Corps.
	Sun. 9 Mar.	Zulus open fire on road party. Death of Pte Stack, 'The Buffs'.
DAY 47.	Mon. 10 Mar.	Second signalling screen erected. Zulus attempt to surround road party, which is withdrawn. Runner arrives with fourteen day-old message, and is arrested as a spy.
	Tue. 11 Mar.	Lt Lewis of 'The Buffs' wounded while out with road party; torpedo exploded to deter Zulus from interfering with work. Attack on vedette post; Pte Brooks saved by Capt Shervinton. Large numbers of Zulus seen moving towards Nyezane to oppose relief column.
	Wed. 12 Mar.	More Zulus seen in direction of Nyezane: death of Capt Williams, 'The Buffs'.
	Thu. 13 Mar.	Road completed. Message received postponing relief until 1/4.
	Fri. 14 Mar.	Regular two-way communications established.
	Sat. 15 Mar.	Zulus observed retiring from Nyezane.
	Sun. 16 Mar.	Heavy thunderstorms herald three days of rain. Deaths of Pte Tubb, 99th, Marine Stagg and Midshipman Coker of HMS *Active*.
DAY 54.	Mon. 17 Mar.	Cattle laager relocated: Pte Kent, 99th (MI) killed on vedette duty. Death of Pte Venn, 99th.
	Tue. 18 Mar.	Bad weather prevents work.
	Wed. 19 Mar.	Runner arrives at Eshowe with news that relief column will march on 29/3.
	Thu. 20 Mar.	Raid on *umuzi* close to fort.
	Fri. 21 Mar.	Death of Pte Coombes, 99th.
	Sat. 22 Mar.	Rain prevents work in afternoon.
	Sun. 23 Mar.	Two Zulu envoys arrested as spies.
DAY 61.	Mon. 24 Mar.	Private sun-flash messages prohibited. Wagons withdrawn from fort and replaced with sod traverses.
	Tue. 25 Mar.	Work on new sod traverses continues.
	Wed. 26 Mar.	Death of Pte Roden, 99th.

	Thu. 27 Mar.	Second wattle hut completed. Death of Lt Davison, 99th and Pte Tarrant, 'The Buffs'.
	Fri. 28 Mar.	Two heavy rainstorms prevent work in afternoon. Death of Pte Lewis, 99th.
	Sat. 29 Mar.	Pearson receives request from Chelmsford to sally out and support his advance. Pearson replies that garrison is not fit enough. Runners arrive with medicine and newspapers.
	Sun. 30 Mar.	Relief column observed at amaTigulu river. Death of Lt Evelyn, 'The Buffs'.
DAY 68.	Mon. 31 Mar.	Cavalry scouts observed ten miles distant.
	Tue. 1 Apr.	Relief column forms laager about ten miles from Eshowe.
	Wed. 2 Apr.	Relief column defeats Zulus at battle of Gingindlovu. Death of Able Seaman Smith, HMS *Active*.
	Thu. 3 Apr.	The siege of Eshowe lifted.
DAY 72.	Fri. 4 Apr.	The garrison at Eshowe begins its return march to the Thukela. Death of Pte Monk, 'The Buffs'.

Appendix Two

British Casualties in the Eshowe Campaign:

(1) The Battle of Nyezane

Killed

Pte 1266 John Bough, 2/3rd Regt

Pte 766 James Kelleher, 2/3rd Regt

Lt J.L. Raines, 1/2nd NNC

Lt Gustav Plattner, 1/2nd NNC

Sgt Emil Unger, 1/2nd NNC

Cpl Wilhelm Lieper, 1/2nd NNC

Cpl Edward Miller, 1/2 NNC

Cpl Carl Goesch, 1/2 NNC

Five unnamed Privates, 1/2nd NNC

Wounded

Pte 1100 William Dunne*, 2/3rd Regt, dangerously wounded, gunshot abdomen; died 23/1/79.

Pte 865 John Corble, 2/3rd Regt, dangerously wounded, gunshot head.

Pte 1244 F. Smith, 2/3rd Regt, severely wounded, gunshot.

Pte 716 F. Clifford, 2/3rd Regt, severely wounded, gunshot left arm.

Pte 548 Henry Walker, 2/3rd Regt, severely wounded, gunshot.

QMS 1554 Kelly, 1st Sqd MI, (90th Regt), severely wounded, gunshot left arm.

Pte W. Devenport, 1st Sqd MI, (2/24th), severely wounded, gunshot breast.

Able Seaman H. Gosling, Naval Brigade, seriously wounded, gunshot right hand.

Ord Seaman G. Berryman, Naval Brigade, seriously wounded, gunshot left leg.

Ord Seaman George Doran, Naval Brigade, dangerously wounded, gunshot upper left thigh.

Able Seaman T. Butler, Naval Brigade, slightly wounded, gunshot.

Ord Seaman E. White, Naval Brigade, slightly wounded, gunshot left thigh.

Ord Seaman (Krooman) Jack Ropeyarn, Naval Brigade, slightly wounded, gunshot left chest.

Ord Seaman (Krooman) Jack Lewis, Naval Brigade, slightly wounded, gunshot upper arm.

Lt Harry Webb, 1/2nd NNC, slightly wounded, gunshot.

Sgt O. Hydenburg*, 1/2nd NNC, dangerously wounded, gunshot knee; died 26.1.1879.

The number of wounded from the ranks of the 1/2nd NNC is not recorded.

* The spelling of Dunne and Hydenburg varies between the rolls and their graves; the authors are of the opinion that the spellings on the grave are the most likely to be

accurate. Dunne's initial is listed as J. in Pearson's dispatch; presumably an error. There are a number of discrepancies in spelling between the various rolls; for example, Pte 766 of the Buffs is listed as Kelliher in Pearson's dispatch of 23.1.1879, Kelleher in the *Natal Mercury* report of 28.1.1879, and Kelleker on the current battlefield monument. A misprint in Krooman Jack Lewis's name has sometimes led to the inclusion in some lists of a spurious casualty, various rendered Able Seaman Ockleweis or Duckleweis! This is indicative of the uncertainty which inevitably surrounds any casualty roll, including those offered here.

(2) The Battle of Gingindlovu

Killed

Lt G.C. Johnson, 99th Regt

Pte J. Pratt, 60th Rifles

Pte R. Marshall, 91st Highlanders

Pte J. Lawrence, 99th Regt

Pte J. Smith, 99th Regt

Mortally Wounded

Lt Col F.V. Northey, 3/60th Rifles, gunshot wound, right shoulder.

Pte T. Perkins, 57th Regt, gunshot wound back. D.O.W. 19.4.1879.

Pte P. Armstrong, 99th Regt, gunshot wound, buttock and right ankle.

Pte G. Baker, 99th Regt, gunshot wound, neck.

Wounded

Col J.N. Crealock, Staff, slight wound, gunshot abrasion of upper third right arm.

Major P.H.S. Barrow, 19th Hussars (Mounted Infantry), slight wound, gunshot abrasion (?) right thigh.

Capt H.C. Hinxman, 57th Regt, slight wound, gunshot of right thigh.

S Surg Longfield, RN, dangerous wound, gunshot of right shoulder.

Pte Flannery, 2/3rd Regt, serious wound, gunshot of head.

Pte Deacon, 57th Regt, slight wound, gunshot abrasion of nose.

Pte Harris, 57th Regt, slight wound, gunshot of scalp.

Col Sgt E. Dallard, 3/60th Rifles, slight wound, gunshot of head.

Pte Aylett, 3/60th Rifles, slight wound, gunshot of left hand.

Pte W. Poplett, 3/60th Rifles, dangerously wounded, gunshot of left thigh.

Pte E. Traney, 3/60th Rifles, slight wound, gunshot of neck.

Pte W. Lowkiff, 3/60th Rifles, dangerous wound, gunshot of left elbow.

Pte H. Richards, 91st Regt, severe wound, gunshot of leg.

Pte Staridge, 91st Regt, slight wound, gunshot of thigh.

Pte Bryan, 91st Regt, dangerous wound, gunshot of head.

Pte Malley, 91st Regt, dangerous wound, gunshot of head.

Pte Hanlon, 91st Regt, dangerous wound, gunshot of abdomen.

Sgt McIntyre, 91st Regt, serious wound, gunshot of left eye.

Pte Sutton, 91st Regt, severe wound, gunshot of left arm.

Pte Gillespie, 91st Regt, severe wound, gunshot of right ear.

Pte J. Blackwell, 99th Regt, slight wound, gunshot of left shoulder.

Pte Drew, 99th Regt, serious wound, gunshot of right shoulder (compound fracture).

Pte P. Bryan, Mounted Infantry (88th Regt), dangerous wound, gunshot abrasion of right thigh.

Pte A. Hartley, Mounted Infantry, (90th Regt), serious wound, gunshot of right shoulder and back.

Able Seaman E. Bird, HMS *Shah*, serious wound, gunshot abrasion of left side (arm).

Able Seaman J. Bulgar, HMS *Shah*, serious wound, gunshot of right arm (shoulder).

Capt's Mate P. Condy, HMS *Boadicea*, slight wound, gunshot of right arm.

Boy J. Hinchley, HMS *Boadicea*, dangerous wound, gunshot of right thigh.

Act Bombadier J. Parfitt, RMA, HMS *Boadicea*, dangerous wound, gunshot of right thigh and shoulder.

Pt Officer, J. Porteus, HMS *Tenedos*, slight wound, gunshot of right shoulder.

Sources: Nominal Roll, Surgeon-Major Farrant, *Natal Mercury*, and Chelmsford's roll. There are discrepancies between these rolls; Farrant seems to have reversed the injuries of Ptes Hartley and Bryan (e.g. he gives Bryan as 'severely wounded', but describes his wound as a 'graze').

NNC Casualties

There is considerable confusion regarding the number of NNC men killed and wounded, which varies even on different official rolls. The most comprehensive breakdown suggests that in:

No. 4 Btn. 1 man killed, 2 severely wounded, 3 slightly wounded,
No. 5 Btn. 4 men killed, 8 severely wounded, 4 slightly wounded.

Two men were apparently mortally wounded; it is not clear whether these are included in the killed total above.

Note: A Private J. Dunn is included on the battlefield memorial at Gingindlovu. This has been interpreted as referring to Pte William Dunne of 'The Buffs' who died at Eshowe, and is, therefore, apparently buried in two places! No Pte Dunn was killed at Gingindlovu; the authors suggest that the grave is in fact that of the member of Dunn's scouts, killed in the scare at eMvutsheni mission, 6.4.1879.

(3) Casualties in the Scare Near eMvutsheni ('Imfuchini') Mission, 6.4.1879

D Company, 3/60th Rifles (Gunshot Injuries):

No. 1982 Pte F. Lambert, compound comminuted fracture of left elbow.

No. 1939 Pte W. Bruton, severe flesh wound penetrating left thigh and inside right leg.

No. 783 Pte J. Barker, penetrating flesh wound left thigh.
No. 3279 Pte J. Crowdson, wound, left shoulder.
No. 2033 Pte R. Winter, penetrating bullet wound, gluteal region.

Note: The roll adds that Pte Lambert was twenty-two years old with two years' service, whilst Pte Bruton was twenty, with one and a half years' service.

Dunn's Scouts

8 men wounded, 2 dangerously, 1 since dead.

(4) Deaths at Eshowe

The following is a list by unit of those buried in the military cemetery at Eshowe during the period of occupation, 23 Jan–4 April 1879. The date of deaths can be found in *Appendix 1: Diary of a Siege.*

2/3rd Regiment, 'The Buffs'

Capt H.J.N. Williams	Pte W. McLeod
Lt G.R.J. Evelyn	Pte J. Monk
Lce Cpl T. Taylor	Pte E. Oakley
Drummer A. Mortimer	Pte J. Stack
Pte W. Dunne (buried in fort)	Pte A. Tarrrant
Pte A. Kingston	

99th Regiment

Lt A.S.F. Davison	Pte J. Paul
Pte C. Coombes	Pte P. Roden
Pte W. Kent	Pte J. Shields
Pte W. Knee	Pte W. Tubb
Pte B. Lewis	Pte T. Venn

Army Hospital Corps

Pte W. Barber

HMS *Active*

Midshipman L.C. Coker	Able Seaman A. Smith
Artificer J. Moore	Marine W. Stagg
Leading Seaman J. Radford	

Natal Native Contingent

Sergeant O. Hydenburg (buried in fort)

Glossary

Note: Zulu names have been listed alphabetically according to stem rather than prefix (e.g. ibutho/ amabutho under 'b').

abatis/abattis: a defence formed from fallen trees placed lengthways, with their branches facing towards the enemy.

banquette: a step built inside a rampart to enable troops to fire over the rampart: a firing step.

bastion: a structure projecting from the corners of a fortification, so as to enable fire to be directed along the outside face of the walls of a fortification.

ibutho, pl. **amabutho**: a group of youths of a common age, organised into a guild to give service to the Zulu king; in its military context, a regiment.

caponnier: a covered passage across a defensive ditch.

counterscarp: the vertical side of a defensive ditch nearest the enemy.

donga: a run-off gully, caused by soil erosion.

drift: the crossing point of a river.

embrasure: an opening in a parapet, normally one through which a gun can be fired.

gallery: an underground passage.

glacis: the parapet of a defensive ditch extended in a slope to meet the natural surface of the ground, so that every part of it can be fired upon from the ramparts.

ka; 'of', usually used in the sense of 'born of', e.g. Cetshwayo kaMpande.

ikhanda, pl. **amakhanda**: royal homesteads, belonging to the king; the centres of royal authority, which served as barracks for the amabutho.

kwa: prefix for Zulu place names, meaning 'at the place of'.

laager: Afrikaans terms for a defensive wagon-circle: used by the British to mean a temporary fortified camp.

impi: Zulu term for a body of armed men.

impondo zankomo: 'the beast's horns', the Zulu attack formation.

imuzi, pl. **imizi**: an ordinary Zulu civilian homestead.

induna, pl. **izinduna**: a state official of the Zulu kingdom.

parapet: the defensive wall which serves to provide cover for the defenders.

rampart: a bank of earth around a fortified place, usually built on the inside of a ditch, with soil taken from the ditch.

ravelin: an outwork raised across the ditch at the top of the counterscarp to protect the space between two bastions.

redoubt: a roughly constructed strongpoint.

revetment: a wall built to prevent earthen ramparts, parapets and ditches from collapsing.

traverse: a parapet built within an earthwork to prevent any enemy flanking fire, or fire from higher ground, striking the defenders of the parapets.

vlei: a patch of low-lying ground, marshy in wet weather.

Sources

Unpublished Papers, Diaries, Memoirs etc

Backhouse, Lt J.B., 2/3rd Regt: Personal diary, National Army Museum, London.

Carroll, Gunner J., RMA: Personal diary (family collection).

Cato Papers: letter from G.C. Cato to Richards, 2.2.1893, describing Nyezane. Killie Campbell Africana Library.

Chelmsford Papers 68-386-7: Letters and telegrams between Lt General Lord Chelmsford and Col Pearson, Major Barrow, Commander Campbell, Lt Dowding and others, National Army Museum, London.

Courtney, Lt D.C., RE: Private diary. Royal Engineers Museum, Chatham.

Davison, Lt A.S.F., 99th Regt: Personal diary. Private collection.

Hamilton, Lt W. des V., HMS *Active*: Letters to his father, National Army Museum, London.

Hargreaves, Pte, 3/60th Regt: Personal diary. Royal Greenjackets Museum, Winchester.

Hempstead, Pte A, 99th Regt: Personal account. Private collection.

Hymas, Pte C.A., 3rd Regt: Personal account.

Main, Ltd T.R., RE: Personal memoirs, Royal Engineers Museum, Chatham.

Message Book, St Andrew's mission signal station, March 1879. Royal Engineers Museum, Chatham.

Robarts, Lt W., VMR: Personal letters, collection of Mr Bill Robarts, Empangeni.

Shervinton, Capt C. St. L., 2nd NNC: Personal letters and papers (including statements from Lord Chelmsford, Col Pearson and Pte Brooks, 99th, regarding claim for VC). Keith Reeves Collection.

Sparks, Colonel Harry: *Chelmsford's Ultimatum to Cetewayo*, Killie Campbell Africana Museum (KCM 42329).

Wynne, Capt R.C.: Letters and diary, family collection. Also ms. report of Nyezane, dated 'Ekowe, 23rd January 1879', in Royal Engineers Museum, Chatham.

Published Contemporary Accounts

Barrow, Major P.H.S.: Report on battle of Nyezane, British Parliamentary Papers (C. 2367).

Chelmsford, Lt Gen Lord: Correspondence with Secretary of State for War, British Parliamentary Papers (C. 2318).

Coates, Lt Col C., 99th Regt.: *The First Phase Of The Zulu War*, London, 1879.

Courtney, Capt D.C., RE: *Report on Fort Ekowe*, British Parliamentary Papers (C. 2367) April 9th 1879.

Molyneux, Major W.C.F.: 'Notes On Hasty Defences As Practised In South Africa', *Journal of the Royal United Services Institution*, vol. xxiv, London 1881.

Mynors, Lt A.C.: *Letters and Diary*, privately published, 1879.

Pearson, Col C.K.: Correspondence in British Parliamentary Papers, (C. 2260).

Various: Accounts by correspondents with Pearson's column (chiefly unidentified Volunteers) and the Relief Column (including C.L. Norris-Newman), in the Zulu War supplement to the *Natal Mercury*, Jan–June 1879.

Later Published Memoirs (including edited works)

A Natal Volunteer: *The Zulu War*, United Services Magazine, November 1897.

Clarke, Sonia (ed): *Zululand At War 1879*, Houghton, 1984.

Davitt, Napier: *Galloping Jack – The Reminiscences of Brig. Gen. J.R. Royston*, London, 1937.

Dawnay, Guy C.: *Campaigns: Zulu 1879, Egypt 1882, Suakim 1885*, private publication c. 1886, reprinted London, 1989.

Dunn, John: (ed. D.C.F. Moodie), *John Dunn, Cetywayo and the Three Generals*, Pietermaritzburg, 1886.

Emery, Frank: *The Red Soldier*, London, 1978. (Includes accounts by Lts Wilkinson and Hutton of the 60th, the unidentified NNC officer, Pte Powis, MI, Lt Dowding, RM, Cpl F.W. License.)

French, Major Hon G.: *Lord Chelmsford and the Zulu War*, London, 1939.

Hall, H.L.: *With Assegai and Rifle: Reminiscences of a Transport Conductor in the Zulu War*, South African Military History Journal, Vol. 4, 5, June 1979.

Hamilton-Browne, Commdt G.: *A Lost Legionary in South Africa*, London, c. 1911.

Knight, Capt H.R.: *Reminiscences of Ethshowe*, United Services Magazine, Vol. VIII New Series, Oct 1893, April 1894. London, 1894.

Lloyd, Lt W.N., RHA: *The Defence of Ekowe*, Royal Artillery Institution, Woolwich, 1881 (Reprinted *Natalia* V, December 1975).

Ludlow, Capt W.R.: *Zululand And Cetewayo*, London, 1882 (reprinted Pretoria 1969).

Mackinnon, J.R. and S.H. Shadbolt: *The South African Campaign, 1879*, London, 1880, reprinted 1980.

Mitford, Bertram; *Through The Zulu Country: Its Battlefields and Its People*, London, 1883, reprinted 1975, 1992.

Molyneux, Maj Gen W.C.F.: *Campaigning in South Africa and Egypt*, London 1896.

Norbury, Fleet-Surgeon H.F.: *The Naval Brigade in South Africa During the Years 1877–78–79*, London, 1880.

Norris-Newman, C.L.: *In Zululand With the British Throughout the War of 1879*, London, 1880, reprinted London, 1988.

One Who Was There (believed to be Capt Pelly Clarke, 103rd Regt): *The Zulu War: With Colonel Pearson at Ekowe*, Blackwood's Magazine, Vol. CXXVI, July 1879.

Samuelson, R.C.: *Long, Long Ago*, Durban, 1929.

Shervinton, Kathleen: *The Shervintons – Soldiers of Fortune*, London, 1899.

Sihlahla, uMxapho ibutho: Account in supplement to *Natal Mercury*, 22.1.1929.

Webb, C. de B., and J.B. Wright, (eds): *A Zulu King Speaks: Statements Made by Cetshwayo kaMpande on the History and Customs of His People*, Pietermaritzburg and Durban, 1978.

Webb, C. de B., and J.B. Wright, (eds): *The James Stuart Archive of Recorded Oral Evidence Relating to the History of the Zulu and Neighbouring People*, Pietermaritzburg and Durban, Vols 1–4, 1976, 1979, 1982, 1986.

E. & H.W., *Soldiers of the Cross in Zululand*, (includes Reverend Robertson's account of Nyezane), London and Derby, 1905.

War Office, Intelligence Branch (Rothwell, J.S. comp.): *Narrative of Field Operations Connected With The Zulu War of 1879*, London, 1881 (reprinted 1906, 1989).

Zimema, Chief, uMxapho ibutho: Account in supplement to *Natal Mercury*, 22.1.1929.

Regimental Histories

Dunn-Pattison, R.P.: *The History of the 91st Argyllshire Highlanders*, London, 1910.

Hare, Stuart: *Annals of the King's Royal Rifle Corps*, Vol. IV, London, 1929.

Woolwright, H.H.: *History of the Fifty-Seventh (West Middlesex) Regiment of Foot, 1855–1881*, London, 1893.

Recent Books

Ballard, Charles: *John Dunn: The White Chief of Zululand*, Craighall, 1985.

Duminy, Andrew and Charles Ballard: *The Anglo-Zulu War; New Perspectives*, Pietermaritzburg, 1981.

Knight, Ian: *Brave Men's Blood*, London, 1990.

Knight, Ian (ed.): ' *By the Orders of the Great White Queen*', London, 1992.

Knight, Ian and Ian Castle, *The Zulu War: Then and Now*, London, 1993.

Laband, John: *Kingdom in Crisis – The Zulu Response to the British Invasion of 1879*, Manchester, 1992.

Laband, John and Paul Thompson, *Kingdom and Colony at War*, Pietermaritzburg and Cape Town, 1990.

Laband, John and Paul Thompson: *Field Guide to the War in Zululand and the Defence of Natal, 1879*, revised edition, Pietermaritzburg, 1987.

Laband, John: *Fight Us in the Open*, Durban, 1985.

Wilkinson-Latham, Robert: *From Our Special Correspondent: Victorian War Correspondents and Their Campaigns*, London, 1979.

Index

252